Prehistoric Man and His Environments

A Case Study in the Ozark Highland

STUDIES IN ARCHEOLOGY

Consulting Editor: Stuart Struever

Department of Anthropology
Northwestern University
Evanston, Illinois

Prehistoric Man and His Environments

A Case Study in the Ozark Highland

edited by

W. Raymond Wood

University of Missouri
Columbia, Missouri

R. Bruce McMillan

Illinois State Museum
Springfield, Illinois

ACADEMIC PRESS   New York   San Francisco   London

A Subsidiary of Harcourt Brace Jovanovich, Publishers

ACADEMIC PRESS, INC.
111 Fifth Avenue, New York, New York 10003

United Kingdom Edition published by
ACADEMIC PRESS, INC. (LONDON) LTD.
24/28 Oval Road, London NW1

Library of Congress Cataloging in Publication Data
Main entry under title:

Prehistoric man and his environments.

    (Studies in archeology series)
    "Contains contributions 10 through 24 . . . of the
Archaeological and Quaternary Studies Program,
Illinois State Museum."
    Bibliography: p.
    Includes index.
    1.   Indians of North America--Ozark Mountains–
Antiquities.   2.   Ozark Mountains--Antiquities.
3.   Human ecology--Ozark Mountains.   I.   Wood, W.
Raymond.   II.   McMillan, Robert Bruce, (date)
E78.09P73   977.8'49'00497   75-3578
ISBN 0–12–762950–5

To the people of Benton and Hickory counties, Missouri

Contents

II QUATERNARY ENVIRONMENTS

III THE QUESTION OF MAN'S ANTIQUITY

IV   MAN AND HIS ENVIRONMENT

List of Contributors

Numbers in parentheses indicate the pages on which the authors' contributions begin.

Stanley A. Ahler (123, 163), Quaternary Studies Center, Illinois State Museum, Springfield, Illinois

William M. Bass III (201), Department of Anthropology, University of Tennessee, Knoxville, Tennessee

C. Vance Haynes (47), Department of Anthropology, University of Arizona, Tucson, Arizona

Frances B. King (141, 249, 261), Quaternary Studies Center, Illinois State Museum, Springfield, Illinois

James E. King (63, 241), Quaternary Studies Center, Illinois State Museum, Springfield, Illinois

Everett H. Lindsay (63), Department of Geosciences, University of Arizona, Tucson, Arizona

R. Bruce McMillan (13, 81, 111, 141, 163, 211, 235, 241) Assistant Museum Director, Illinois State Museum, Springfield, Illinois

Paul W. Parmalee (141), Department of Anthropology, University of Tennessee, Knoxville, Tennessee

William L. Rhule II (201), 2003 Shaw, Grissom Air Force Base, Indiana

W. Raymond Wood (3, 97, 235, 241), Department of Anthropology, University of Missouri, Columbia, Missouri

Acknowledgments

This volume represents a decade of field work and laboratory analysis by scores of individuals. In the course of an interdisciplinary research program the project personnel become indebted to many people, directly or indirectly. Individuals to whom we are indebted number in the hundreds, and it is impossible to name all of them. Some individuals have played exceptionally important roles in the research, a number of whom are named below. For the many others who have contributed to this research we offer our sincere gratitude and thanks.

The research reported here has been supported by contracts with the National Park Service, Midwest Region, and by National Science Foundation grants GS-1185, 1604, and 2112 to W.R. Wood, and National Science Foundation Grant GB-24710 to R.B. McMillan and E.H. Lindsay. This support is gratefully acknowledged.

We deeply appreciate the assistance of Carl H. Chapman during the first year of the research, when he acted as overall director of the project. The assistance of Wilfred D. Logan and Dale R. Henning in getting the project under way was largely responsible for much of our subsequent success.

Landowners deserve very special mention. The gracious cooperation of Jack Rodgers, the original owner of Rodgers Shelter, is deeply appreciated, as well as the generosity and tolerance of Ivan Trolinger during the fieldwork at the Trolinger Spring. The assistance of the U.S. Army Corps of Engineers and the National Park Service in expediting the excavation permits to conduct our investigations on federally owned land is gratefully acknowledged.

Many individuals contributed not only labor in the field, but numerous ideas to the project. Three of the field supervisors deserve special mention: Stanley A. Ahler, Marvin Kay, and Robert W. Biggs. Nearly 100 workers were employed during the project in both the field and laboratory. The devotion and labor they brought to their tasks made working with them a real pleasure.

During the years of laboratory and library research, individuals too numerous to mention contributed time, space, and ideas to the project. The facilities of the Department of Anthropology, Division of American Archaeology, University of Missouri-Columbia; the Illinois State Museum; the Department of Anthropology, University of Colorado; the Department of Geosciences, University of Arizona; the Department of Geological Sciences, Southern Methodist University; and the Department of Anthropology, University of Kansas bore the brunt of the research. Finally, we are grateful to Violet Jones and Judi Johnson for typing the final draft of the manuscript.

Assistance in radiocarbon dating was provided Haynes by James B. Griffin, University of Michigan; Austin Long, University of Arizona; and E. Mott Davis, Texas Memorial Museum. A special word of appreciation is due Sam Valastro of the last-named organization for his special handling of many of the smaller samples in order to increase the precision of measurement. All specimens illustrated in Chapters 6 and 10 were coated with ammonium chloride before they were photographed.

This volume contains contributions 9 through 24 (Chapters 1–14; Appendices A–B) of the Archaeological and Quaternary Studies Program, Illinois State Museum.

I

The Program

1

Interdisciplinary Studies in the Pomme de Terre River Valley

W. Raymond Wood

It is the purpose of the present study to offer a preliminary model for the paleoecology of the western Ozark Highland for the last 35,000 years and an interpretation of how man has adapted to and exploited the Ozarks for the 10,500 years he is known to have lived in the area. The model, a set of hypotheses that offer a putative explanatory framework for our numerous observations (Clarke 1968: 32), is based on more than a decade of interdisciplinary fieldwork by a score of individuals. It is, nevertheless, a tentative statement needing a great deal of revision and elaboration, in spite of a rather broad data base. The research has centered on the postglacial deposits in a deep rock shelter—Rodgers Shelter—and on five nearby spring bogs, each of which contained the bones of extinct mammals, pollen, and other material dating from late Pleistocene and early Holocene times. Chapters 2 through 12 detail the investigations and subsequent analyses of these sites. A concise statement summarizing the overall conclusions developed here is offered in Chapter 13. The epilogue, Chapter 14, describes the direction of our present and future research— lines of inquiry by which we propose to test aspects of the model developed herein.

The Ozark Highland, or Plateau, is a distinct physiographic province which, together with the Ouachita Mountains, provides the major area of upland relief in the mid-southern United States. These uplands lie nearly midway between the southern Appalachian Mountains and the southern Rocky Mountains, on the boundary between the Coastal Plain and the Central Lowlands (Fenneman 1938). To the south and east are deciduous and coniferous forests extending to the Gulf and Atlantic coasts; to the west, vast prairie and plains areas extend nearly 800 km to the mountains.

Geographers, geologists, and botanists, especially, have long been attracted by the unique features to be found in the Ozarks. Paleontological studies, described later, began in the 1830s with the work of Albert Koch, but the Pleistocene fauna of the area is still very poorly known today (Mehl 1962). By the mid-1890s the physiography of the area had been described by Hershey (1895) and Marbut (1896), but the first geography of the area was not to appear for another 25 years (Sauer 1920). Other aspects of the area have been studied intensively even more recently. Useful studies of the vegetation, for example, postdate 1940 (Steyermark 1940, 1963), and archaeological studies of lasting significance did not begin to appear until the 1930s. Information on Ozark biogeography and prehistory has therefore been accumulating for more than a century. Various technical studies, however, even by recent specialists, have depended largely on the concepts and data from individual disciplines, and no general overview of Ozark ecology or paleoecology has been available.

The Ozarks are south of the areas blanketed by ice during the Pleistocene epoch (Flint 1971: Fig. 2.1), but they were significantly affected by the advancing and retreating ice to the north during that time. Throughout the Pleistocene the vegetation along and south of the glacial fronts was extremely unstable, repeatedly adjusting to changes in glacial masses and climate. Our study locality (described in Chapter 2) is only 400 km southwest of the maximum Wisconsinan ice sheet, well within this zone of vegetational instability. Pleistocene megafauna, including mastodon, muskox, horse, tapir, giant beaver, and ground sloth, and associated vegetational records were recovered from late Pleistocene spring deposits in our study locality—but none of them is known to be contemporaneous with early man (Chapter 6).

The earliest radiocarbon dates for human occupancy of the Ozarks are 10,500 to 10,200 years ago, these dates coming from early levels in Rodgers Shelter. Archaeological remains in this area from that time to about the time of Christ (or a little earlier) are referred to the Archaic Period. Cultural groups of the Early, Middle, and Late Archaic were hunters and gatherers, depending principally on deer and other modern small game, on shellfish and other riverine resources, and on local vegetal produce. These populations underwent a long period of adaptation to the changing postglacial environmental conditions in the western Ozarks and in the nearby prairie areas (described in Chapter 12).

The succeeding Woodland Period may be locally bracketed approximately within the first millennium A.D. Early Woodland subsistence, settlements, and tools are not very different from those of Late Archaic groups, but there is the addition of pottery to their household inventories. Woodland groups probably cultivated some crops, but they were still essentially hunters and gatherers. The Woodland groups were replaced, about a millennium ago, by peoples of the Mississippian Period. These horticultural people, in western Missouri, were the predecessors and probable ancestors of the historic Osage Indians. The Osage lived along the middle reaches of the Osage River when the first European explorers entered western Missouri. They were moved to Kansas and Oklahoma in 1823, about the time the area was first being settled by Europeans. This, then, is the skeleton outline of the story we hoped to flesh out by our work in and around Rodgers Shelter.

The team research reported here began in the early 1960s, commencing, modestly enough, with limited archaeological salvage at Rodgers Shelter. The University of Missouri–Columbia, in cooperation with the National Park Service, Midwest Region, was at that time conducting an archaeological reconnaissance of the Harry S. Truman (then Kaysinger Bluff) Reservoir area.[1] This impoundment, a project of the U.S. Army Corps of Engineers, will eventually inundate at full flood pool 847 km² of bottomland along the Osage River and up the lower reaches of its tributaries in southwestern Missouri. The dam, to be built near the town of Warsaw, will back water nearly to the Kansas–Missouri boundary, and some 29 airline km up the valley of the Pomme de Terre River. Rodgers Shelter was discovered during a routine reconnaissance of the lower Pomme de Terre valley by Rolland E. Pangborn in the spring of 1962. The site will be permanently inundated when the Harry S. Truman Reservoir reaches full pool level, as will several of the nearby spring bogs.

Rodgers Shelter is near the north edge of a large river bottomland area, part of which was formed by an old cut-off meander of the Pomme de Terre River. The old meander, locally referred to as "Breshears Bottoms," is enclosed by the relatively undissected, prairie uplands of the western Ozark Highland, into which the river has cut a trench 90 to 100 m deep. A varied environment is present within a short distance of the shelter, since riverbottom forest and prairie, and upland forest and prairie biomes all occur within a few kilometers of the site. The prairie–forest dichotomy in part reflects the fact that the shelter is near the ecotone between the oak–hickory forests of the Ozark Highland and the prairie areas of western Missouri.

---

[1] Since Harry S Truman had no middle name, there properly should be no period after his middle initial. However, a period was inadvertently placed after his middle initial when the reservoir was ratified by Congress. Today, legally and officially, the lower Pomme de Terre basin will be inundated by the Harry S. Truman Reservoir.

The shelter appeared to be a choice location in which to seek stratified archaeological deposits within the reservoir, for it faced directly south, and its earthen floor was well above river flood levels. Both conditions were favored by prehistoric rock shelter inhabitants. The first tests were dug in the shelter in 1963, with work continuing under and in front of the overhang for the next 5 years, through 1968. Nearly 13 months were eventually spent in the field there.

The first excavations beneath the overhang were made by William E. Sudderth and Sidney Denny, then graduate students at the University of Missouri–Columbia. They dug a 10.7 m long trench to an average depth of 60 cm, penetrating a rich Late Archaic and Woodland deposit. Excavations were halted when a thick deposit of sterile gravel-sized colluvium was reached. Because of the richness of the deposits, and because they contained material that was then poorly known in the area, more extensive excavations were planned the following year. R.B. McMillan assumed charge of the work the next season, in 1964, and continued as field director for the duration of the project. Responsibility for the overall direction of the research, initially under the guidance of Carl H. Chapman, was assumed by W. R. Wood in 1965.

The surficial Late Archaic and Woodland deposits were investigated in 1964, and a test pit, dug to determine the depth of the deposits, penetrated the sterile layer of colluvium. Beneath it was a thick, very rich Middle to Late Archaic midden averaging about 1.5 m thick. This midden deposit was tested extensively in 1965 by means of a large block excavation, and the test pit begun the previous year was dug to the water table, 7 m below the surface. Just above the water table McMillan discovered chipped stone tools in charcoal-flecked occupational levels, clear evidence of human habitation much earlier in time than the Middle to Late Archaic deposits some 3.5 m higher.

By 1968 the block excavation had been taken to the base of the deposits, exposing Early Archaic features in several occupational levels, with sufficient associated charcoal to date them. By this time, Rodgers Shelter had yielded one of the longest and most nearly complete cultural sequences in the Midwest. The thickness of the deposits greatly enhance its significance, for cultural material that is often compressed into thin layers in most Ozark rock shelters is separated at Rodgers by thick layers of alluvium and colluvium. The various cultural components, therefore, are more readily separable, yielding a clearer picture of the cultural sequence than had previously been available. This sequence is described and interpreted in Chapters 7 through 12.

Other, and concurrent, work was also planned in the locality. There are a number of spring bogs in old alluvial terraces along the south side of the old meander to the south of the shelter, and there are others west of Rodgers Shelter, and further south along the Pomme de Terre River.

One of these, the Koch Spring, had been investigated in 1840 by Albert Koch (Chapter 5), who claimed to have found cultural remains associated with mastodon bones in the spring deposits (Koch 1857). These springs were slated for reinvestigation before they, also, were to be inundated by the reservoir.

Specialists in a variety of disciplines, however, were required for this work, as well as for specialized studies being initiated at Rodgers Shelter, for the project by this time had greatly transcended a routine salvage operation. In 1966 C. Vance Haynes, Jr. began geochronological studies in the valley (Chapter 3), and Peter J. Mehringer, Jr. and James E. King began pollen work about the same time. Paul W. Parmalee and William M. Bass III were working on the animal and human bone, respectively, from the shelter. Everett H. Lindsay began paleontological work in 1968, assisted in 1971 by Jeffrey J. Saunders. Each of these specialists participated directly in the fieldwork, especially that devoted to the investigation of the Quaternary deposits in the spring bogs.

Although excavations in the springs had been planned to explore the possibility that they might contain cultural remains associated with extinct mammals, they were tested in 1966 and 1967 for an additional reason. Several attempts were made to recover pollen from the deposits at Rodgers Shelter, but it was too poorly preserved to be useful. Consequently, since pollen is often well preserved in spring deposits, the springs were tested to obtain pollen profiles that we then hoped to correlate, using radiocarbon determinations, with the deposits at Rodgers Shelter. Boney Spring, only 2.5 km west of the shelter, was sampled with a piston corer by Mehringer and Wood in 1966. The core revealed a spruce-dominated pollen record, spruce and larch macrofossils, and bone and tusk fragments—clearly documenting a boreal forest environment (Mehringer *et al.* 1968). The pollen spectrum came from a bone bed about 4 m below the surface.

Boney Spring, so named because local residents said that pieces of bone boiled to the surface at times of heavy spring discharge, consists of a funnel-shaped conduit or feeder overlain by a heavy mat of vegetation. It is surrounded by marshy ground supporting a heavy growth of lush aquatic plants. It had not been disturbed by previous excavations, but the conduit was choked with limbs and lumber that had been thrust into it to determine its depth.

Boney Spring was to become the most intensively excavated of the five local springs. Attempts were made to excavate the bone bed in 1967 and 1968, but it was almost impossible to obtain fossil bones and sample associated sediments because of the heavy artesian discharge. Working under controlled conditions was all but impossible, for the water could not be disposed of adequately. In 1971 wells were drilled around the edge of the spring, and pumps were used to draw the water table down below the bone bed. It was then possible to dry out and expose completely the bone bed and to excavate it systematically. Trenches were later cut to bedrock below the bone bed, yielding a 7-m-deep, intermittent depositional and associated vegetal record from about 28,000 to 4200 years ago. Archaeological investigations around the edges of the spring revealed an Early Woodland component dating to about the time of Christ.

The Koch Spring is about 5 km south of Rodgers Shelter, set on the edge of a low terrace on the west bank of the river, overlooking the river bottomlands. When work was begun there in 1971 it was a marshy depression rimmed by Koch's old backdirt piles, with the spring discharge flowing over the terrace edge to the east. Koch presumably dug into the center of the spring and removed or disturbed the upper 1.5 m of sediment above the bones, but he left extensive peat beds and other sediments intact below and to the sides of his excavation.

Several test pits were dug around the margin of the spring to determine the nature and extent of archaeological remains in the vicinity. Three wells were then drilled around the spring, and the water table was lowered by pumping, as at Boney Spring. Matrix, pollen, and radiocarbon samples were taken from trenches dug in and near the spring. Trenches into the center of Koch's nineteenth-century excavation proved that he had completely excavated the spring's original bone bed. Because of the prior disturbance no attempt was made to drain the spring completely and excavate the remainder of the peat deposit.

There are three other springs along the south edge of the old abandoned meander: Trolinger, Jones, and Kirby springs Each of them was tested, but only Trolinger Spring was extensively investigated.

Trolinger Spring had been an artesian spring of low volume discharge until 1964, when its flow ceased and the surface over the conduit became dry. There was no apparent surface indication of its former presence in 1966 except for a small stake driven in the ground above the center of the conduit. In spite of appearances, an initial trench across the spring revealed there was still moisture less than 1 m deep. A bone-laden peat deposit, saturated with water, was only 1.5 m below the surface. It was eventually practical to excavate Trolinger Spring under controlled conditions by cutting a trench from the conduit and draining water into a nearby sump. Most of the conduit was excavated in 1967 and 1968.

A few hundred meters west of Trolinger Spring is another artesian spring, Jones Spring. Some years past, a pond had been dug above it, although this apparently had little effect on the discharge. In 1971 a short trench was cut to drain the pond. A trench cut into its floor exposed a rich peat beneath alluvial terrace deposits, yielding tusk fragments, remains of two kinds of large turtles, and plant macrofossils.

A few hundred meters west of Jones Spring is Kirby Spring. This spring had been dug in the mid-1800s by local residents, probably inspired by Koch's earlier success in obtaining mastodon bones in 1840. The apparent center of the spring was disturbed to an uncertain depth, and is today ringed by a pile of backdirt containing tusk and bone fragments. Because of its disturbed nature, no attempt was made to dig there, but a trench was cut into undisturbed deposits near the west side of the spring. A peat deposit was exposed, yielding plant macrofossils, pollen (but no vertebrate fossils), and radiocarbon samples.

There are now nearly 40 radiocarbon dates from the spring deposits, and another 11 dates from Rodgers Shelter. The radiocarbon dating program is being coordinated by Haynes. All of the faunal remains, pollen profiles, significant plant macrofossils, radiocarbon samples, and the stratigraphy of each site have been studied and mapped. The faunal and floral remains have been placed in a stratigraphic sequence in each of the springs. Using radiocarbon data and pollen analyses for control, the stratigraphic sequence in the different springs has been correlated, providing the first comprehensive outline of the late Quaternary biogeography and geologic history of the area.

The geological setting of the Pomme de Terre valley and the late Quaternary biogeography of the area are summarized in Chapters 3 and 4. The late Quaternary events chronicled in these springs, from about 35,000 to 12,000 years ago, set the stage for the appearance of man in the area—for in none of the springs was there clear evidence of the contemporaneity of man with any of the extinct faunas.

The same team has conducted the field and laboratory work for the past decade, so there is a high level of continuity in the research. Various individuals and combinations of individuals have, indeed, acted as principal investigators for the project as one or another research tactic was emphasized, but the overall research strategy and field plans have not changed: to outline the past environments of the Ozarks, and to understand how man adapted to, and perhaps modified, those environments.

This continuity in personnel is very important, for we have labored under the handicap that most of us are in different institutions. We are consequently widely separated, making it possible for us to meet only in the summers when fieldwork is in progress, although we have been able to get together at national and regional meetings. A great deal of correspondence, therefore, has been necessary to collate field plans and results, and we have been deprived of the stimulation gained from the constant interaction possible between individuals at the same institution. Our long association, however, has made it possible for us in part to negate this fractionation, for we know how other members operate and how they are likely to approach problems. We have not always agreed, but our disagreements have always been minor, and the problems quickly resolved so that what was really important—the research—could move along efficiently. We were exceptionally fortunate in being able to assemble a team capable of weathering the vicissitudes of a decade of close association.

The story that this team details in the chapters to follow, then, begins in the late Pleistocene, near the middle of the fourth and last glacial stage, and chronicles the fluctuating climate and vegetation along the western margin of the Ozark Highland, and man's entrance into and long history in the area. It is a story of success and of failure: success in piecing together a long story of the late Quaternary events in the area, but a failure in that (so far) it has not been possible to overlap this climatic–vegetational sequence with the very long cultural sequence from Rodgers Shelter. It is a story nevertheless well worth the telling, even in its incomplete form, and it provides a model that must be tested and elaborated by workers in many disciplines.

Early in the work it was realized that the nature and depth of the deposits at Rodgers Shelter, the fact that it lay on a major ecotone, and the fact that springs known to be rich in biogeographical data were in the vicinity combined to make the study area an ideal one for late Quaternary environmental studies. Although the early work was salvage oriented, the program expanded rapidly as the research potential of the area was realized. It would, in fact, be difficult to have chosen in advance an area as rich in potential for late Quaternary studies as our study locality. These happy circumstances are, unfortunately, marred by the fact that Rodgers Shelter—and most of the nearby springs—will be permanently inundated by the Harry S. Truman Reservoir.

The remains that will be lost in the lower Pomme de Terre River valley are a national asset, not only to archaeology, but to all of those disciplines concerned with reconstructing the past so that we may better understand the present. Rodgers Shelter, for example, has been placed on the National Register of Historic Places because of the significance of its deposits. We have, in brief, developed a cultural and biogeographical model for the late Quaternary of western Missouri rich in detail. As fresh evidence has been unearthed, the model (and related hypotheses) has changed, converging on "an increasingly small number of increasingly more powerful hypotheses [Clarke 1968:435]." Models of any sort must be continually tested, especially those built on a limited number of cases. The tragedy in this case is that those sites most ideally suited to test the model will be lost beneath the waters of the Harry S. Truman Reservoir.

REFERENCES

Clarke, D.L.
1968 *Analytical archaeology*. London: Methuen & Co., Ltd.
Fenneman, N.M.
1938 *Physiography of eastern United States*. New York: McGraw-Hill.

Flint, R.F.
1971 *Glacial and Quaternary geology*. New York: Wiley.
Hershey, O.H.
1895 River valleys of the Ozark plateau. *American Geologist* **16:** 338–352.
Koch, A.C.
1857 Mastodon remains in the State of Missouri, together with evidence of the existence of man contemparaneously with the mastodon. *Transactions of the Academy of Science*, St. Louis **1:** 61–64.
Marbut, C.F.
1896 Physical features of Missouri. *Missouri Geological Survey* **10:** 11–109.
Mehl, M.G.
1962 Missouri's ice age mammals. State of Missouri, Division of Geological Survey and Water Resources, *Educational Series* No. 1.
Mehringer, P.J., C.E. Schweger, W.R. Wood, and R.B. McMillan
1968 Late-Pleistocene boreal forest in the western Ozark highlands? *Ecology* **49:** 567–568.
Sauer, C.O.
1920 The geography of the Ozark highland of Missouri. *The Geographic Society of Chicago*, Bulletin 7. Chicago, Illinois: Univ. of Chicago Press.
Steyermark, J.A.
1940 Studies of the vegetation of Missouri—I, natural plant associations and succession in the Ozarks of Missouri. Field Museum of Natural History, Pub. 485, *Botanical Series* **9:** 349–475.
1963 *Flora of Missouri*. Ames, Iowa: Iowa State Univ. Press.

2

The Pomme de Terre
Study Locality:
Its Setting

R. Bruce McMillan

The lower Pomme de Terre River drainage constitutes a part of the western border of the Ozark Highland where this dissected plateau merges with Missouri's unglaciated prairie region. This is approximately 95 km north of Springfield, Missouri and 150 km southeast of Kansas City. This river, where our research program is centered, is an affluent of the Osage River, which in turn is one of the larger tributaries of the lower Missouri River.

Locally, the area studied is about half the distance between the communities of Warsaw, on the north, and Wheatland, to the south. The latter, where our field camp was headquartered for 5 years, is famous in the anthropological literature as *Plainville, U.S.A.* (West 1945; Gallaher 1961).

Within the next few years the area under consideration will be inundated beneath the waters of the Harry S. Truman Reservoir, an impoundment authorized by Congress under the United States Flood Control Act of 1954 (United States Army 1967). The proposed 225-km² conservation-power pool, bordered by a shoreline of over 1500 km, will destroy by inundation or lake-inspired development most of the antiquities of the Osage River basin between Warsaw, Missouri and the Missouri counties that border the Kansas state line. This will surely be the *coup de grace* to

be perpetrated on the region's landscape following the many changes that
have transpired since pioner settlement.

The most important geographic consideration of the study locality is its
location on the border between two major biogeographical and physical
provinces. Physiographically, the locality is in an area where the hilly
Ozark Plateau merges with the rolling residual plains of the Mid-Continent Lowland. The eastern deciduous forest also meets the tall grass
prairie here, and forms a mosaic of forest and grassland habitats (Küchler
1964:82). Although there is a general correspondence between the biota,
surficial landscape features, and the subsurface geology, there is not
always a one-to-one correlation. As a result, geographers have found it
difficult to delineate definite borders between these complex physiographic and biotic provinces.

Sauer (1920:66) characterized this border region as historically and
physiographically part of the Ozarks, although resembling eastern
Kansas. This was apparently true in prehistoric times as well. The
primeval environment offered all the major resources—floral, faunal, and
geological—found in the central Ozarks; per contra, a much greater percentage of the Pomme de Terre landscape was covered with tall grass
prairie than were areas to the east.

GEOGRAPHY AND GEOLOGY

The lower Pomme de Terre River forms a sinuous border between
what has variously been called the Salem Plateau (Fenneman 1938:647;
Bretz 1965:30-31) or Central Plateau (Sauer 1920:70) on the east and the
Springfield Plain to the west (Sauer 1920:66-67) (Figure 2.1). The former
is moderately dissected with steep relief along its deeply incised streams.
Between basins on the Salem surface there are numerous small plateaus.
The least dissected region of the Ozarks is the Springfield Plain.

Most physiographers delineate the Springfield Plain as a physiographic
region distinguishable from the residual Cherokee Plains of eastern
Kansas, Oklahoma, and extreme western Missouri (Marbut 1896:60-67;
Fenneman 1938:652–655; Sauer 1920:66–67). This separation is principally based on differences in the subsurface geology, as the underlying
formations become progressively younger as one moves west. The older,
uplifted Ordovician rocks exposed throughout the central Ozarks are
overlain by Mississippian limestones in the Springfield Plain (Branson
1944:351; McCracken 1961). To the west, the Cherokee Plains are formed
on younger Pennsylvanian shales (Fenneman 1938:613).

Basing the distinction between the Springfield Plain and the plains to
the west simply on underlying formations has not been satisfactory to
some observers. Branson (1944:350–351) observed that the hilly regions
of the Springfield Plain grade almost imperceptibly into the surrounding

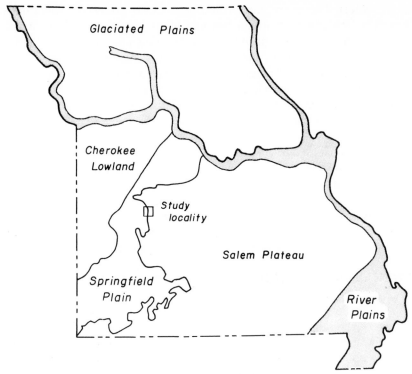

Figure 2.1 The study locality, showing its intermediate location between the Salem Plateau and the Cherokee Lowland. (Adapted from Fenneman 1938: Pl.6; and Marbut 1896: Pl.2.)

plains regions, and contends that "there is no structural, geologic, or topographic feature to set off the Springfield Structural Plains from the old plains further west. . . ." Following this reasoning, the Missouri Geological Survey presently does not include the Springfield Plain under the general term of "Ozarks" (Bretz 1965:95).

The undissected upland plateaus of the study areas lie some 100 m above the valley floors and about 300 m above mean sea level; closer to the streams, the bordering hills normally rise 60 m above the valley floor. Exposures of Lower Ordovician Jefferson City dolomite form many bluffs along stream meanders (McCracken 1961; McMillen 1950:14); the uplands are formed on limestone and dolomites of Mississippian age. Chert is abundant in both of these systems.

The Pomme de Terre River is typical of most Ozark streams, flowing northward along its winding path for over 160 km, from northwest of the city of Springfield to its confluence with the Osage River near the former streamside village of Fairfield. The stream's steepest gradient is near its source where there are numerous small pools connected by rapids. Gradually, the gradient diminishes and in its lower portion the stream slows to a more sluggish pace with longer eddies and fewer riffles. The clear water, augmented by numerous springs along its course, flows over a bed floored with chert fragments weathered and eroded from the surrounding hills. The stream bottom is much more resistant to cutting than the banks, causing considerable lateral shifting of the stream's course. Consequently, the stream bed is often many times wider than the stream itself.

The meandering course of the Pomme de Terre usually has one steep side on the outer or convex part of the curve; the inner or concave side of meanders is usually reached by long, gradual, "slip-off" slopes, often terraced near the stream. These slopes provide easy access from the valleys to the uplands. Meanders are sometimes cut off, leaving abandoned valleys encircling a "lost hill," as illustrated by the Breshears Bottoms near the center of the study locality (Chapter 3).

MINERAL RESOURCES

There are a number of rocks and minerals that occur on or near the surface of the landscape in the lower Pomme de Terre area that would have been readily available to prehistoric man. Vegetation, or the lack thereof, and erosion may have influenced the availability of these resources at various times during the Holocene.

Chert is ubiquitous throughout the area where it weathers from the lower Ordovician Jefferson City dolomite. Most of it is dark or light gray and blue–gray, and is mottled or banded with white. Few fossils occur in these cherts although much of it is öolitic. Although chert occurs abundantly on the surfaces of the hills and slopes and in the stream beds, most of it is frost fractured and weathered. With little difficulty, however, one can find large rounded to oblong nodules or small boulders buried in the hillside residuum just below the frost line; this source is far more satisfactory for the manufacture of chipped stone tools. Because of the widespread occurrence of the Jefferson City cherts and their proximity to the surface, no aboriginal quarrying operations are known in connection with this formation.

A second geologic formation rich in chert is the Mississippian-aged Burlington formation, which generally encircles the Ozark Highland in Missouri (Branson 1944:Fig. 6; Klippel 1971b:11–13). Although Burlington limestone outcrops in a few places at the very hilltops in the study locality, the closest known source of the characteristic fossiliferous chert of this formation is some 40 km upstream from the study area. At that location in Polk County were extensive aboriginal quarries in the residuum above the Burlington formation. They are still visible today

(Turner 1954:10). In general, however, the Burlington cherts do not appear to have been as important a resource in the lower Pomme de Terre valley as the more common varieties from the Jefferson City formation.

Lower Ordovician dolomites suitable for tool manufacture are available throughout the area. Sandstone, while not as common, does occur in beds in the Jefferson City formation, sometimes as much as 1 m thick (Branson 1944:50). It can be found in the lower Pomme de Terre today on hilltops and in stream beds.

A soft and very fine-grained argillaceous siliceous dolomite, called "cottonrock" (Branson 1944:50), occurs in the Jefferson City formation and can be found on the hillsides and in the beds of hollows. Because it can be easily worked, this white, gray, yellow, or buff mineral was a useful resource to aboriginal craftsmen.

Hematite and galena, sources of pigment in prehistoric times, are abundant throughout the Pomme de Terre valley. The first mineral surveys of Benton and Hickory counties record the presence of both of these minerals on many upland exposures as well as in the beds of streams (Shumard 1867; Broadhead 1880). Broadhead (1880:6) stressed that the "iron ore" was found in many places where "it is chiefly found in clay and chert masses overlying the solid limestone beds and sometimes in crevices in the limestone. The ores are specular and limonite, the latter including some ochrey beds."

Galena, or lead ore, was observed in gash veins or pockets in the local dolomites associated with barite, calcite, limonite, malachite, chalcopyrite, and iron pyrites (Broadhead 1880:3). One stream bed only 2 km from Rodgers Shelter was described as being littered with float galena. Shumard (1867:21), in describing this source, observed that "the masses of ore are well rounded, and from a few grains to several pounds in weight, and they are so abundant that I could have gathered several hundred pounds in a couple hours."

SOILS

Pedologists recognize five basic environmental variables that interact during soil formation—climate, organisms, topography, parent material, and time (Holowaychuk 1960:6–19; Ruhe 1969:11). Given the varying degrees of interrelationships among these variables, a pedologist can, within reason, predict the soil type that will be produced under a specified set of conditions. Conversely, the analysis of a given soil affords information on the past processes that led to its formation.

When attempting to elicit past conditions from present soils, two of the above factors, topography and parent material, are relatively constant. A third factor, time, is a variable related to the interaction of the other four variables. The factors that tend to oscillate most, but whose past may still be reflected in present soils, are the biota (organisms) and climate.

Soil color is an important criterion in attempting to educe the past biota from a soil. Prairie soils are usually darker and distinguishable from the lighter red, gray, or brown forest soils (Thorp 1968: Fig. 1). Bottomland soils are notable exceptions in that they are dark colored even under forest (Krusekopf 1962:6).

The study area is positioned between the major regions of darker prairie to the west and lighter forest soils to the east. Unfortunately, detailed soil surveys have not been made of Benton and Hickory counties; the best available maps show only a generalized distinction between the two zones (Krusekopf 1962:1; Scrivner *et al.* 1966:4). The maps do, however, show that the prairie and forest soils generally correspond with the prairie–forest regions presented by Steyermark (1963: xix), and with the topographically different Salem Plateau (forest) and Springfield Plain (prairie).

The soils east of the Pomme de Terre River are characterized by Scrivner *et al.* (1966:25) as forested, highly weathered pediments, developed from cherty dolomite, limestone, and sandstone. These are the Lebanon–Nixa–Clarksville and Hobson–Clarksville associations. West

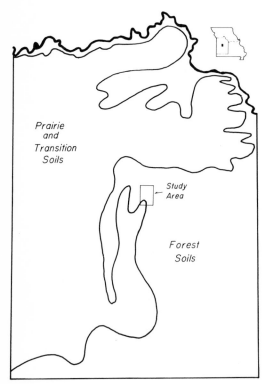

Prairie
and
Transition
Soils

Study
Area

Forest
Soils

Figure 2.2 Location of the study locality along the boundary between forest soils, and prairie and prairie-forest transition soils. (After Scrivner *et al.* 1966:4.)

of the Pomme de Terre basin, soils are generally classified as the Gerald–Craig–Eldon and Baxter–Newtonia associations. They are formed from cherty limestones, and for the most part are dark-colored prairie soils (Scrivner *et al.* 1966:21). Baxter soils, the one exception, occur on the steeper slopes where they developed under forest conditions.

Describing the Pomme de Terre basin as the approximate dividing line between these major soil associations is an oversimplification of a complex distribution of soil types. But because detailed soils maps do not exist, it is impossible to plot the distribution of native vegetation known for the study area against soil types as Howell and Kucera (1956: Fig. 4) did for Boone County, Missouri.

Even in the absence of detailed soils maps, it is evident that the distribution of soil associations tend to corroborate our maps for the native vegetation (Figure 2.2).

CLIMATE

The contemporary climate of west–central Missouri is highly variable, and to describe it in terms of averages or means inadequately expresses its complexity. The principal usefulness of citing means is to indicate the average type weather expected during different time periods (Metcalf and Klingner 1963:18). The climatic means that characterize the contemporary weather patterns have been included for the study area (Table 2.1), but one should keep in mind Transeau's (1935:436) warning that "the extremes of factors are vastly more important than the means . . . an extreme drought marked by lower precipitation, higher evaporation, higher temperatures, and more intensive light can change vegetation more in a few years than a century of favorable weather conditions."

TABLE 2.1 Contemporary Climatic Data for the Study Locality[a]

TEMPERATURE (centigrade)	
Mean maximum temperature—January	6.5° to 7.5°C
Mean minimum temperature—January	−5.5° to −4.4°C
Mean maximum temperature—July	32°C
Mean minimum temperature—July	20°C
PRECIPITATION	
Mean annual precipitation	101.6 cm
Spring	30.48 cm
Summer	30.48 cm
Autumn	25.4 cm
Winter	15.24 cm
GROWING SEASON	
Average date for last killing frost	April 5
Average date for first killing frost	October 30

[a]Adapted from Metcalf and Klingner (1963) and Decker (1955).

Most precipitation in the study area occurs in the spring and summer. Although it occurs in approximately equal amounts during this time (Table 2.1) the effective moisture pattern is substantially different. Spring rains are usually light, but are effective since they last for some time. By comparison, summer precipitation usually comes in the form of heavy, infrequent thunderstorms of short duration that provide less effective moisture and are potentially erosive (Metcalf and Klingner 1963:16–18).

The study area is today in a region affected by both the continental mild Pacific air masses and the Maritime airflow from the Gulf of Mexico. The warm moist Gulf air, which creates the conditions for abundant winter precipitation in the Southeastern United States, decreases as it moves northward and thus has a minimal effect in this part of Missouri.

The weather patterns are basically those described by Borchert (1950:29) for his Climatic Region IV, the wedge-shaped midcontinent area of tall grass prairies, often called the Prairie Peninsula. The major characteristics for the region are:

1. low winter rainfall and snowfall;
2. occasional major summer droughts with a tendency for major summer droughts to occur synchronously within the region;
3. a continental source and trajectory of the mean airstream which blankets the region during dry periods.

These weather patterns produce frequent droughts that have tremendous ecological impact on ecotones such as the one being considered. Since droughts tend to favor grasses over arboreal species, there is a tendency for a forest–prairie border to shift, with the grasslands expanding and contracting in relation to the fluctuating climate. The dynamics of these vegetational perturbations and their implications for human adaptation are discussed later (Chapter 12).

FLORA

In any treatment of the relationship between prehistoric man and his environment, the composition and distribution of the vegetation is pivotal to understanding the culture process itself. Since subsistence strategies of human groups at a technological level comparable to those considered in later chapters are directly dependent on local plant and animal resources, it is essential that we have some understanding of the locality's past biota.

The principal plant regions of Missouri generally correspond to the location of the physiographic areas previously described, but the boundaries are not quite identical (Figure 2.3). Viewed broadly, the floral cover of the Ozark Plateau is a deciduous oak–hickory climax forest. The community, with its associated herbaceous plants, belongs to the Carolinian flora (Dice 1943:18), and is floristically intermediate between the austral and boreal phases (Steyermark 1963:xx). Along the western border of the Ozarks, the region that includes the study area, a post oak–black jack oak association is commonly widespread (Figure 2.4) because of increased xerophytism (Braun 1950:167; Sauer 1920:58). By contrast, the Springfield Plain and Cherokee Lowland are dominated by grasses of Dice's (1943:22) Illinoian biotic type.

This characterization can only be applied in general terms, however. Many prairie outliers occur throughout the Ozarks, where wedgelike extensions of grassland plants penetrate the region. Colonies of prairie plants also occupy cedar glades and other forest openings (Figure 2.5) that have xeric environments (Steyermark 1963:xviii). Sauer (1920:52) notes that grass was usually coextensive with level land, growing on the undissected plateau remnants (Figure 2.6). Further west into the prairie, woody oak–hickory communities can be found on some dissected areas, and along stream valleys arboreal bottomland species continue into the tall grass prairie.

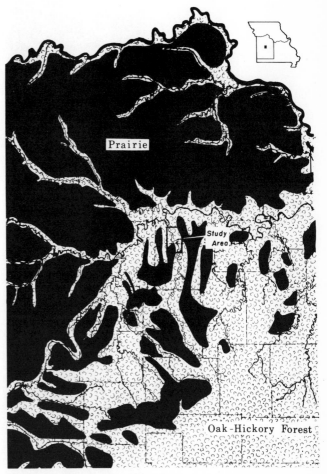

Figure 2.3 Location of the study locality along the oak–hickory (Ozark Highland)–Prairie Peninsula border. (Prairie-forest distribution after Transeau 1935.)

Figure 2.4 Oak-hickory forest along the Pomme de Terre.

Figure 2.5 Cedar glades and barrens east of Rodgers Shelter.

Figure 2.6 Undissected plateau south of Wheatland. It originally supported native prairie.

Although Steyermark (1959, 1963) has extensively described the Missouri Ozark's flora, the distribution and composition of modern vegetation is not the same as it was at the time of pioneer settlement. Sauer (1920:59) notes the following changes:

1. a greater density of trees and more undergrowth, a result of cutting the large timber and the cessation of fires;
2. a great decrease in the bottomland forest because of clearing;
3. a relative increase of those species that have the most efficient means of propagation. For example, the oaks and elms, with their coppicing habits; and in the bottoms, the sycamores and cottonwood, with windblown seeds.

HISTORICAL MODELS

In order to develop data on the distribution and composition of past plant communities one has to turn to historical records from the nineteenth century. This is essential because of the marked biogeographic changes that have transpired during the relatively brief Euro–American Period. For example, Terasmae (1967:209) estimates that only about one-tenth of one percent of the eastern woodlands remains in primeval conditions, and even smaller relicts of the original prairie exist today (Gordon 1969:54; Evers 1955:367).

Modern flora can be used to glean some information on past phytogeography and the composition of plant communities—if one recognizes the many pitfalls. When using modern botanical data one has to be cognizant not only of the effect of the many introduced Old World species, but also of the great extent to which the native vegetation has been altered by timbering, cultivation, and fire control. Bourdo (1956:754), for one, stressed that "second-growth stands and scattered old-growth remnants cannot, without great hazard, be used alone to delineate original vegetation, much less to provide information on its composition."

The problem of constructing past phytogeographical models, while of relatively recent interest in archaeology, has been a concern of botanists since the early part of this century. Sears (1970:556) has pointed out that once ecology moved from its descriptive phase to an emphasis on dynamic and genetic problems, an interest in time and process led to a concern for establishing some kind of datum against which change could be measured.

A number of historical lines of evidence contribute data for constructing models of the native vegetation. Perhaps the most instructive are the United States Federal Land Surveys, available for most areas of the United States. The use of land survey data for mapping native vegetation was first outlined by Paul B. Sears in 1921; subsequently, he demonstrated their usefulness by mapping Ohio's vegetation (Sears 1921, 1925,

1926). Since then many botanists have used the technique (for example, bibliographies in Bourdo 1956; Gordon 1969).

Few studies in Missouri have employed the land surveys for mapping the presettlement flora. Steyermark (1959:60–92) consulted the land surveys to support his argument that forestation in the Ozarks is not a recent phenomenon, as contended by Beilman and Brenner (1951a, b), but I can find only one Ozarks county in which there has been an actual attempt to map the native vegetation. In Dade County, about 80 km southwest of the study area, Howell and Kucera (1956) mapped the composition and distribution of the pioneer vegetation using data from the Federal Land Surveys. Recently, Klippel (1971a:30–43), in his ecologically oriented analysis of the changing Archaic subsistence patterns at Graham Cave, Missouri, used the plats and notes from the land surveys to model the pioneer flora.

Use of the Federal Land Surveys

The potential of the Federal Land Surveys as a source of historical data for mapping the pioneer flora is enhanced by the fact that they were written on location according to a preconceived plan. Moreover, they are usable for quantitative work as well as qualitative analyses since they constitute a definite sample of vegetation (Bourdo 1956:754). Types of information that the surveyors were instructed to record in their field notes, helpful in demarcating the boundaries and character of vegetation types as well as other geographic features, are listed in Table 2.2.

TABLE 2.2   Vegetation Details Recorded in the United States Federal Land Surveys[a]

1. The species, diameter, distance, and bearing of two to four witness trees at every section corner.

2. The species, diameter, distance, and bearing of two witness trees at every quarter section.

3. The species, diameter, and distance of all trees occurring on section lines.

4. All rivers, creeks, and smaller streams of water, with their right-angled width, the type of current, and their course where the lines of the survey intersected or crossed them.

5. All lakes and ponds, with the description of banks surrounding them, and whether the water was deep or shallow and pure or stagnant.

6. All prairies, swamps, and marshes.

7. All coal banks or beds, and peat or turf grounds.

8. All precipices, caves, stone quarries, and ledges of rock, with the kind of stone found in them.

9. The tracks of tornadoes, commonly called windfalls or fallen timber, showing the direction of the wind, as indicated by the fallen trees.

10. The distance the surveyors entered and left every lake, bay, pond, creek, bottom, windfall, grove, prairie, ravine, marsh, and swamp, with the course of the same at both points of intersection.

[a]Adapted from Bourdo (1956).

There may have been some bias in the selection of witness trees (Bourdo 1956:761; Gordon 1969:19), but the overall distortion caused by nonrandom selection is probably not great enough to affect our overall model. Sears (1970:556), for example, assures us that "a tree had to be present to be noted." So for most types of vegetation, species preferences will not prove to be important because the choice of trees adjacent to a corner was limited (Bourdo 1956:767).

Pre-Settlement Vegetation

The 18-x-15-km study locality paralleling the lower Pomme de Terre valley in Townships 38N and 39N, Range 22W, was mapped using the notes and plats from the original land surveys on file at the Missouri State Archives, Jefferson City. All witness trees and line descriptions were plotted on working maps and, from these, a model was compiled locating and delineating the borders of the major vegetational zones as they appeared during the early nineteenth century (Figure 2.7).

For many places the plats from the land surveys define the boundaries of forests, prairies, barrens, etc., but the plats for the study area failed to show the limits of the vegetational zones. Thus, the major floral areas had to be mapped from the surveyors' notes. Using the descriptions in the notes, it was possible to plot the distances from the section corners on a scaled working map each time the surveyors recorded a change in vegetation (i.e., prairie to forest). The points on various section lines were then connected to construct the outlines of the vegetational zones. Five major areas were defined using this method: upland prairie, bottomland prairie, oak barrens, oak–hickory forest, and bottomland forest.

The surveyors' notes contained two sets of data that could be subjected to quantitative treatment. The more objective, and most satisfactory for quantification, were the records of witness trees at quarter sections and section corners (Table 2.2:1–2). These records provided a uniform sample at one-half mile (.8 km) intervals in every direction. The frequency of occurrence for each species was then calculated for each of the vegetational zones (Table 2.3; Figure 2.8).

The surveyors' line descriptions provided a less objective set of data, but one that afforded a check on the witness tree sample. At the end of each mile (1.6 km), the surveyors gave an impressionistic evaluation of the land along the section line they had just passed. For example: "Land on this line mostly rolling and rich with open woods of post oak, black oak, and black hickory [James 1844:67]." Each time a plant was mentioned in a line description, it was counted, and the frequency of the different species computed for all zones (Table 2.4; Figure 2.8).

By employing these techniques, the land surveys provided a valuable insight into the composition of the arboreal plant communities. Unfortunately, this was not the case with the prairie communities; only their

TABLE 2.3 Comparison of the Frequency of Witness Trees in the Major Vegetation Zones [a]

Common names recorded (species interpreted)	Barrens		Oak – Hickory		Bottomland		Total
	Number	Percentage	Number	Percentage	Number	Percentage	
Post oak							
(*Quercus stellata*)	131	58.0	104	45.6	—	—	235
Black oak							
(*Quercus velutina*)	43	19.0	40	17.6	9	19.0	92
Black jack oak							
(*Quercus marilandica*)	11	4.8	8	3.5	—	—	19
White oak							
(*Quercus alba*)	12	5.2	49	21.5	—	—	61
Northern red oak							
(*Quercus rubra*)	1	0.4	5	2.2	1	2.15	7
Bur oak							
(*Quercus macrocarpa*)	4	1.8	2	0.9	2	4.3	8
Pin oak							
(*Quercus palustris*)	2	0.9	3	1.3	—	—	5
Chinquapin oak							
(*Quercus prinoides* var. acuminata)	6	2.6	5	2.2	3	6.3	14
Black hickory							
(*Carya texana*)	7	3.1	8	3.6	2	4.3	17
White hickory							
(*Carya tomentosa*)	—	—	1	0.4	2	4.3	3
Shellbark hickory							
(*Carya laciniosa*)	1	0.4	1	0.4	1	2.15	3
Hickory							
(*Carya* spp.)	3	1.3	1	0.4	—	—	4
Black walnut							
(*Juglans nigra*)	—	—	1	0.4	1	2.15	2

[a]Taxonomy based on Steyermark (1963)

limits could be adduced since the surveyors were not instructed to describe the plants they observed there.

Upland Prairie

Outliers of the Prairie Peninsula originally covered the interfluves on both the eastern and western flanks of the Pomme de Terre River basin (Transeau 1935: Fig. 1). The long narrow band of prairie east of Rodgers Shelter extended for almost 80 km along the upland between the Pomme de Terre and Niangua River basins. Southwest of Rodgers Shelter, a trilobed prairie outlier, centering on the undissected plateau near Wheatland (Figure 2.6), came within 5 km of the site. Only the edges of these large prairies extend into the area we mapped in detail (Figure 2.7).

As indicated earlier, the surveyors made no attempt to record the types of herbs and grasses they observed growing on the upland prairies. Kucera (1961:226), in describing the modern flora, listed the principal grass species of Missouri's prairie association as "the bluestems, *Andropogon Gerardi* and *A. scoparius;* Indiana grass, *Sorghastrum nutans;* wild rye, *Elmyus canadensis;* Junegrass, *Koeleria cristata;* dropseed,

TABLE 2.3   (continued)

Common names recorded (species interpreted)	Barrens		Oak – Hickory		Bottomland		Total
	Number	Percentage	Number	Percentage	Number	Percentage	
White walnut							
(Juglans cinerea)	—	—	—	—	1	2.15	1
Walnut							
(Juglans spp.)	1	0.4	—	—	—	—	1
White elm							
(Ulmus americana)	1	0.4	—	—	5	10.6	6
Red elm							
(Ulmus rubra)	—	—	—	—	2	4.3	2
Elm							
(Ulmus spp.)	2	0.9	—	—	—	—	2
White ash							
(Fraxinus americana var. americana)	—	—	—	—	1	2.15	1
Ash							
(Fraxinus spp.)	—	—	—	—	1	2.15	1
Box elder							
(Acer negundo)	—	—	—	—	1	2.15	1
Sugar maple							
(Acer saccharum)	1	0.4	—	—	1	2.15	2
River maple							
(Acer saccharinum)	—	—	—	—	1	2.15	1
Maple							
(Acer spp.)	—	—	—	—	3	6.3	3
Hackberry							
(Celtis occidentalis)	—	—	—	—	5	10.6	5
Sycamore							
(Platanus occidentalis)	—	—	—	—	4	8.5	4
Willow							
Salix spp.)	1	0.4	—	—	1	2.15	2
Totals	227	100.0	228	100.0	47	100.0	502

Sporobolus heterolepis; switchgrass, *Panicum virgatum;* sloughgrass, *Spartina pectinata;* and sideoats grama, *Boutelous curtipendula.*"

Bottomland Prairie

Two prairies were recorded in the bottomland of the lower Pomme de Terre River basin; both were in abandoned meander loops above the modern floodplain (Figure 2.7). The larger, Breshears Bottoms, just 1.6 km south of Rodgers Shelter, contained some wet marshes or bogs formed by poorly drained artesian springs. The second bottomland prairie was also on the Pomme de Terre about 3.2 km downstream from Rodgers Shelter.

Small prairie patches in the upper reaches of Prairie and Whig creeks northeast of Rodgers Shelter are near, and probably closely related to, the upland prairies.

One can only speculate on the vegetational composition of these fluvial grasslands, but some of the same species listed by Kucera (1961:226) for the prairie association in Missouri probably occurred there.

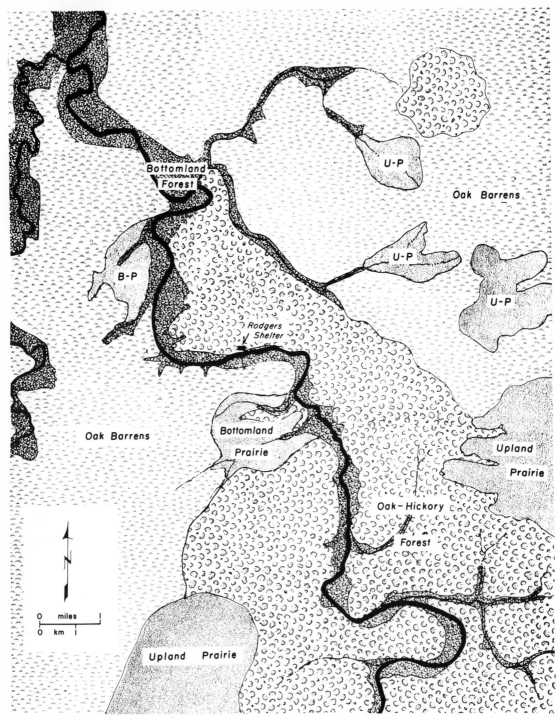

Figure 2.7 Model of the major vegetational communities in the study locality, constructed from plats and notes of the original United States Land Surveys.

28

Oak Barrens

The hilly country in the northern and western portions of the study area supported a floral community referred to by the surveyors as "barrens." Their descriptions suggest that this was primarily a grassland, but one containing varying densities of scattered trees and brush. In one locality Shields (1834:434) described the countryside as "high, rocky, and stony hills, with poor soil, [containing] no timber . . . except a few scattering post oak trees; [and] in places a thick undergrowth of low bushes." There is evidence, however, that in some areas heavier growths of trees occurred on the north-facing slopes, in contrast to the mostly grass-covered southern hillsides. For examples:

> land this mile open barrens. Timber scattering black oak, white oak, [and] post oak, mostly confined to north side of hills. The vallies [sic] and southern slopes being prairie or very open barrens with scarce any undergrowth but grass [description for line between Sections 3 and 10, T39N, R22W; James 1844:57].

> land barrens in the vallies [sic] and on the southern slopes of the hills, the northern sides of the hills [are] open post oak and black oak woods, undergrowth oak shrubs, grape vines, and prairie grass [description for line between Sections 5 and 6, T39N, R22W; James 1844:87].

Quantitative treatment of the witness trees suggests that the woody vegetation the surveyors found growing in the barrens was a post oak–black oak association with lesser numbers of white oak, black jack oak, and black hickory. This interpretation, based on a sample of 227 witness trees, is corroborated by the more subjective, qualitative line descriptions given by the surveyors (Figure 2.7). A complete list of species recorded as witness trees or mentioned in the line descriptions is given in Tables 2.3 and 2.4.

Some indication of the brushy nature of the barrens as well as its herbaceous vegetation can be gained from the line descriptions. The "prairie grass" is often described as interspersed with "oak sprouts." Other descriptions report the presence of sumac, hazel, rose, grape, and strawberry (Table 2.4). Unfortunately, as with the prairie, the surveyors made no attempt to identify any of the grasses. Broadhead (1880:2), a half century later, did write that "the open woods [barrens] were covered with a luxuriant growth of wild grasses, including three species of excellent native grass." It is probable that the grasses Broadhead alluded to are three of those listed by Kucera (1961:226).

Oak–Hickory Forest

The southeastern quarter of the study area, extending down the north side of the Pomme de Terre River to the mouth of Prairie Creek, was generally forested (Figure 2.7). The relief of this area is slightly more rugged than other parts of the locality.

TABLE 2.4   Comparison of Vegetation Listed in the Land Surveys Line Descriptions[a]

Common names recorded (species interpreted)	Barrens		Oak – Hickory		Bottomland		Total
	Number	Percentage	Number	Percentage	Number	Percentage	
Post oak							
(*Quercus stellata*)	60	26.0	65	23.0	2	1.6	127
Black oak							
(*Quercus velutina*)	45	19.5	52	18.4	8	6.2	105
Black jack oak							
(*Quercus marilandica*)	16	6.9	22	7.8	—	—	38
White oak							
(*Quercus alba*)	13	5.6	23	8.2	2	1.6	38
Northern red oak							
(*Quercus rubra*)	—	—	1	0.35	—	—	1
Bur oak							
(*Quercus macrocarpa*)	—	—	—	—	12	9.3	12
Pin oak							
(*Quercus palustris*)	—	—	1	0.35	—	—	1
Chinquapin oak							
(*Quercus prinoides* var. acuminata)	—	—	2	0.7	—	—	2
Oak sprouts							
(*Quercus* spp.)	30	13.0	34	12.1	—	—	64
Black hickory							
(*Carya texana*)	6	2.6	20	7.1	2	1.6	28
White hickory							
(*Carya tomentosa*)	—	—	—	—	1	0.75	1
Shellbark hickory							
(*Carya laciniosa*)	—	—	—	—	1	0.75	1
Hickory							
(*Carya* spp.)	13	5.6	14	5.0	11	8.5	38
Black walnut							
(*Juglans nigra*)	1	0.4	—	—	5	3.9	6
Walnut							
(*Juglans* spp.)	—	—	1	0.35	10	7.8	11
White elm							
(*Ulmus americana*)	—	—	—	—	1	0.75	1
Red elm							
(*Ulmus rubra*)	—	—	—	—	1	0.75	1
Elm							
(*Ulmus* spp.)	3	1.3	1	0.35	11	8.5	15
Ash							
(*Fraxinus* spp.)	—	—	—	—	1	0.75	1
Box elder							
(*Acer negundo*)	—	—	—	—	4	3.1	4

[a]Taxonomy based on Steyermark (1963).

Post oak was the dominant arboreal species, with secondary numbers of white oak and black oak. Smaller frequencies of black jack oak and black hickory were reported along with even lesser numbers of other species (Table 2.3).

The line descriptions suggest that even in the forest there were openings, perhaps on southern exposures, and that much of the wooded area contained grasses and other herbaceous vegetation. Oak sprouts

TABLE 2.4   (continued)

Common names recorded (species interpreted)	Barrens		Oak – Hickory		Bottomland		Total
	Number	Percentage	Number	Percentage	Number	Percentage	
Sugar maple (*Acer saccharum*)	–	–	2	0.7	–	–	2
Red maple (*Acer rubrum*)	–	–	–	–	1	0.75	1
Maple (*Acer* spp.)	–	–	–	–	2	1.6	2
Mulberry (*Morus rubra*)	–	–	–	–	3	2.3	3
Hackberry (*Celtis occidentalis*)	–	–	–	–	9	6.95	9
Black cherry (*Prunus serotina*)	–	–	–	–	1	0.75	1
Sycamore (*Platanus occidentalis*)	–	–	–	–	4	3.1	4
Pawpaw (*Asimina triloba*)	–	–	–	–	3	2.3	3
Haw (*Viburnum* spp.)	1	0.4	–	–	1	0.75	2
Buckeye (*Aesculus glabra*)	–	–	–	–	2	1.6	2
Dogwood (*Cornus* spp.)	2	0.9	1	0.35	3	2.3	6
Red cedar (*Juniperus virginiana*)	–	–	3	1.1	–	–	3
Sumac (*Rhus* spp.)	3	1.3	–	–	1	0.75	4
Hazel (*Corylus americana*)	12	5.2	4	1.4	8	6.2	24
Rose (*Rosa* spp.)	1	0.4	–	–	1	0.75	2
Grape (*Vitis* spp.)	2	0.9	1	0.35	2	1.6	5
Strawberry (*Fragaria virginiana*)	–	–	–	–	1	0.75	1
Spice bush (*Lindera Benzoin*)	–	–	–	–	4	3.1	4
Prairie grass, spp.	10	4.3	23	8.2	–	–	33
Vines, spp.	7	3.1	6	2.1	6	4.7	19
Briers, spp.	6	2.6	6	2.1	5	3.9	17
Totals	231	100.0	282	100.0	129	100.0	642

were cited often enough to suggest that at least parts of the woodland were brushy. Although there was no attempt to calculate density of the tree stand for the forested area, it is apparent that the stand of mature trees was not dense. For example, in a wooded area described by James (1844:49) as timbered with post oak, black hickory, and black jack oak, the distances to the four witness trees were: 67 links (134.8 m), 113 links (227.4 m), 103 links (207.2 m), and 190 links (382.3 m).

Qualitatively, there is little difference between the composition of the oak–hickory forest and the oak barrens (Figure 2.8). A quantitative treatment of witness trees, however, demonstrates a much higher frequency of white oaks in the forested portions than in the barrens. White oaks occur in 4% greater frequency than black oaks, a species that far outnumbered the former in the barrens. Interestingly, the surveyors' subjective line descriptions failed to make this distinction between the two zones.

Bottomland Forest

The floodplain supported the most diversified flora and series of microhabitats of any of the major plant communities defined. The ecological niches include the narrow zone paralleling the base of the bluffs, the floodplain proper, the riparian habitat bordering the streams, gravel bars, spring and slough borders, and aquatic communities. Although there is great variety in these microzones, they are very close to one another, and will be considered together as contiguous units that constitute the bottomland forest.

A variety of trees was listed for the bottoms; the most common were bur oak, black oak, chinquapin oak, hackberry, sycamore, black walnut, box elder, and several species of hickory, elm, and maple (Figure 2.8; Tables 2.3 and 2.4). The rich alluvial bottomland soils also produced a luxuriant undergrowth of smaller bushes, vines, and briers as evidenced by this typical description of the floodplain flora where a survey line transected the bottoms:

> the bottom is covered with heavy timber [including] walnut, burr oak, hickory, elm, mulberry, black oak, [and an] undergrowth [of] hazle [sic], greenbrier, rose bush, black haw, grape vines, etc., in thickets which are hard to penetrate [description for line between Sections 19 and 20, T39N, R22W; James 1844:57].

Nineteenth-Century Vegetational Trends

The land surveys have provided data for the construction of a vegetational model—one that simulates the floral distribution and composition as it appeared in the early to mid-nineteenth century. This provides a satisfactory datum against which to measure former changes, but for the model to help us successfully in predicting past changes, we must decide if this border was stable at the time of European settlement, or if it was fluctuating, with an encroachment of plants from one of the major biomes into the other.

Many authors have referred to the general tendency of woody vegetation to invade the prairies subsequent to the time of Euro–American settlement (Sauer 1920:52; Steyermark 1940:388; Borchert 1950:35; Howell and Kucera 1956:216). Steyermark (1940:388), for example, has observed that according to early travelers' and settlers' records, much of

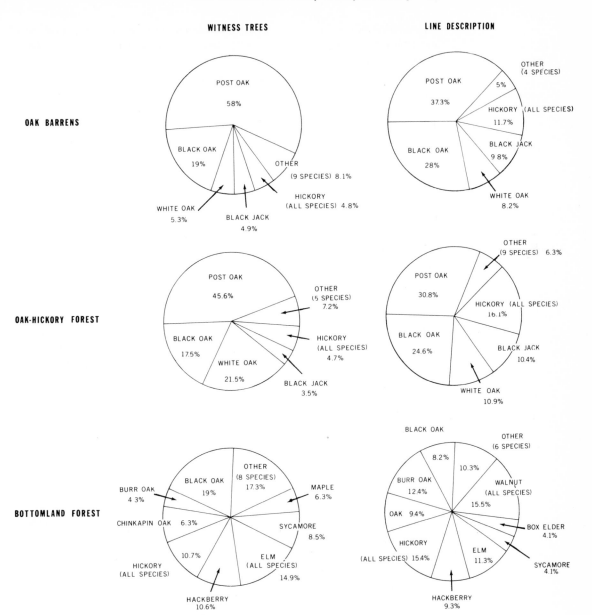

Figure 2.8 The frequency of dominant arboreal species in three floral communities: the oak barrens, oak–hickory forest, and bottomland forest.

the Ozark Plateau that is now forested was originally prairie, arguing that, under a climatic mesophytic climax, the natural tendency is for open barrens and prairie habitats to succeed to forest. Transeau (1935) and Borchert (1950) have countered that the prairie was a climax community, that the tendency for woody vegetation to invade the borders of the grassland would take place only during cycles of increased precipitation, and that during drought years the Prairie Peninsula would enlarge at the expense of the forest.

Evidence from land surveys indicates that at the period of Euro–American settlement, the oak–hickory forest was invading the grassland near Rodgers Shelter. As a working hypothesis, it is suggested that the areas described as barrens were sections of the broad border between the Ozark forests and the Prairie Peninsula where arboreal species were invading the grassland, a trend that has continued to the present, excepting temporary reversals during drought years such as those of the 1930s.

Beyond the historical evidence concerning this process, the composition of woody species in the barrens indicates they were succeeding to forest and were in what Steyermark (1940) considered to be the third stage of succession from prairie to oak–hickory woodland (Table 2.5). Steyermark (1940:388–390) observes that after initial colonization of grassland by woody shrubs, black jack and post oaks are the first trees to invade. Black oaks appear about a dozen years later (Drew 1942), soon followed by white oaks (Table 2.6). Since black jack and post oaks are light-demanding types, they begin to lose ground with the incursion of black oaks. The faster-growing black oaks eventually attain greater heights, shading the black jack and post oaks, and thus create the conditions for the next successional stage (Steyermark 1940:390).

Comparison of the topography and soils of the areas described as

TABLE 2.5   Stages of Woody Plant Succession during Forest Invasion of Ozark Prairies[a]

Stage	Species	Remarks
1	sassafras	initial invaders
	(Sassafras albidum var. molle)	
	winged sumac	
	(Rhus copallina var. latifolia)	
	fragrant sumac	less frequent
	(Rhus aromatica)	
	persimmon	sometimes initial invader
	(Diospyros virginiana)	instead of sassafras-sumac
2	black jack oak	major arboreal pioneers
	(Quercus marilandica)	
	post oak	
	(Quercus stellata)	
3	black oak	follow and compete with
	(Quercus velutina)	above oaks
	Ozark hickory	
	(Carya Buckleyi van arkansana)	
	white oak	usually later, but sometimes
	(Quercus alba)	with black oak

[a]After Steyermark (1940:388-390).

TABLE 2.6 Succession of Plants on Bare Ground in Boone and Callaway Counties, Missouri[a]

Year	Plant cover	Year	Plant cover
0	bare ground	12	black oak (Quercus velutina)
1-4	grasses and forbs	15	white oak (Quercus alba)
5	woody shrubs and sumac (Rhus spp.)		
6	post oak (Quercus stellata) shagbark hickory (Carya ovata)		

[a]After Drew (1942).

barrens with those supporting forest indicates that the topographic, edaphic, and climatic conditions should not have been greatly different between these areas. By and large, the rolling hill country paralleling the Pomme de Terre River is relatively homogeneous. On this basis it is reasonable to hypothesize that we are observing an expanding forest along this prairie–woodland ecotone. At the time of the original land surveys, the barrens were in a younger stage of succession than the forest, containing a 20% greater frequency of the pioneering post oaks and black jack oaks than did the latter.

Had the locality been surveyed a hundred years earlier, much of the area shown as forest might have been barrens. On the other hand, a modern botanical survey should find portions of the land described as barrens during the 1840s covered with forest, if not affected by modern lumbering and agriculture.

FAUNA

The fauna of a biotic community is largely attendant on the local flora. In an area that is transitional between two or more diverse communities as, for example, between the forest and grassland of the study locality, there is often a tendency for increased variety and density of species because of the "edge effect." Odum (1971:157) explained this ecological principle when he wrote:

> The ecotonal community commonly contains many of the organisms of each of the overlapping communities and, in addition, organisms which are characteristic of and often restricted to the ecotone. Often, both the number of species and the population density of some of the species are greater in the ecotone than in the communities flanking it.

Past densities are difficult to calculate, but certainly there was a wide variety of species inhabiting the Ozark Highland–Prairie border. Species adapted to both the forest and grassland biomes as well as a number of species preferring the ecotone or edge-community have been reported.

TABLE 2.7 Modern Mammalian Fauna Native to the Study Locality and Their Preferred Habitats

Species	Prairie	Forest border (barrens)	Oak-hickory forest	Bottomland forest	Bottomland prairie	Aquatic
Opossum (Didelphis marsupialis)		O	O	X		
Short-tailed shrew (Blarina brevicauda)			O	X		
Least shrew (Cryptotis parva)	X	O				
Eastern mole (Scalopus aquaticus)	X	O				
Little brown bat (Myotis lucifugus)		O	O	X	O	
Gray bat (Myotis grisescens)		O	O	X	O	
Keen's bat (Myotis keenii)		O	O	X	O	
Indiana bat (Myotis sodalis)		O	O	X	O	
Least bat (Myotis subulatus)		O	O	X	O	
Silver-haired bat (Lasionycteris noctivagans)		O	O	X	O	
Eastern pipistrelle (Pipistrellus subflavus)		O	O	X	O	
Big brown bat (Eptesicus fuscus)		O	O	X	O	
Red bat (Lasiurus borealis)		O	O	X	O	
Hoary bat (Lasiurus cinereus)		O	O	X	O	
Evening bat (Nycticeius humeralis)		O	O	X	O	
Black-tailed jack rabbit (Lepus californicus)	X					
Eastern cottontail rabbit (Sylvilagus floridanus)		X				
Woodchuck (Marmota monax)		O	X	O		
Thirteen-lined ground squirrel (Spermophilous tridecemlineatus)	X	O				
Eastern chipmunk (Tamias striatus)		O	X			
Eastern gray squirrel (Sciurus carolinensis)		O	O	X		
Eastern fox squirrel (Sciurus niger)		X	O	O		
Southern flying squirrel (Glaucomys volans)			X	O		
Plains pocket gopher (Geomys bursarius)	X	O				
Beaver (Castor canadensis)[b]						X
Western harvest mouse (Reithrodontomys megalotis)	X	O				

[a]Key: X represents preferred habitat; O represents secondary habitats.
[b]Extirpated, reintroduced.
[c]Extirpated species.

TABLE 2.7 (continued)

Species	Prairie	Forest border (barrens)	Oak–hickory forest	Bottomland forest	Bottomland prairie	Aquatic
Fulvous harvest mouse (*Reithrodontomys fulvescens*)	X	O			O	
Prairie white-footed mouse (*Peromyscus maniculatus*)	X	O				
White-tailed deer (*Odocoileus virginianus*)		X	O	O	O	
Gray wolf (*Canis lupus*)[c]		O	X	O		
Mountain lion (*Felis concolor*)[c]		O	X	O		
Elk (*Cervus canadensis*)[c]			X	O	O	
Bison (*Bison bison*)[c]	X					
Woodland white-footed mouse (*Peromyscus leucopus*)		O	X	O		
Common cotton rat (*Sigmodon hispidus*)	O	X				
Eastern wood rat (*Neotoma floridana*)		O	X	O		
Southern bog lemming (*Synaptomys cooperi*)				O	X	
Prairie vole (*Microtus ochrogaster*)	X	O				
Meadow vole (*Microtus pennsylvanicus*)[c]					X	
Pine mouse (*Microtus pinetorum*)		O	X			
Muskrat (*Ondatra zibethicus*)						X
Meadow jumping mouse (*Zapus hudsonius*)				O	X	
Coyote (*Canis latrans*)	X	O	O			
Red fox (*Vulpes fulva*)		X	O			
Gray fox (*Urocyon cinereoargenteus*)		O	X			
Black bear (*Ursus americanus*)[c]			O	X		
Raccoon (*Procyon lotor*)			O	X	O	
Long-tailed weasel (*Mustela frenata*)	O	O	X			
Mink (*Mustela vison*)				X		
Badger (*Taxidea taxus*)[c]	X	O				
Spotted skunk (*Spilogale putorius*)	X	O				
Striped skunk (*Mephitis mephitis*)		X	O	O		
Bobcat (*Lynx rufus*)		O	X	O		

37

Modern Faunal Diversity

Faunal surveys presenting the distribution of the various classes of modern vertebrate fauna demonstrate that most of the species present during the pioneer period occur in varying numbers today. Some animals have been extirpated from their former ranges since Euro–American settlement, and now either occur in regions outside Missouri or are extinct. The main classes of vertebrates—mammals, birds, amphibians, reptiles, and fish—are discussed in the following sections.

Mammals

The diversity of fauna along the prairie border is indicated by the 54 mammalian species resident to the area during the Historic Period (Table 2.7). All but 7 of these are still present today, although the present population of modern beaver, *Castor canadensis*, was derived from individuals that were reintroduced to the state.

Schwartz and Schwartz (1959:331–333) and McKinley (1960a, b, 1961, 1962b, 1964) cite six species of larger animals that have been extirpated from the Pomme de Terre locality, three of which no longer occur in the state. Species that are no longer part of Missouri's fauna are the gray wolf, *Canis lupus;* elk, *Cervus canadensis;* and bison, *Bison bison.* The mountain lion, *Felis concolor*, and black bear, *Ursus americanus*, occur only rarely in the densely forested regions of the interior Ozark Highland. The badger, *Taxidea taxus*, although presently extending its range across greater sections of Missouri (McKinley 1960b), is not yet a part of the local fauna.

Birds

Birds are so wide ranging that no attempt has been made to give a complete list of the species whose ranges include the study area. The reader is referred to Peterson (1947) for reference to the avifauna that regularly occur in southwestern Missouri.

Species of potential economic importance observed when we were in the field are the forest-dwelling wild turkey, *Meleagris gallopavo;* the bobwhite, *Colinus virginanus*, inhabiting the edge areas; and the prairie chicken, *Tympanuchus cupido.* A population of the latter today occupies the treeless, undissected plateau area around Wheatland, about 19 km south of Rodgers Shelter. According to McKinley (1960c), the ruffed grouse, *Bonasa umbellus*, may also have been present in the forested regions during the nineteenth century. Once found in great flocks, the passenger pigeon, *Ectopistes migratorius*, was eradicated from Missouri even before it became extinct (McKinley 1960d).

Waterfowl indigenous to the Mississippi Valley Flyway frequent the locality during migration periods, especially the overflow ponds and sloughs of the expansive Osage River bottoms near the mouth of the Pomme de Terre River. The trumpeter swan, *Olor buccinator*, native to the area in the past, has been extirpated from Missouri (McKinley 1962a).

Amphibians and Reptiles

A variety of amphibian and reptilian species have ranges that include the study locality. In all, 22 species of amphibians (Wiley 1968) and 43 species of reptiles (Anderson 1965) are reported (Table 2.8). There is a large number of nonvenomous snakes (21 species), but they are excluded from the table. A list of those native to the area can be found in Anderson (1965:124–161). Three venomous species—the copperhead, *Agkistrodon contortrix*, cottonmouth, *Agkistrodon piscivorus*, and timber rattlesnake, *Crotalus horridus horridus*—are part of the local herpetofauna.

Of the species included in Table 2.8, the two terrestrial box turtles (*Terrapene carolina* and *Terrapene ornata*) and the several species of aquatic turtles would probably have been most important in the prehistoric food economy.

Fish

Pflieger (1971) has listed 98 species of fish that inhabit the streams along the Ozark border area (Table 2.9). These include a few species that are native only to Missouri's larger streams (e.g., the lake sturgeon, *Acipenser fulvescens*), but they are included here since they are available in the Osage River proper only 11 km north of Rodgers Shelter.

Mussels

The bed of the modern Pomme de Terre River contains a large freshwater mussel (naiad) population. The stream has provided numerous

TABLE 2.8 Modern Amphibians and Reptiles

AMPHIBIANS	REPTILES
Hellbender *(Cryptobranchus a. alleganiensis)*	Common snapping turtle *(Chelydra serpentina serpentina)*
Spotted salamander *(Ambystoma maculatum)*	Stinkpot *(Sternothaerus odoratus)*
Marbled salamander *(Ambystoma opacum)*	Three-toed box turtle *(Terrapene carolina triunguis)*
Ringed salamander *(Ambystoma annulatum)*	Ornate box turtle *(Terrapene ornata ornata)*
Eastern tiger salamander *(Ambystoma t. tigrinum)*	Map turtle *(Graptemys geographica)*
Central newt *(Notophthalmus viridenscens louisianensis)*	Mississippi map turtle *(Graptemys kohni)*
Dark-sided salamander *(Eurycea l. melanopleura)*	Ouachita map turtle *(Graptemys pseudogeographica ouachitensis)*
Cave salamander *(Eurycea lucifuga)*	Western painted turtle *(Chrysemys picta belli)*
Slimy salamander *(Plethodon g. glutinosus)*	Red-eared turtle *(Pseudemys scripta elegans)*
Redbacked salamander *(Plethodon c. cinereus)*	Western spiny soft-shelled turtle *(Trionyx spinifer hartwegi)*
Waterdog *(Necturus m. maculosus)*	Smooth soft-shelled turtle *(Trionyx mutica mutica)*
American toad *(Bufo a. americanus)*	Eastern collared lizard *(Crotaphytus collaris collaris)*
Dwarf American toad *(Bufo a. charlesmithi)*	Northern fence lizard *(Sceloporus undulatus hyacinthinus)*
Fowler's toad *(Bufo w. fowleri)*	Western slender glass lizard *(Ophisaurus attenuatus attenuatus)*
Blanchard's cricket frog *(Acris crepitans blanchardi)*	Six-lined racerunner *(Cnemidophorus sexlineatus)*
Western chorus frog *(Pseudacris t. triseriata)*	Ground skink *(Lygosoma laterale)*
Northern spring peeper *(Hyla crucifer crucifer)*	Five-lined skink *(Eumeces fasciatus)*
Gray treefrog *(Hyla v. versicolor)*	Broad-headed skink *(Eumeces laticeps)*
Bullfrog *(Rana catesbeiana)*	Southern coal skink *(Eumeces anthracinus pluvialis)*
Green frog *(Rana clamitans melanota)*	
Pickerel frog *(Rana palustris)*	
Southern leopard frog *(Rana p. sphencephala)*	

TABLE 2.9 Modern Fish of the Ozark Border Region

LAMPREYS (Petromyzonidae)

  Northern brook lamprey *(Ichthyomyzon fossor)*
  Chestnut lamprey *(Ichthyomyzon castaneus)*

STURGEONS (Acipenseridae)

  Lake sturgeon *(Acipenser fulvescens)*
  Shovelnose sturgeon *(Scaphirhynchus platorynchus)*

PADDLEFISHES (Polyodontidae)

  Paddlefish *(Polyodon spathula)*

GARS (Lepisosteidae)

  Shortnose gar *(Lepisosteus platostomus)*
  Longnose gar *(Lepisosteus osseus)*

EELS (Anguillidae)

  American eel *(Anguilla rostrata)*

HERRINGS (Clupeidae)

  Skipjack herring *(Alosa chrysochloris)*
  Gizzard shad *(Dorosoma cepedianum)*

MOONEYES (Hiodontidae)

  Goldeye *(Hiodon alosoides)*
  Mooneye *(Hiodon tergisus)*

PIKES (Esocidae)

  Northern Pike *(Esox lucius)*

MINNOWS (Cyprinidae)

  Golden shiner *(Notemigonus crysoleucas)*
  Creek chub *(Semotilus atromaculatus)*
  Southern redbelly dace *(Chrosomus erythrogaster)*
  Hornyhead chub *(Hybopsis biguttata)*
  Silver chub *(Hybopsis storeriana)*
  Gravel chub *(Hybopsis x-punctata)*
  Speckled chub *(Hybopsis aestivalis)*
  Suckermouth minnow *(Phenacobius mirabilis)*
  Emerald shiner *(Notropis atherinoides)*
  Rosyface shiner *(Notropis rubellus)*
  Redfin shiner *(Notropis umbratilis)*
  Bleeding shiner *(Notropis zonatus)*
  Striped shiner *(Notropis chrysocephalus chrysocephalus)*
  Wedgespot shiner *(Notropis greenei)*
  Bigeye shiner *(Notropis boops)*
  Red shiner *(Notropis lutrensis)*
  Sand shiner *(Notropis stramineus)*
  Blacknose shiner *(Notropis heterolepis)*
  Ghost shiner *(Notropis buchanani)*
  Ozark minnow *(Dionda nubila)*
  Bluntnose minnow *(Pimephales notatus)*
  Fathead minnow *(Pimephales promelas)*
  Largescale stoneroller *(Campostoma oligolepis)*
  Central stoneroller *(Campostoma anomalum pullum)*

SUCKERS (Catostomidae)

  Blue sucker *(Cycleptus elongatus)*
  Bigmouth buffalo *(Ictiobus cyprinellus)*
  Black buffalo *(Ictiobus niger)*
  Smallmouth buffalo *(Ictiobus bubalus)*
  Quillback *(Carpiodes cyprinus)*
  River carpsucker *(Carpiodes carpio carpio)*
  Highfin carpsucker *(Carpiodes velifer)*
  White sucker *(Catostomus commersoni)*
  Northern hog sucker *(Hypentelium nigricans)*
  Black redhorse *(Moxostoma duquesnei)*
  Golden redhorse *(Moxostoma erythrurum)*
  Silver redhorse *(Moxostoma anisurum)*
  Northern redhorse *(Moxostoma macrolepidotum)*
  River redhorse *(Moxostoma carinatum)*

CATFISHES (Ictaluridae)

  Black bullhead *(Ictalurus melas)*
  Yellow bullhead *(Ictalurus natalis)*
  Channel catfish *(Ictalurus punctatus)*
  Blue catfish *(Ictalurus furcatus)*
  Tadpole madtom *(Noturus gyrinus)*
  Freckled madtom *(Noturus nocturnus)*
  Slender madtom *(Noturus exilis)*
  Stonecat *(Noturus flavus)*
  Flathead catfish *(Pylodictis olivaris)*

CAVEFISHES (Amblyopsidae)

  Southern cavefish *(Typhlichthys subterraneus)*

KILLIFISHES (Cyprinodontidae)

  Northern studfish *(Fundulus catenatus)*
  Plains topminnow *(Fundulus sciadicus)*
  Blackspotted topminnow *(Fundulus olivaceus)*
  Blackstripe topminnow *(Fundulus notatus)*

LIVEBEARERS (Poeciliidae)

  Mosquitofish *(Gambusia affinis affinis)*

SILVERSIDES (Atherinidae)

  Brook silverside *(Labidesthes sicculus sicculus)*

BASSES (Percichthyidae)

  White bass *(Morone chrysops)*

SUNFISHES (Centrarchidae)

  Smallmouth bass *(Micropterus dolomieui)*
  Largemouth bass *(Micropterus salmoides salmoides)*
  Warmouth *(Chaenobryttus gulosus)*
  Green sunfish *(Lepomis cyanellus)*
  Orangespotted sunfish *(Lepomis humilis)*
  Longear sunfish *(Lepomis megalotis megalotis)*
  Bluegill *(Lepomis macrochirus)*
  Rock bass *(Ambloplites rupestris)*
  Black crappie *(Pomoxis nigromaculatus)*
  White crappie *(Pomoxis annularis)*

TABLE 2.9 (continued)

PERCHES (Percidae)

Walleye *(Stizostedion vitreum vitreum)*
Sauger *(Stizostedion canadense)*
Bluestripe darter *(Percina cymatotaenia)*
Slenderhead darter *(Percina phoxocephala)*
Logperch *(Percina caprodes)*
Johnny darter *(Etheostoma nigrum)*
Bluntnose darter *(Etheostoma chlorosomum)*
Missouri saddled darter *(Etheostoma tetrazonum)*
Banded darter *(Etheostoma zonale)*
Greenside darter *(Etheostoma blennioides)*
Niangua darter *(Etheostoma nianguae)*

Stippled darter *(Etheostoma punctulatum)*
Rainbow darter *(Etheostoma caeruleum)*
Orangethroat darter *(Etheostoma spectabile)*
Fantail darter *(Etheostoma flabellare)*
Slough darter *(Etheostoma gracile)*
Least darter *(Etheostoma microperca)*

DRUMS (Sciaenidae)

Freshwater drum *(Aplodinotus grunniens)*

SCULPINS (Cottidae)

Mottled sculpin *(Cottus bairdi bairdi)*
Banded sculpin *(Cottus carolinae)*

TABLE 2.10   Modern Naiad Fauna Collected from the Pomme de Terre River in 1966

Scientific name	Vernacular name	Frequency
Actinonaias carinata	mucket	abundant
Actinonaias ellipsiformis	ellipse	common
Alasmidonta marginata	elk-toe	common
Amblema costata	three-ridge	common
Cyclonaias tuberculata	purple warty-back	common
Elliptio dilatatus	spike	uncommon
Fusconaia flava	pig-toe	common
Fusconaia undata	pig-toe	uncommon
Lampsilis anadontoides	yellow sand-shell	uncommon
Lampsilis fallaciosa	slough sand-shell	uncommon
Lampsilis ventricosa	pocketbook	abundant
Lasmigona complanata	white heel-splitter	uncommon
Leptodea fragilis	fragile paper-shell	common
Leptodea laevissima	pink paper-shell	uncommon
Ligumia recta	black sand-shell	uncommon
Megalonaias gigantea	washboard	uncommon
Obliquaria reflexa	three-horned warty-back	common
Plagiola lineolata	butterfly	common
Plethobasus cyphyus	bullhead	uncommon
Pleurobema cordatum	—	uncommon
Proptera alata	pink heel-splitter	common
Quadrula metanevra	monkey-face	uncommon
Quadrula pustulosa	pimple-back	abundant
Strophitus rugosus	squaw foot	common
Tritogonia verrucosa	buckhorn	common

habitats for pelecypod fauna since at least the mid-postglacial, since they are present in considerable numbers in the deposits of that age and later at Rodgers Shelter. Presently, there are few data to indicate whether or not there were substantial naiad populations in the Pomme de Terre earlier than this time.

A recent attempt to collect the range of species inhabiting the stream in the vicinity of the shelter was made during the 1966 field season by Paul W. Parmalee of the Illinois State Museum. This study provided individuals of at least 25 species (Table 2.10).

REFERENCES

Anderson, P.
   1965 *The reptiles of Missouri.* Columbia, Missouri: Univ. of Missouri Press.
Beilman, A.P., and L.G. Brenner
   1951 The recent intrusion of forests in the Ozarks. *Annals of the Missouri Botanical Gardens* 38: 261–282.
   1951b Changing forest flora in the Ozarks. *Annals of the Missouri Botanical Gardens.* 38: 283–291.
Borchert, J.R.
   1950 The climate of the central North American grassland. *Annals of the Association of American Geographers* **40:** 1–39.
Bourdo, E.A., Jr.
   1956 A review of the General Land Office Survey and of its use in quantitative studies of former forests. *Ecology* 37: 754–768.
Branson, E.B.
   1944 The geology of Missouri. *The University of Missouri Studies* 19(3).
Braun, E.L.
   1950 *Deciduous forests of eastern North America.* Philadelphia, Pennsylvania: The Blakiston Company.
Bretz, JH.
   1965 *Geomorphic history of the Ozarks of Missouri.* Rolla, Missouri: Missouri Geological Survey and Water Resources.
Broadhead, G.C.
   1880 *Geological report upon the mineral lands of Major R.H. Melton.* Sedalia, Missouri: Eagle Print.
Decker, W.L.
   1955 Late spring and early fall killing freezes in Missouri: Agricultural Experiment Station, University of Missouri: *Bulletin* **649.**
Dice, L.R.
   1943 *The biotic provinces of North America.* Ann Arbor, Michigan: Univ. of Michigan Press.
Drew, W.B.
   1942 The revegetation of abandoned cropland in the Cedar Creek area, Boone and Callaway counties, Missouri. Agricultural Experiment Station, University of Missouri *Bulletin* **344:** 3–52.
Evers, R.A.
   1955 Hill prairies of Illinois. *Bulletin of the Illinois Natural History Survey* **26:** 367–446.
Fenneman, N.M.
   1938 *Physiography of eastern United States.* New York: McGraw-Hill.
Gallaher, A., Jr.
   1961 *Plainville fifteen years later.* New York: Columbia Univ. Press.
Gordon, R.B.
   1969 The natural vegetation of Ohio in pioneer days. *Bulletin of the Ohio Biological Survey* (new series) 3(2).
Holowaychuk, N.
   1960 Soil formation factors in the North Central Region. In Soils of the North Central Region of the United States. *Agricultural Experiment Station Bulletin* **544.** Madison, Wisconsin: Univ. of Wisconsin. Pp. 6–19.
Howell, D.L., and C.L. Kucera
   1956 Composition of presettlement forests in three counties of Missouri. *Bulletin of the Torrey Botanical Club* 83: 207–217.

James, E.
1844 Surveyors field notes (for section lines, Townships 38N and 39N, Range 22W). *United States Federal Land Surveys.* Jefferson City, Missouri: Missouri State Archives.

Klippel, W.E.
1971a Prehistory and environmental change along the southern border of the Prairie Peninsula during the Archaic Period. Ph.D. dissertation, Department of Anthropology, University of Missouri, Columbia.
1971b Graham Cave revisited, a reevaluation of its cultural position during the Archaic Period. *Memoir* 9, Missouri Archaeological Society, Columbia.

Krusekopf, H.H.
1962 *Major soil areas of Missouri, 1962.* Columbia, Missouri: Agricultural Experiment Station, University of Missouri.

Kucera, C.L.
1961 The grasses of Missouri. *University of Missouri Studies* 35: 1–241.

Küchler, A.W.
1964 *Potential natural vegetation of the conterminous United States* (Map and Manual). American Geographical Society Special Publication 36. New York.

Marbut, C.F.
1896 *Physical features of Missouri.* Missouri Geological Survey 10:11-109.

McCracken, M.H.
1961 *Geologic map of Missouri.* Rolla, Missouri: Missouri Geological Survey and Water Resources.

McKinley, D.
1960a The American elk in pioneer Missouri. *Missouri Historical Review* 54(4):356–365.
1960b The badger in pioneer Missouri. *The Bluebird* 27:3–7.
1960c History of the ruffed grouse in Missouri. *The Bluebird* 27:3–11.
1960d A history of the passenger pigeon in Missouri. *The Auk* 77:399–420.
1961 The mountain lion, a history of Missouri's big cat. *The Bluebird* 28:6–12.
1962a The trumpeter swan in Missouri. *The Bluebird* 29:2–7.
1962b The history of the black bear in Missouri. *The Bluebird* **29:2–16.**
1964 The American bison in pioneer Missouri. *The Bluebird* 31:3–14.

McMillen, D.E., Jr.
1950 Geology of the Shawnee Bend quadrangle, Benton County, Missouri. M.A. thesis, Department of Geology, University of Missouri, Columbia.

Metcalf, V.A., and C.E. Klingner
1963 *Agriculture in Missouri.* Columbia, Missouri: University of Missouri Extension Division.

Odum, E.P.
1971 *Fundamentals of ecology*, 3rd edition. Philadelphia, Pennsylvania: W.B. Saunders.

Peterson, R.T.
1947 *A field guide to the birds*, 2nd revised edition. Boston, Massachusetts: Houghton Mifflin.

Pflieger, W.L.
1971 A distributional study of Missouri fishes. *University of Kansas Publications, Museum of Natural History* 20:225–570.

Ruhe, R.V.
1969 *Quaternary landscapes in Iowa.* Ames, Iowa: Iowa State Univ. Press.

Sauer, C.O.
1920 *The geography of the Ozark Highland of Missouri.* Chicago, Illinois: Univ. of Chicago Press.

Schwartz, C.W., and E.R. Schwartz
1959 *The wild mammals of Missouri.* Columbia, Missouri: Univ. of Missouri Press.
Scrivner, C.L., J.C. Baker, and B.J. Miller
1966 *Soils of Missouri, a guide to their identification and interpretation.* Columbia, Missouri: Univ. of Missouri Extension Division.
Sears, P.B.
1921 Vegetation mapping. *Science* 53:325–327.
1925 The natural vegetation of Ohio, I. A map of the virgin forest. *Ohio Journal of Science* 25:139–149.
1926 The natural vegetation of Ohio, II. The prairies. *Ohio Journal of Science* 26:128–146.
1970 Ohio vegetation when first surveyed. *Ecology* 51:556–557.
Shields, W.
1834 Surveyors field notes (for township and range lines, Townships 38N and 39N, Range 22W). *United States Federal Land Surveys.* Jefferson City, Missouri: Missouri State Archives.
Shumard, B.F.
1867 *A geological report on the mineral lands belonging to R.H. Melton, Esq. in Benton and Hickory counties, Missouri.* St. Louis, Missouri: R.P. Studley and Company.
Steyermark, J.A.
1940 Studies of the vegetation of Missouri, I, natural plant associations and succession in the Ozarks of Missouri. *Field Museum of Natural History Botanical Series* 9:349–475.
1959 Vegetational history of the Ozark forest. *The University of Missouri Studies* No. 31.
1963 *Flora of Missouri.* Ames, Iowa: Iowa State Univ. Press.
Terasmae, J.
1967 Paleoecology: A practical viewpoint and general considerations. In *Life, land, and water,* edited by W.J. Mayer-Oakes. Winnipeg, Manitoba: Univ. of Manitoba Press. Pp. 207–215.
Thorp, J.
1968 The soil—a reflection of Quaternary environments in Illinois. In *Quaternary of Illinois,* edited by R.E. Bergstrom. Urbana, Illinois: University of Illinois College of Agriculture.
Transeau, E.N.
1935 The Prairie Peninsula. *Ecology* 16:423–437.
Turner, C.H.
1954 Indian quarries. *Missouri Archaeologist* 16(2):6–24.
United States Army
1967 *Kaysinger Bluff Dam and Reservoir, Missouri.* United States Army Corps of Engineers, Kansas City District.
West, J.
1945 *Plainville, U.S.A.* New York: Columbia Univ. Press.
Wiley, J.R.
1968 Guide to the amphibians of Missouri. *Missouri Speleology* 10:132–172.

II

Quaternary Environments

3

Late Quaternary Geology of the Lower Pomme de Terre Valley[1]

C. Vance Haynes

The lower Pomme de Terre valley, for purposes of this report, consists of bottomlands along the Pomme de Terre River 3 to 5 km either side of the Benton–Hickory county line in southwestern Missouri (Figure 3.1), and includes what is locally referred to as the Breshears Bottoms and the now abandoned community of Avery. The area, first described physiographically by Hershey (1895) and Marbut (1896), lies near the western edge of the Ozark Plateaus Province of Fenneman (1938) and near the boundary between the Salem and Springfield Plateaus (Bretz 1965; Knox 1966). Three geomorphic surfaces in the Ozark Plateaus are ascribed to either (1) peneplanation resulting from Paleozoic–Mesozoic erosional cycles (Bretz 1965) or (2) Pleistocene pedimentation correlated with interglacial episodes (Quinn 1956). In addition, two strath terraces have been recognized in some parts of the Ozarks (Hershey 1895), and surfaces in the Breshears Bottoms could be related to one or both of these.

Bedrock in the area, chiefly the Jefferson City dolomite of Lower Ordovician age, containing abundant chert, is entrenched 100 m or more by meanders of the Pomme de Terre River (Tarr 1924). Undercutting has in some places formed steep bluffs, some of them with rock overhangs such as Rodgers Shelter, which has been intermittently occupied by man for the past 10,500 years (Chapters 7–12).

[1] This work was supported in part by National Science Foundation grants GA-12772 and GA-35625 to the author.

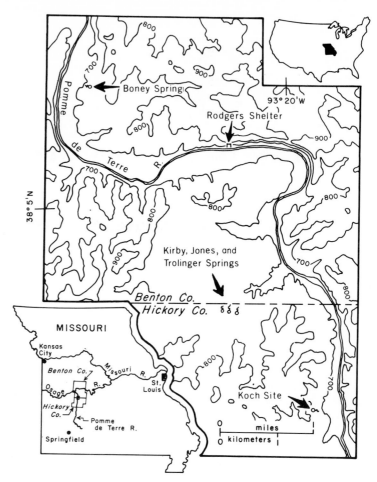

Figure 3.1   Map of the lower Pomme de Terre River area, showing the location of sites.

Breshears Bottoms is a horseshoe-shaped valley underlain by alluvial sediments, including stream-rounded chert gravels, indicating that it is an ancient abandoned meander scar of the main river, and probably related to one of the two erosional stages represented by straths elsewhere in the Ozark Highland (Bretz 1965: 106). Within this ancient alluvium and along terraces of the Pomme de Terre River are numerous spring bogs containing bones of extinct vertebrates, plant macrofossils, and fossil pollen of late Pleistocene age (Koch 1857; Mehringer *et al.* 1970; King 1973). These deposits and those of Rodgers Shelter are the subject of current paleoecological investigations along the western margin of the Ozark Highland, and the objective of this chapter is to present preliminary results of the stratigraphic and geochronologic investigations in support of this project.

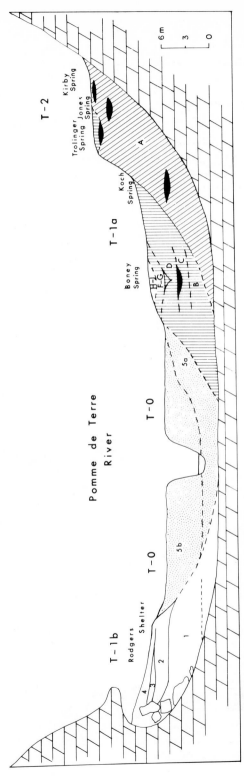

Figure 3.2 Diagrammatic cross section of the Pomme de Terre valley, showing generalized stratigraphic relationships of spring deposits (black lenses) to alluvial terraces (no horizontal scale).

49

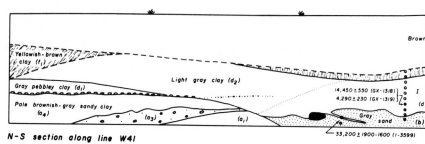

Figure 3.3 Cross-section of Trolinger Spring at line W41 (1967), showing the location of pollen profiles and radiocarbon samples. (See scale and key in Figure 3.4.)

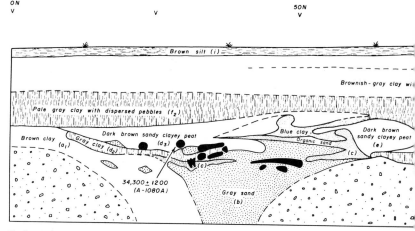

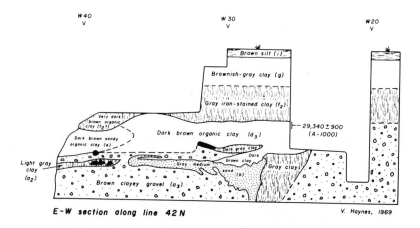

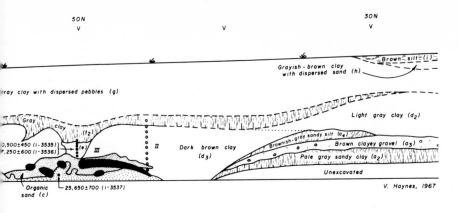

50N
∨

30N
∨

Brown silt (i)

Grayish - brown clay
with dispersed sand (h)

ray clay with dispersed pebbles (g)

Light gray clay (d₂)

Gray clay (f₂)

0,500±450 (I-3535)

₇,250±600 (I-3536)

(e) III

II

Dark brown clay
(d₃)

Brownish-gray sandy silt (a₄)

Brown clayey gravel (a₃)

Pale gray sandy clay (a₂)

Unexcavated

Organic sand (c)

25,650±700 (I-3537)

V. Haynes, 1967

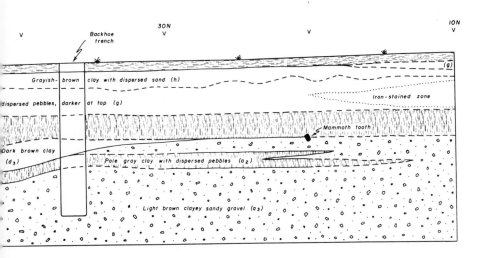

∨

Backhoe trench

30N
∨

∨

ION
∨

(g)

Grayish - brown clay with dispersed sand (h)

Iron-stained zone

dispersed pebbles, darker at top (g)

Mammoth tooth

Dark brown clay (d₃)

Pale gray clay with dispersed pebbles (a₂)

Light brown clayey sandy gravel (a₃)

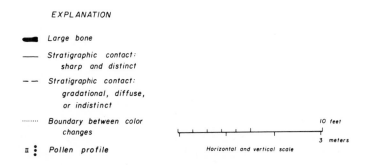

EXPLANATION

▬ Large bone

—— Stratigraphic contact:
sharp and distinct

— — Stratigraphic contact:
gradational, diffuse,
or indistinct

········ Boundary between color
changes

II ⫶ Pollen profile

10 feet

3 meters

Horizontal and vertical scale

Figure 3.4 Cross-section of Trolinger Spring at line W38 (1968), showing the location of pollen profile V and radiocarbon samples.

OLDER TERRACE DEPOSITS

Two terraces (T-1 and T-2) can be recognized above the floodplain (T-0) in the area (Figure 3.2), but the highest, T-2, is best preserved in the Breshears Bottoms, where it stands 12 to 13.5 m above the bed of the Pomme de Terre River. Spring bog deposits within the T-2 fill are yielding important paleoecological records. Trolinger Spring (Figure 3.1) has provided fossil pollen, mammal bones, and plant remains dated between 35,000 and 20,000 B.P., and indicates an interstadial to stadial climatic shift (Mehringer *et al.* 1970; Chapter 4). The stratigraphy and radiocarbon dates are shown here in cross sections (Figures 3.3 and 3.4) and in the stratigraphic column (Figure 3.5).

Prior to 1964, Trolinger Spring was reportedly a low-discharge spring or seep, but since then it has remained as only a small boggy area on the edge of a field on T-2. A few meters southwest of the bog, Terrace 2 is partly dissected by a small gulley whose walls reveal interbedded alluvial clay, silt, and thin gravel lenses that are hereafter referred to as unit *a*.

These floodplain deposits, laid down by the Pomme de Terre River when it still occupied the Breshears meander, are truncated by the springlaid deposits, units *b* to *h*, dated 35,000 to 20,000 B.P.

Buried spring deposits of this type are characterized by a feeder or conduit that has been cut by water ascending along cracks or other weaknesses of the host deposit, the feeder expanding in average diameter as it approaches the surface. With time, as the conduit is enlarged by erosive or sapping action, the sediment is broken down and sorted by the winnowing action of the ascending water. As a result, the sediments within the conduit are graded from coarsest at depth to finer near the top, where there is commonly an admixture of mineral sediment and more buoyant organic debris and peat. Trolinger Spring exhibits all of these features, which were exposed by mechanical excavation of trenches cut through it.

Referring to Figures 3.3 and 3.4, the spring feeder sand, unit *b*, the organic sand, unit *c*, and the overlying peats, units d_3 and *e*, could all be penecontemporaneous in that they reflect sorting due to vertical decrease in velocity of ascending water. However, at the early high discharge state the "eye" of a spring commonly consists of a pool of clear roiling water surrounded by a vegetation mat that becomes a mixture of peat and clay, thickening as growth and decay of plants continues. As discharge declines, the mat encroaches upon and eventually covers the "eye" to form a bog. Large animals could become trapped in the spring at any time in its history, but the absence of abrasion and rounding on the animal bones from Trolinger Spring suggests that the animals did not fall into the spring at the open pool stage with roiling sand and water, but instead became mired and eventually sank into the bog after the vegetation mat had at least partly covered the conduit.

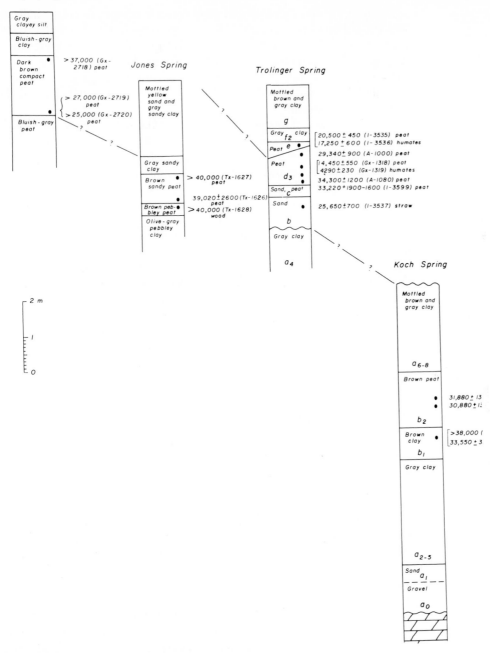

Figure 3.5 Correlation chart for stratigraphic columns from Terrace 2. Date Gx-1318 is considered too young because of the recent age of the humic acid fraction (Gx-1319).

Radiocarbon dates on peat and plant fragments from Trolinger indicate that the period of peat accumulation occurred between 34,000 and 20,000 years ago, but the lack of chronostratigraphic order among them suggests that there has been mixing within the deposits. This is not surprising considering the complexity of the microstratigraphy (Figures 3.3 and 3.4) and the fact that mastodons have thrashed and churned the deposits on occasion.

If the hypothetical model of the history of the spring suggested here is correct, the central part of the peat (that is, the peat overlying the "eye" or conduit) should be younger than peat farther out. At Trolinger, the radiocarbon dates on peat show no systematic order from youngest to oldest with depth (Figure 3.5), but sample Gx-1318 should be omitted because of acute humic acid contamination, as indicated by Gx-1319, run on the same sample. If this is done, the model is now consistent in that unit e is younger, with a date of 20,500±450 (I-3535). Unit e is an irregular mass of peat surrounded by older clayey peat of unit d_3, the top of which dated 29,340±900 (A-1000). Below the peats is a variegated mixture of dark brown plant fragments and pale gray sand (unit c) created by an overlapping of microlenses of plant fragments and sand, apparently the result of intermittent variations in discharge. During lesser discharges, water-logged plant fragments settled out on inactive parts of the feeder sand, only to become covered by feeder sand during subsequent episodes of greater discharge or when the loci of activity of subsidiary feeders changed within the main feeder. This intermediate period of activity took place around 34,000 to 32,000 years ago, as indicated by dates on a thin peat lens in the feeder sand (Figure 3.3) and on peat filling the nerve cavity of a mastodon tusk in unit d_3.

Many of the mammal bones are in unit c and are probably contemporaneous with it, but some occur on it and in the basal part of unit d_3, indicating younger ages. However, horizontal stratigraphic separation according to age of burial is not to be expected because of disturbance by the animals in their attempts to extract themselves from the bog. Evidence in support of this is suggested by the occurrence of irregular streak-like concentrations of short fragments of straw and twigs in the sand of unit b and below unit c. These plant fragments have the appearance of masticated vegetation as it might appear in the bowels of a mastodon, and could be preserved gut contents. In any case, the date of 25,650±700 (I-3537) is considerably younger than unit d and indicates intrusion from above.

The progressive reduction of spring discharge indicated by the sediments at Trolinger Spring may reflect either a lowering of the local water table as a result of the abandonment of the Breshears Bottoms by the Pomme de Terre River or a reduction in recharge accompanying a reduction in precipitation. In either case, this occurred sometime before 34,000 years ago when the peat began forming. If the radiocarbon dates on peat are correct, then the clays of units f_2 and g formed after 20,000 years ago as either backwater deposits (a clay plug) or springlaid pond deposits, or a combination thereof. On the other hand, because of the proximity of the Trolinger peat deposit to the modern surface bog there is the distinct possibility of contamination from younger organic matter, and the overlying units, f_2 and g, could represent the final phases of T-2 aggradation before the river abandoned this level or, if the dates are correct, they could be the result of high flood stage overbank deposition at the time of T-1a aggradation. The radiocarbon dates support the latter hypothesis, but more work will be required to settle this question.

The top of a peat stratum at the Kirby Spring (Figure 3.1), approximately 400 m west of Trolinger and 2 m higher, produced a radiocarbon date of >37,000 B.P. (Gx-2718) (Figure 3.5) and is overlain by a meter of clay. From our preliminary investigations, it is not clear if this clay is related to the bog or to unit a, but the date and elevation suggest that the peat itself is within unit a, making the entire unit 37,000 years old or older.

Jones Spring, less than 150 m from Trolinger (Figure 3.1), has been dated at >40,000 (Tx-1627, Tx-1628) and 39,020±2600 (Tx-1626). These dates, plus its depth below the T-2 tread and the fact that it is within the alluvium of unit a, make it older than Trolinger (Figure 3.2). Preliminary pollen evidence is consistent with an interstadial vegetation for both the Kirby and Jones peat deposits (Chapter 2).

The Koch Spring (Figure 3.1), a spring from which Albert Koch removed bones of a mastodon in 1840 (Koch 1857), was reopened in 1971. The work revealed a bone-bearing peat deposit within alluvial sediments believed to be equivalent to unit a in the Breshears Bottoms. If this interpretation is correct, the peat and the Koch mastodon are older than similar deposits at Trolinger, Jones, and Kirby springs because these are stratigraphically higher than the Koch peat (Figure 3.2), the lower part of which is dated as >38,000 B.P. (Tx-1457). This is consistent with the interpretation, but an overlying date of 31,800±1340 B.P. (Tx-1412) is not (Figure 3.5) and is probably contaminated, because it would require less than 2% of modern carbon to produce the discrepancy.

INTERMEDIATE TERRACE DEPOSITS

Several remnants of T-1 separate the floodplain terrace from the base of the dolomite bluffs, but examination and dating of the stratigraphy of these remnants at Boney Spring and at Rodgers Shelter (Figure 3.1) reveal that T-1 is a compound terrace representing two cycles of degradation and aggradation. The earlier period of alluvial deposition is represented by overbank accretion and spring deposits (T-1a) enveloping the bone bed at Boney Spring, whereas the later period is represented by the alluvium (T-1b) at Rodgers Shelter (Figure 3.2). Dates pertaining to the formation of T-1a are middle to late Wisconsinan dates of 16,500 and 13,500 years ago from the bone bed at Boney Spring, and dates of between 28,000 and 20,000 years ago from underlying strata (Figure 3.6).

At Boney Spring the matrix of the bone bed is clay, containing some fragments of spruce and larch wood approximately 16,500 years old, as well as clumps of moss. There is no penecontemporaneous peat deposit as there is at Trolinger Spring. The feeder extending below the bone bed is

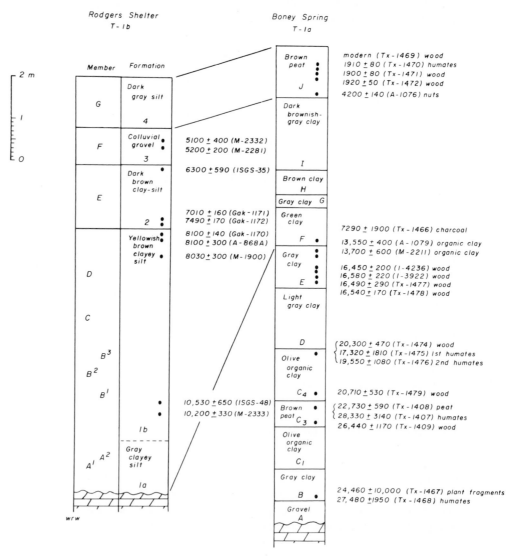

Figure 3.6 Correlation chart of stratigraphic columns for Terrace 1.

filled with granular tufa representing calcareous pseudomorphic over-growths on moss. These observations suggest that at the time of animal entrapment Boney Spring was either an open pool surrounded by a mat of moss or was covered by a moss mat, much of which later decayed. The granular tufa probably resulted from algal overgrowths that sank into the conduit and accumulated as older parts of the mat became inactive and broke up on decay. A date of 28,230± 940 B.P. (Tx-1473) on carbonate from the tufa is 12,000 years too old, indicating that 75% of the carbonate in the spring water is from the Paleozoic carbonates in the bedrock or from CO_2 in ancient soil gas.

Beneath the bone bed at Boney Spring are organic clays and a clayey peat deposit, all dating between 28,000 and 20,000 B.P. (Figure 3.6), indicating that T-1a began forming approximately 28,000 years ago and was abandoned after 13,000 years ago but before 11,000 B.P., when sediments of T-1b began forming. The underlying chert gravel is probably a lag deposit derived from the reworking of the gravel at the base of the T-2 fill, which crops out 30 m east of the spring and contains a reddish-brown relict B-horizon of a paleosol, most of which has been eroded away. The deposits of this T-2 remnant are correlated with unit *a* of the Breshears Bottoms.

At Rodgers Shelter, alluvial silts and colluvial gravels contain a record of 10,500 years of human occupation during postglacial aggradation of the Pomme de Terre floodplain (Chapter 8). Analyses of the sediments by Ahler (1973; Chapter 8) suggest an eolian source for silt of Strata 1 and 2 dated 10,500 to 6000 years ago. From 6000 to 3000 years ago there was the accumulation of colluvial gravel on T-1b, indicating that aggradation had ended by 6000 years ago. Abandonment of T-1b occurred before a date of 840± 60 (Tx-1454) years ago, based on wood from the middle of the T-0 deposits at Koch Spring (Figure 3.7).

Perched on both T-1a and T-0 are spring deposits that are wet today and contain accumulated peat and organic sediments dating back to at least 4000 B.P., but their discharge seeps back into the alluvium within a few meters of the "eye." One of these overlies the older peat at Boney Spring, and both the radiocarbon dating and archaeology indicate a temporal overlap between this Holocene deposit and Stratum 3 at Rodgers Shelter.

Between the Holocene peat layer and the bone bed at Boney Spring is a conformable sequence of clays (Figure 3.6) that fill the gap between the 13,500-year-old dates from the bone bed and the 4200-year-old date from the Holocene peat. There is a radiocarbon date from the clay beneath the peat of 7290± 1900 (Tx-1466). The date is from a very small sample of charcoal but it confirms the interpretation that these beds are in part correlative with Strata 1 and 2 at Rodgers Shelter, and may indicate that there is a thicker buried remnant of the T-1b immediately west of the spring and toward the river. Woodland artifacts were found in unit J during archaeological testing of Boney Spring (Chapter 6).

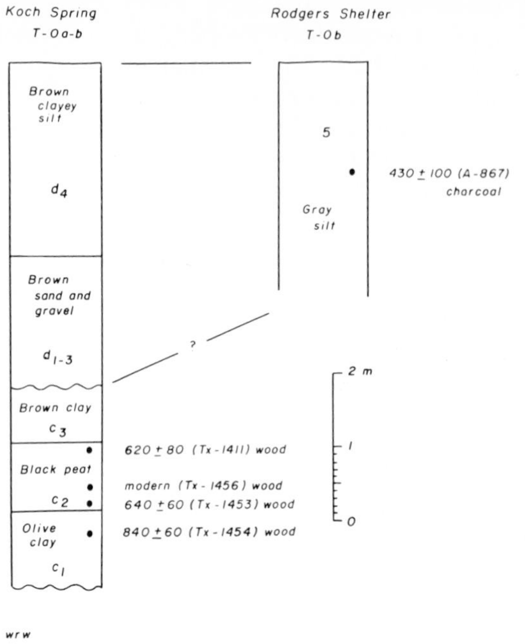

Figure 3.7   Correlation chart for Terrace   O.

FLOODPLAIN DEPOSITS

Terrace 1b is not present at Koch Spring, at least on the west side of the river, and the Holocene peat bog there is part of the modern floodplain, T-0. Dates within the peat indicate that T-0 began forming before 800 B.P. and continued to aggrade until after 600 B.P., when downcutting occurred, but a return to conditions of net aggradation must have taken place before 400 B.P. as evidenced by a charcoal date from T-0 at Rodgers Shelter (Figure 3.7). Thus, T-0, like T-1, is a compound fill with a younger floodplain deposit (T-0b) inset against another older one (T-0a).

Local farmers say that annual flooding kept the floodplain naturally fertile, but since the Pomme de Terre dam above the village of Hermitage was closed in 1961, T-0 has been abandoned and requires artificial fertilization to yield as well as it did before damming.

SUMMARY AND CONCLUSIONS

From the preliminary work in the lower Pomme de Terre valley, we can construct a tentative chronology of geologic–climatic events over at least the past 38,000 years. Before 38,000, the river had incised its meandering channel some 100 m into the Paleozoic rocks of the Ozark Plateau. By 38,000, a cycle of net aggradation had begun and continued until approximately 30,000 years ago when, after depositing at least 12 m of clay, silt, and gravel, the Pomme de Terre River cut off the Breshears meander and may have begun a period of net degradation throughout the system. Precisely when this period of downcutting began and ended is not clear, but it occurred sometime between 32,000 and 29,000 years ago—near the end of peat formation at Trolinger Spring—and 28,000 B.P.—by which time alluvial deposition had begun at Boney Spring. The degradation after abandonment of T-2 resulted in from partial to complete removal of T-2 in some parts of the valley.

The period of T-1a net aggradation was interrupted by a period of quasi-stability between 26,000 and 23,000 years ago, during which the lower peat deposit (unit C_3) at Boney Spring formed. This was followed by slow aggradation until about 16,500 years ago when another period of stability set in, and spruce grew at the site of Boney Spring. By 13,000 years ago, the bones of trapped mastodons, ground sloths, giant beavers, horses, etc. had been buried by organic clay, and T-1a reached its maximum height of 10 m.

Sometime after 13,000 B.P., but before 11,000 years ago, the Pomme de Terre again downcut its channel and left T-1a as evidence of its former floodplain. By 10,500 B.P., the river again aggraded as Paleo–Indians entered the area and began occupation of Rodgers Shelter. By 6000 B.P., aggradation had all but ceased, and Terrace 1b stabilized at essentially the same level as T-1a, thus forming a compound terrace. Except for colluvial deposition and occasional flooding, T-1 remained stable for possibly as much as 4000 years, but sometime before about 1000 B.P. T-1 was abandoned and a new floodplain was established 5 m above the present stream bed. This erosional–depositional cycle repeated itself again between 600 and 400 B.P., and final abandonment of T-0 came after completion of the Pomme de Terre dam.

In comparing the Pomme de Terre geochronology with the continental glaciation of North America we can see that the period of net aggradation represented by T-1a correlates very closely with the late Woodfordian substage of Frye and others (1968) in Illinois. The period of net degradation between T-1a and T-1b correlates with the Twocreekan substage and Terrace 1b with the Valderan substage. These correlations indicate a correspondence between net aggradation and glaciation even though the Pomme de Terre drainage is in the Ozark Highland, an unglaciated area over 400 km south of Wisconsinan moraines.

The earlier events are more difficult to correlate because of less reliability and confidence in radiocarbon dates in excess of 25,000 years. Furthermore, continental glacial events beyond this age are not as well established as are the younger events, partly for the same reason and partly because of poorer exposure and poorer preservation of tills. If radiocarbon dates from the older peat deposits are correct, then Terrace 2 would correlate with the Altonian substage in Illinois, and the evidence from fossil pollen would relate to periods of quasi-stability when peat deposits formed in spring bogs on the aggrading floodplain. That these periods were cooler and moister than today, but not as much so as the full glacial part of the cycle, is attested to by the pollen records from the peat deposits as compared to the fluvial clays such as the blue clay in unit D at Boney Spring. This suggests that there were several climatic cycles within the time represented by T-2, and these might correlate with events in the Lake Ontario and Lake Erie areas (Dreimanis 1969). Units C_1 and C_3 at Boney Spring, for example, might correlate with the Plum Point interstade, and unit c at Trolinger Spring might correlate with the stade between the Plum Point and Port Talbot interstades.

It should be pointed out, however, that these preliminary correlations are quite tenuous because only a percent or two of contamination in the radiocarbon samples would seriously affect the dates and would require significant modification to the interpretations based thereon. Geologic mapping in progress in the lower Pomme de Terre valley will result in more stratigraphic sections and replicate radiocarbon dates that will undoubtedly result in a better understanding of past events than the tentative picture presented here.

REFERENCES

Ahler, S.A.
  1973 Post-Pleistocene depositional change at Rodgers shelter, Missouri. *Plains Anthropologist* **18**: 1–26.
Bretz, JH.
  1965 Geomorphic history of the Ozarks of Missouri. *Missouri Geological Survey and Water Resources* **XLI** (end series).
Dreimanis, A.
  1969 The last Ice Age in the eastern Great Lakes region, North America. Paper presented at the 8th INQUA Congress, Paris.
Fenneman, N.H.
  1938 *Physiography of eastern United States.* New York: McGraw Hill.
Frye, J.C., H.B. Willman, M. Rubin, and R.F. Black
  1968 Definition of Wisconsinan Stage. *U.S. Geological Survey Bulletin,* 1274-E.
Hershey, O.H.
  1895 River valleys of the Ozark Plateau. *American Geologist* **16**: 338–352.
King, J.E.
  1973 Late Pleistocene palynology and biogeography of the western Missouri Ozarks. *Ecological Monographs* **43**: 539–565.
Knox, B.R.
  1966 Pleistocene and Recent geology of the southwest Ozark plateaus. MS., Ph.D. dissertation, Department of Geology, University of Iowa.
Koch, A.C.
  1857 Mastodon remains in the State of Missouri, together with evidence of the existence of man contemparaneously with the mastodon. *Transactions of the Academy of Science,* St. Louis **1**: 61–64.
Marbut, C.F.
  1896 Physical features of Missouri. *Missouri Geological Survey* **10**: 11–109.

Mehringer, P.J., Jr., J.E. King, and E.H. Lindsay.
1970 A record of Wisconsin-age vegetation and fauna from the Ozarks of western Missouri. In *Pleistocene and Recent environments of the Central Great Plains*, edited by W. Dort, Jr., and J. K. Jones, Jr. Lawrence, Kansas: Univ. of Kansas Press. Pp. 173–183.
Mehringer, P.J., Jr., C.E. Schweger, W.R. Wood, and R.B. McMillan
1968 Late-Pleistocene boreal forest in the western Ozark Highlands? *Ecology* 49: 567–568.
Quinn, J.H.
1956 Origin and age of Ozark Plateau surfaces in northwestern Arkansas. *Geological Society of America Bulletin* 67: 1726.
Tarr, W.A.
1924 Entrenched and incised meanders of some streams on the northern slope of the Ozark Plateau in Missouri. *Journal of Geology* 32: 583–600.

4

Late Quaternary Biotic Records from Spring Deposits in Western Missouri[1]

James E. King and Everett H. Lindsay

As part of the paleoenvironmental investigations in the lower Pomme de Terre River valley, a number of spring sediments were sampled in the hope of finding botanical and faunal evidence of past climatic change. Possible postglacial climatic changes are indicated at Rodgers Shelter by faunal shifts and by changing patterns of cultural adaptation (Part IV). The pollen analysis part of this program was initiated by Peter J. Mehringer, Jr., and has been continued by James E. King.

The Pomme de Terre River valley in Missouri was closely associated with fossil hunting and the early development of paleontology in North America. In 1840 Albert Koch excavated mastodon fossils from a spring 5 km southeast of Rodgers Shelter (Koch 1857). Koch, primarily an entrepreneur and showman, exhibited his strange fossils as the "Missouri Leviathan" and ultimately sold them to the British Museum. One of the best preserved specimens of mastodon *(Mammut americanum)* ever recovered was reassembled from this collection.

Several springs, located on terraces of the Pomme de Terre River in the vicinity of Rodgers Shelter (Figure 3.1), were examined by the research team, and two of them were selected for intensive investigation. A preliminary core collected from Boney Spring in 1966 revealed a spruce *(Picea)* dominated boreal pollen record and plant macrofossils of larch

[1] This paper is contribution No. 41, Department of Geosciences, University of Arizona, Tucson, Arizona.

(Larix laricina) and spruce, together with bone scraps and tusk fragments of proboscideans (Mehringer *et al.* 1968). Excavations were thus started in 1967 at Boney Spring to recover its floral and faunal record. At the same time, tests at Trolinger Spring also revealed mastodon bones associated with plant remains.

Trolinger Spring ceased flowing several years before its initial testing in 1967, thereby greatly simplifying its subsequent excavation. The spring margins were trenched with a backhoe, and the spring itself was excavated by hand. In addition to the faunal remains, pollen and plant macrofossil samples were collected from five vertical stratigraphic profiles and from the pulp cavities of several mastodon tusks. The Trolinger Spring excavations were completed in 1968. The excavation of Boney Spring, begun in 1967, was completed in 1971 when the spring's

Figure 4.1 Boney Spring during the 1971 excavations. The bone concentration was 4.2m below the surface and contained the remains of at least 30 mastodons. (By permission of the Illinois State Museum.)

flow was temporarily stopped by drilling wells around it to draw down the water table in the aquifer. As the spring sediments dried, it was possible to expose completely the entire bone deposit (Figure 4.1). Following excavation of the bone concentration, backhoe trenches were cut below it down to the gravel that overlay bedrock, thereby exposing the entire stratigraphic sequences (Chapter 3).

Preliminary results of the Boney and Trolinger springs excavations were reported earlier (Mehringer *et al.* 1970). Further radiocarbon dates, faunal data, pollen profiles, and plant macrofossils are now available. In addition, the excavation of Boney Spring is now complete, preliminary data from two other springs (Jones and Kirby springs) have been analyzed, and Koch's original spring site has been reinvestigated. This additional information has resulted in the construction of a paleoenvironmental chronology from at least 35,000 to 13,500 years B.P. When combined with the environmental data from Rodgers Shelter, the resulting record is one of the longest Quaternary geochronological sequences in the Midwest. For a discussion of these late Pleistocene records see King (1973).

FLORA AND RADIOCARBON DATES

Trolinger Spring

At Trolinger Spring, there is a marked change with depth in both the stratigraphy (Mehringer *et al.* 1970: Fig. 5) and the dominant pollen taxa. The pollen assemblage shifts abruptly from nonarboreal pollen (NAP) and pine dominance in the lower dark organic clay of unit d_3 (Figures 3.3, 3.4, and 3.5) to spruce dominance in the overlying blue–gray clay of unit f_2 (Figure 4.2). This significant change in pollen zones is duplicated in profiles from opposite sides of the spring (Figure 4.3), and is dated at about 23,000 to 25,000 B.P., as discussed later.

The NAP–pine pollen zone is composed principally of pine and Cyperaceae (sedge family) pollen, up to 60% for these two types. Other arboreal pollen types, except for oak *(Quercus)*, birch *(Betula)*, and willow *(Salix)*, are rare. This zone extends to the base of the dark organic clay at the contact with the basal sands of the spring conduit.

Macrofossils in the NAP–pine zone (unit d_3) include seeds of pondweed *(Potamogeton spirillus)*, coneflower *(Rudbeckia)*, sedge *(Carex)*, spike-rush *(Eleocharis)*, and bugleweed *(Lycopus americanus)*, larch needles, moss fragments, and insect parts. The insect remains, identified by John V. Matthews Jr., are those of aquatic beetles.

The pollen spectra from organic debris contained in the pulp cavities of four mastodon tusks were also dominated by NAP–pine (Figure 4.2), and

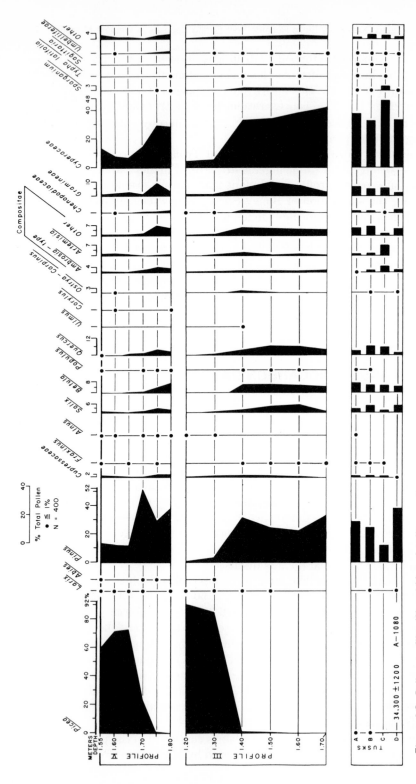

Figure 4.2 Pollen profiles III and V, and pollen spectra from mastodon tusk pulp cavities from Trolinger Spring.

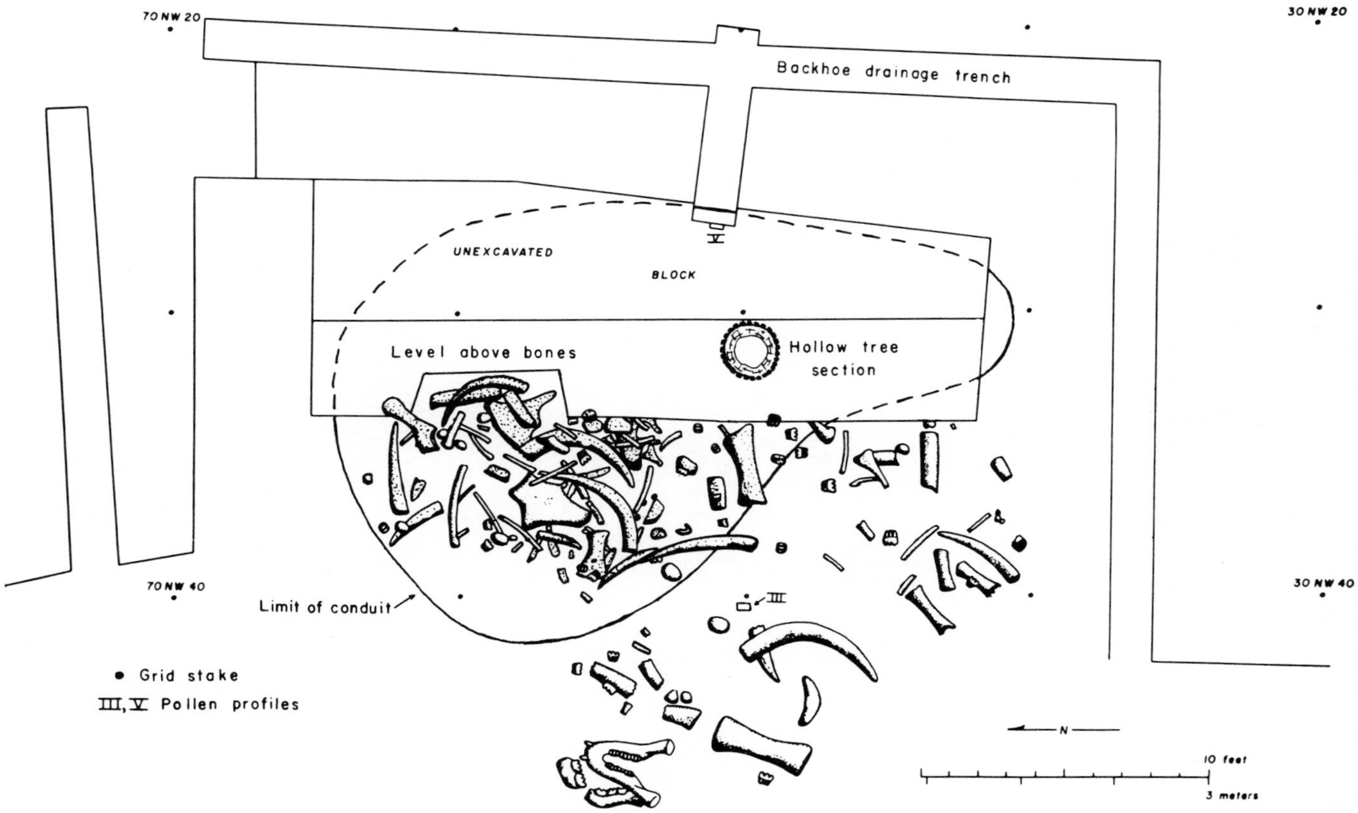

Figure 4.3 Map of Trolinger Spring showing the excavated portions, recovered faunal remains, and the location of pollen profiles.

67

all of the faunal remains in Trolinger Spring were restricted to the NAP–pine zone. Samples of matrix surrounding the mastodon remains did not contain any spruce pollen.

The blue–gray clay (unit f_2) directly overlying the dark organic clay contains spruce pollen percentages ranging from 60 to 92% with pine generally less than 10%. Spruce dominates this pollen zone; all other pollen types are notably absent. These spruce-dominated pollen spectra are similar to other late Wisconsinan-age pollen profiles and compare well with those given by Wright (1970) for the spruce period following deglaciation in the Great Lakes region. Pollen was present for only 30 cm above the shift from the NAP–pine zone to spruce zone. Above this, pollen preservation was too poor for analysis. Unfortunately, no plant macrofossils were associated with the spruce pollen zone.

Two radiocarbon dates from organic debris within the NAP–pine zone are 33,200+1900, −1600 B.P. (I-3599) and 25,650±700 B.P. (I-3537). A radiocarbon date of 34,300±1200 B.P. (A-1080) was obtained from plant detritus in the pulp cavity of mastodon tusk D (Figure 4.2) recovered from the organic sand underlying the dark organic clay. These dates are in proper stratigraphic context. Five other dates, stratigraphically higher in the NAP–pine pollen zone, range from 29,340±900 (A-1000) to 14,540±550 (Gx-1318) B.P. The date of 14,540±550 (Gx-1318) is disregarded by Haynes (Chapter 3) because of contamination by younger humic acids that have been dated at 4,290±230 B.P. (Gx-1319). This variation in the Trolinger Spring dates (excluding samples Gx-1318 and Gx-1319) prohibits a precise determination for the date of the shift from the NAP–pine zone to spruce pollen zone. There are no dates from the spruce pollen zone at Trolinger Spring.

Boney Spring

At Boney Spring, the fossil deposit, unit e (Figure 3.6), is overlain by about 4 m of clay and peat. A layer of peat 1 m thick at the surface of the spring contained no pollen, but there were well-preserved acorns and hickory nuts at its base. The clays between the surface peat and fossil deposit were also devoid of pollen. The fossil deposit, however, contained pollen-bearing sediments, and these, along with four pollen spectra from the pulp cavities of mastodon tusks (Figure 4.4), were dominated by spruce. These spectra are similar to the initial core sample from the conduit taken at a depth of greater than 4 m (Mehringer *et al.* 1968). However, these spruce-dominated pollen spectra differ from the Trolinger Spring spruce zone in the larger amounts of the thermophilus deciduous tree pollen and in the lower values of spruce (26-36%). In the Boney Spring spruce zone, as recorded in the mastodon tusks, *Quercus*, *Alnus*, *Fraxinus*, *Corylus*, and *Ostrya/Carpinus* are constant components.

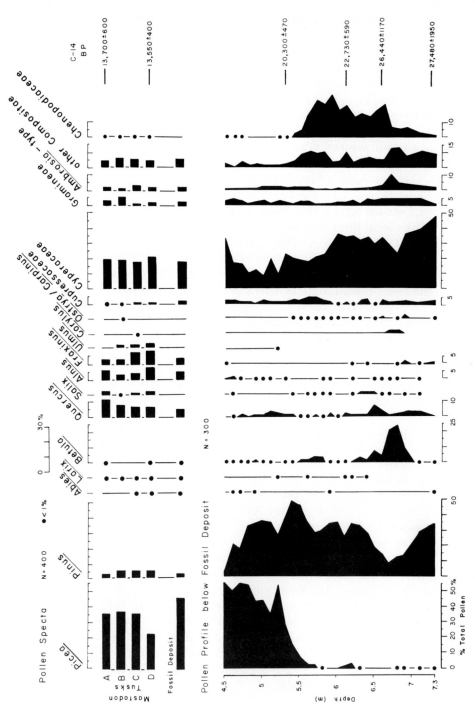

Figure 4.4 Summary pollen diagram from Boney Spring. The pollen profile is from sediments below the fossil deposit; the spectra are from within it. (Adapted from King 1973.)

Plant macrofossils recovered from the faunal deposit at Boney Spring include the wood of spruce (Figure 4.5), larch, and either willow or poplar (Salicaceae). There were also seeds of larch, sedge (*Scirpus*), dogwood (*Cornus racemosa*), pondweed (*Potamogeton spirillus*), sedge (*Carex*), bramble (*Rubus*), bur-marigold (*Bidens*), bugleweed (*Lycopus americanus*), knotweed (*Polygonum pensylvanicum* and *P. sagittatum*), buttercup *(Ranunculus)*, together with needles and cone parts of larch, spruce, and large quantities of mosses. Ostracods and insect fragments were also present. The insect remains (identified by Matthews) were mostly aquatic beetles.

Several radiocarbon dates are available from the fossil deposit at Boney Spring. Organic debris in two mastodon tusk cavities was dated at 13,550±400 B.P. (A-1079, Tusk A) and 13,700±600 B.P. (M-2211, Tusk D). Dates from three spruce logs are 16,450±200 B.P. (I-4236), 16,490±290 B.P. (Tx-1477), and 16,580±220 B.P. (I-3922). Another unidentified log from the fossil deposit was dated at 16,540±170 B.P. (Tx-1478). The hickory nuts from the base of the surface peat, approximately 2.8 m above the fossil deposit, date at 4200±140 B.P. (A-1076). In addition, there are three radiocarbon dates on archaeological specimens from near the center of the surface peat of 1900±80 B.P. (Tx-1471), 1910±80 B.P. (Tx-1470), and 1920±50 B.P. (Tx-1472).

A pollen profile from the trench excavated below the fossil deposit at Boney Spring (Figure 4.4, lower portion) shows the same sequence of pollen zones found at Trolinger Spring: NAP–pine pollen dominating in the lower portions, shifting to spruce dominance above. The overlap between the NAP–pine and the spruce pollen zones (4.5 to 5.5 m, Figure 4.4) probably reflects both a faster rate of sedimentation at Boney Spring and a possible depositional hiatus between these two pollen zones at Trolinger Spring. The pollen assemblages of spruce with deciduous elements are missing in the upper samples from the Boney Spring pollen profile. This indicates there is probably a gap in the pollen record between the top of the Boney Spring pollen profile and that of the fossil deposit. Radiocarbon dates within the pollen profile (Figure 4.4) indicate its age as Wisconsinan.

Analyses of the deposits in Jones and Koch springs have confirmed the NAP–pollen zone described from Trolinger Spring. The lowest levels at both Jones and Koch springs contain NAP–pine pollen spectra associated with mastodons. At a depth of 2 m in Koch Spring, associated with the NAP–pine pollen zone, jack pine (*Pinus banksiana*) cone scales were found. Radiocarbon dates from Koch Spring of >38,000 B.P. (Tx-1457), 33,550±3210 B.P. (Tx-1458), 31,880±1340 B.P. (Tx-1412), and 30,880±1320 B.P. (Tx-1455) confirm the age of NAP–pine pollen zone as greater than 23,000 B.P.

Figure 4.5 Spruce log *in situ* within the fossil deposit at Boney Spring. A tusk is visible on the left and part of a mastodon skull is on the upper right. Scale arrow (in cm) points north; depth of log, 4.8 m.

FAUNA

Faunal remains from both Boney Spring and Trolinger Spring, shown in Table 4.1, include 22 genera of mammals. The mammal fauna at Boney Spring is much better represented (20 genera) than that of Trolinger Spring (7 genera). Four genera *(Blarina, Peromyscus, Synaptomys,* and *Mammut)* are common to both spring deposits. Six of the mammal genera *(Paramylodon, Castoroides, Mammut, Mammuthus, Equus,* and *Symbos)* are extinct or naturally terminated in North America and most (15 of 16) of the extant genera presently inhabit the Ozark Highland.

The fauna was concentrated within a rather narrow stratigraphic interval in both springs. At Boney Spring the bone concentration or fossil deposit was in a gray clay (unit *e*), at a depth of about 4 m. At Trolinger Spring the bone concentration was primarily in the organic sand or the overlying dark organic clay about 2 m beneath the surface (Figure 4.3). Bones adjoining the spring conduit (in fine sand) were displaced in both springs. The bone beds were distinctive and horizontal in undisturbed areas away from the conduit. With the exception of a single *Mammuthus* tooth at Trolinger Spring, the fossil specimens were all taken from the

TABLE 4.1 Vertebrates from Boney Spring and Trolinger Spring, Missouri

	Boney Spring	Trolinger Spring
PISCES		
Teleostei	indeterminate fish	
AMPHIBIA		
Anura	*Rana* sp. (frog)	
REPTILIA		
Lacertilia	lizard	
Ophidia	snake	
MAMMALIA		
Insectivora	*Blarina brevicauda* (short-tail shrew)	*Blarina brevicauda* (short-tail shrew)
	Cryptotis parva (least shrew)	
	Scalopus aquaticus (eastern mole)	
Edentata	*Paramylodon harlani*[a] (ground sloth)	
Lagomorpha	*Sylvilagus floridanus* (eastern cottontail)	
Rodentia	*Marmota* sp. (marmot)	
	Tamias striatus (eastern chipmunk)	
	Glaucomys volans (southern flying squirrel)	
	Geomys bursarius (plains pocket gopher)	
	Castoroides ohioensis[a] (giant beaver)	
	Peromyscus maniculatus (deer mouse)	*Peromyscus* sp. A. (mouse)
		Peromyscus sp. B. (mouse)
	Neotoma floridana (eastern woodrat)	
	Synaptomys cooperi (southern bog lemming)	*Synaptomys cooperi* (southern bog lemming)
	Microtus ochrogaster (prairie vole)	
	Microtus sp. (vole)	
	Napaeozapus insignis (woodland jumping mouse)	
Proboscidea	*Mammut americanum*[a] (American mastodon)	*Mammut americanum*[a] (American mastodon)
		Mammuthus sp.[ab] (mammoth)
Carnivora	*Procyon lotor* (raccoon)	
Perissodactyla	*Equus* sp.[a] (horse)	*Equus* sp.[a] (horse)
	Tapirus sp. (tapir)	
Artiodactyla	*Odocoileus* sp. (deer)	
		Symbos sp.[a] (muskox)

[a] Extinct or naturally terminated in North America.
[b] *Mammuthus* is not associated with the other Trolinger Spring fauna (see text).

bone beds and conduits. The *Mammuthus* tooth came from a strati-graphically lower and peripheral area at Trolinger Spring that predates the main deposit. About 300 kg of sediment matrix were screen-washed from both springs to recover small mammals and this process was especially succesful at Boney Spring.

The most abundant mammal at both Boney and Trolinger springs is *Mammut americanum*, the American mastodon. In 1968 over 100 speci-mens (complete or partial elements) from Boney Spring and about 80 specimens from Trolinger Spring were collected. In 1971 over 600 ad-ditional specimens were collected at Boney Spring (Saunders 1975). There are at least 30 individuals of *Mammut* from Boney Spring and 7 individuals from Trolinger Spring. Mastodon, an herbivorous browser, was apparently a common inhabitant in the open pine parkland (Trolinger Spring) and in spruce forests (Boney Spring) of the Ozark Highland during the late Quaternary.

Other large mammals preserved in the spring deposits include an ex-tinct ground sloth *(Paramylodon harlani)*, an extinct giant beaver *(Castoroides ohioensis)*, an extinct muskox *(Symbos* sp.), a raccoon *(Procyon lotor)*, deer *(Odocoileus* sp.), tapir *(Tapirus* sp.), and horse *(Equus* sp.). The ground sloth, giant beaver, tapir, raccoon, and deer are from Boney Spring; the muskox is from Trolinger Spring. This difference in faunal composition in geographically close but chronologically distinct deposits probably reflects both a shift in local animal populations and selective preservation. The only mammal that is abundant in either spring is the mastodon. Excavation of the bone concentration was meticulous and thorough; it is unlikely that the remains of any large animals were over-looked. *Castoroides* and deer were more common in the disturbed sedi-ments near the spring conduit, hinting that they were added to the de-posit later than the main bone concentration. This is further suggested by the fact that the roots of several mastodon teeth had been gnawed away, apparently by the *Castoroides*. None of the large mammals are especially restricted to cold climates, althouth Pleistocene records of mastodon and *Symbos* are more common in northern, colder regions.

The most common small mammals from Boney Spring are the short-tail shrew *(Blarina brevicauda)*, deer mouse *(Peromyscus maniculatus)*, and prairie vole *(Microtus ochrogaster)*. All of these genera presently live in the Ozark Highland, although this is near the southern limits of distribution for the prairie vole.

Other small mammals relatively common at Boney Spring include the eastern mole *(Scalopus aquaticus)*, marmot *(Marmota* sp.), eastern chipmunk *(Tamias striatus)*, southern flying squirrel *(Glaucomys volans)*, plains pocket gopher *(Geomys bursarius)*, southern bog lem-ming *(Synaptomys cooperi)*, and voles *(Microtus* sp.). All of these taxa are found in the Ozark Highland today, although the eastern chipmunk and the plains pocket gopher are marginal inhabitants, and the southern bog lemming is near the southern limit of its distribution.

Four small mammals very poorly represented at Boney Spring are the least shrew (*Cryptotis parva*), eastern cottontail (*Sylvilagus floridanus*), eastern woodrat (*Neotoma floridana*), and woodland jumping mouse (*Napaeozapus insignis*). The only taxon of this group that does not presently inhabit the Ozark Highland is the woodland jumping mouse.

The small mammal fauna from Trolinger Spring includes *Blarina brevicauda;* two species of *Peromyscus,* one larger and one smaller than *P. maniculatus* from Boney Spring; *Synaptomys* sp., probably *S. cooperi;* and microtine tooth fragments, probably from *Synaptomys.*

Habitat preferences (Schwartz and Schwartz 1959; Hoffman and Jones 1970) of the small mammals are predominately deciduous forest biome, with the gopher and vole preferring a steppe biome, and the bog lemming and jumping mouse preferring a boreal biome.

Small mammals from Rodgers Shelter (Chapter 9) show a dominance of the larger genera, such as *Sylvilagus, Sciurus, Microtus,* and *Geomys,* probably reflecting the selective collection (and preservation) of edible species. Flying squirrel and jumping mouse are absent at Rodgers Shelter.

Notable by their absence in the springs are such carnivorous animals as coyote, dire wolf, fox, skunk, or badger. Other animals we might have expected to see in the springs, based on their present distribution or their record at Rodgers Shelter, are the opossum, gray squirrel, beaver, and muskrat. Late Pleistocene cave faunas of North America commonly include such large mammals as the dire wolf *(Canis dirus),* the short-faced bear *(Arctodus),* and one of the peccaries *(Platygonus* or *Mylohyus),* but none were in the spring deposits. Small mammals are rarely common members of cave faunas, although they dominate the fauna of Crankshaft Cave (Parmalee *et al.* 1969), which also includes mastodon, tapir, and horse. The most common taxa at Crankshaft Cave are the short-tail shrew, cottontail rabbit, marmot, packrat, and vole.

Hoffman and Jones (1970) have ably reconstructed the late Pleistocene distribution of mammals that presently inhabit the North American Great Plains. They identified a Wisconsinan-age steppe fauna, boreal or montane fauna, deciduous forest fauna, and probable immigrant species, based on the present distribution and ecologic niche preference of individual species. Hoffman and Jones followed the climatic chronology of Bryson *et al.* (1970), and considered the interval 40,000 to 25,000 years ago as full glacial, noting the presence of steppe faunas (Dalquest 1962, 1964; Slaughter and Ritchie 1963) with *Blarina brevicauda, Synaptomys cooperi,* and *Microtus ochrogaster* from central Texas. Our pollen analysis indicates, however, that Trolinger Spring was an open pine parkland from at least 34,000 to about 24,000 years ago, and that it should have a forest–bog fauna during a later phase of glacial climate, based on the Boney Spring spectra of 16,500 to 13,500 years ago. Dalquest (1965) noted *B. brevicauda, S. cooperi,* and *M. ochrogaster* from Hardeman

County, Texas, at 16,775 years B.P.—about the same time that Boney Spring was accumulating these species. Lundelius (1967), in his excellent review of late Pleistocene faunas, noted the infrequent record of these same taxa in Texas. Lundelius suggested that taxa now inhabiting forests and bogs may have lived in the canyons of Texas during the late Pleistocene. The wide geographic distribution of these taxa during the late Pleistocene suggests that they had greater ecologic tolerances at that time than they now have. Apparently, small mammals did not change their geographic distribution along with plant communities as the climate fluctuated during the late Pleistocene. The data consequently indicate that great care must be exercised in drawing climatic–ecologic conclusions from mammalian paleogeography in the late Pleistocene.

DISCUSSION AND SUMMARY

The Trolinger Spring deposits record an NAP–pine pollen zone from at least 34,000 to about 24,000 years ago associated with a mastodon-dominated fauna with horse and muskox. This is the first record of mastodon associated with pine-dominated pollen spectra in unglaciated North America. Mastodon has previously been considered a spruce forest inhabitant. This same pollen zone has been found at Boney Spring and Koch Spring; at Koch Spring it was also associated with mastodon remains.

The NAP–pine zone equates with the mid-Wisconsinan interstade that preceded the late Wisconsinan glaciation. This lengthy interstade, a period of relatively mild climatic conditions during which the continental glaciers retreated northward, is recorded from deposits in the Lake Erie region of Canada dated between more than 48,000 to 24,000 B.P. (Dreimanis *et al.* 1966; Dreimanis and Karrow 1972) and in a core from southern Illinois dated at more than 22,000 B.P. (E. Grüger 1972). The Ozark NAP–pine pollen zone is interpreted as an open pine parkland; we previously noted (Mehringer *et al.* 1970) that the NAP–pine spectra are similar to the aspen parkland of southern Manitoba (Lichti-Federovich and Ritchie 1965, 1968). The absence of aspen *(Populus)* pollen from the Ozark pollen record does not alter this comparison as aspen pollen does not preserve well. *Pinus banksiana* macrofossils, present in the NAP–pine pollen zone with mastodon, indicate the Ozark interstadial pine was the jack pine of the Great Lakes region and not one of the southern pines such as *P. echinata,* which presently grows in southern Missouri. The change from NAP–pine to spruce-dominated pollen spectra reflects the onset of late Wisconsinan glacial conditions at the end of the mid-Wisconsinan interstade. While precise dating of this transition has not been obtained, our data indicate that it occurred 23,000 to 25,000 years ago.

The Boney Spring fossil deposit is more diverse than the one at Trolinger Spring: It consists of a mastodon-dominated fauna with giant beaver, ground sloth, tapir, deer, and horse. Associated with this fauna is a late Wisconsinan floral record of spruce with deciduous elements, radiometrically dated between 16,500 and 13,500 years ago. Except for the low percentage of pine pollen, the Boney Spring spruce zone resembles the present southern boreal forest or mixed coniferous–broad-leaved deciduous forest (Lichti-Federovich and Ritchie 1968). The sediments below the late Wisconsinan fossil deposit contain NAP–pine-dominated pollen assemblages and radiocarbon dates that indicate a mid-Wisconsinan interstadial age. The radiocarbon dates, flora, and fauna from these Ozark springs are summarized in Table 4.2.

TABLE 4.2   Summary of the Inferred Dominant Vegetation and Faunal Assemblages from Spring Deposits in the Western Missouri Ozarks

Inferred dominant vegetation	C^{14} years B.P.	Megafaunal assemblages
oak–hickory forest	2,000	
- - - - - - - - - - - - - - - - - - - -	- 6,000	(no data)
(no data)		
- - - - - - - - - - - - - - - - -	- 10,000 -
spruce with deciduous trees	14,000	mastodon, tapir, ground sloth, deer, giant beaver, horse
	18,000	- - - - - - - - - - - - - - - - - - -
spruce forest		(no data)
	22,000	- - - - - - - - - - - - - - - - - - -
	26,000	
open pine parkland	30,000	mastodon, horse, muskox
	34,000	

The first report of a boreal pollen record in the mid-continent area was by Horr (1955) from Muscotah Marsh, northeastern Kansas. He found a basal spruce zone [which was unfortunately misidentified as *Abies* in the original counts (Wells 1970: note 6) dated at 15,000±1500 B.P. (McGregor 1968)]. Recent studies at Muscotah Marsh (J. Grüger 1973) show a spruce pollen zone from at least 23,000 to about 12,000 B.P., when it was replaced by a NAP-dominated zone that is interpreted to be of prairie origin. The dates on the Muscotah Marsh profiles and their lack of a basal mid-Wisconsinan NAP–pine zone identify them as younger than the older deposits at Trolinger Spring, Boney Spring and Koch Spring.

The Ozark postglacial paleoenvironmental record from spring deposits is as yet a meager one, although some conclusions are evident. The decline of the spruce forest apparently occured after 13,550 B.P., the latest date on the spruce pollen zone, but before 11,300 B.P., which is the earliest date on prairie vegetation at Muscotah Marsh, Kansas (J. Grüger 1973).

Whether deciduous forest or prairie followed the spruce is unknown, although an oak–hickory forest was definitely present by 4200 B.P., as evidenced by hickory nuts and acorns at Boney Spring. Extrapolating from Muscotah Marsh, it would appear that the Ozark spruce forest ended about 12,000 years ago.

From the evidence contained in the Ozark springs and from the literature cited, the following sequence of events can be constructed. From at least 34,000 to around 24,000 years ago, during the mid-Wisconsinan interstade, an open pine parkland existed in the western Missouri Ozarks. With the onset of full-glacial climatic conditions around 23,000 to 24,000 years ago, dominant spruce forest replaced the pine parkland. Spruce was present from this time until at least 13,500 B.P., although it declined in dominance and deciduous elements appeared in the later phases. Spruce disappeared from the Ozark Highland about 12,000 years ago.

REFERENCES

Bryson, R.A., D.A. Baerreis, and W.M. Wendland
  1970 The character of Late-Glacial and Post-Glacial climatic change. In *Pleistocene and Recent environments of the Central Great Plains*, edited by W. Dort, Jr., and J.K. Jones, Jr. Lawrence, Kansas: Univ. of Kansas Press.
Dalquest, W.W.
  1962 The Good Creek Formation, Pleistocene of Texas, and its fauna. *Journal of Paleontology* 36:568–582.
  1964 A new Pleistocene local fauna from Motley County, Texas. *Transactions of the Kansas Academy of Science* 67:499–505.
  1965 New Pleistocene formation and local fauna from Hardeman County, Texas. *Journal of Paleontology* 39:63–79.
Dreimanis, A., and P.F. Karrow
  1972 Glacial history of the Great Lakes—St. Lawrence region, the classification of the Wisconsin(an) stage, and its correlatives. *International Geological Congress*, 24th Session, Section 12:5–15.
Dreimanis, A., J. Terasmae, and G.D. McKenzie
  1966 The Port Talbot interstade of the Wisconsin glaciation. *Canadian Journal of Earth Science* 3:305–325.
Grüger, E.
  1972 Late Quaternary vegetation development in south-central Illinois. *Quaternary Research* 2:217–231.
Grüger, J.
  1973 Studies on the late Quaternary vegetation history of northeastern Kansas. *Geological Society of America Bulletin* 84:239–250.
Hoffman, R.S., and J.K. Jones, Jr.
  1970 Influence of Late-Glacial and Post-Glacial events on the distribution of Recent mammals on the northern Great Plains. In *Pleistocene and Recent environments of the Central Great Plains*, edited by W. Dort, Jr., and J.K. Jones, Jr. Lawrence, Kansas: Univ. of Kansas Press.

Horr, W.H.
  1955 A pollen profile study of the Muscotah Marsh. *Univ. of Kansas Science Bulletin* **37**:143–149.

King, J.E.
  1973 Late Pleistocene palynology and biogeography of the western Missouri Ozarks. *Ecological Monographs* **43**:539–565.

Koch, A.C.
  1857 Mastodon remain in the State of Missouri, together with evidence of the existence of man contemparaneously with the mastodon. *Transactions of the Academy of Science*, St. Louis **1**:61–64.

Lichti-Federovich, S., and J.C. Ritchie
  1965 Contemporary pollen spectra in central Canada. II: The forest–grassland transition in Manitoba. *Pollen et Spores* **7**:63–87.
  1968 Recent pollen assemblages from the western interior of Canada. *Review of Palaeobotany and Palynology* **7**:297–344.

Lundelius, E.L.
  1967 Late Pleistocene and Holocene faunal history of central Texas. In *Pleistocene extinctions, the search for a cause*, edited by P.S. Martin, and H.E. Wright, Jr. New Haven, Connecticut: Yale Univ. Press.

McGregor, R.L.
  1968 A C-14 date for the Muscotah Marsh. *Transactions of the Kansas Academy of Science* **71**:85–86.

Mehringer, P.J., Jr., J.E. King, and E.H. Lindsay
  1970 A record of Wisconsin-age vegetation and fauna from the Ozarks of western Missouri. In *Pleistocene and Recent environments of the Central Great Plains*, edited by W. Dort, Jr., and J.K. Jones, Jr. Lawrence, Kansas: Univ. of Kansas Press.

Mehringer, P.J., Jr., C.E. Schweger, W.R. Wood, and R.B. McMillan
  1968 Late-Pleistocene boreal forest in the western Ozark Highlands? *Ecology* **49**:567–568.

Parmalee, P.W., R.D. Oesch, and J.W. Guilday
  1969 Pleistocene and Recent faunas from Crankshaft Cave, Missouri. *Illinois State Museum, Reports of Investigations* No. 14.

Saunders, J.J.
  1975 Late Pleistocene vertebrates of the western Ozark Highlands, Missouri. Ph.D. dissertation, Department of Geosciences, University of Arizona, Tucson.

Schwartz, C.W., and E.R. Schwartz
  1959 *The wild mammals of Missouri.* Columbia, Missouri: Univ. of Missouri Press.

Slaughter, B.H., and R. Ritchie
  1963 Pleistocene mammals of the Clear Creek local fauna, Denton County, Texas. *Journal of the Graduate Research Center*, Southern Methodist University **31**:117–131.

Wells, P.V.
  1970 Postglacial vegetational history of the Great Plains. *Science* **167**:1574–1582.

Wright, H.E., Jr.
  1970 Vegetational history of the Central Great Plains. In *Pleistocene and Recent environments of the Central Great Plains*, edited by W. Dort, Jr., and J.K. Jones, Jr. Lawrence, Kansas: Univ. of Kansas Press.

III

The Question of
Man's Antiquity

5

Man and Mastodon: A Review of Koch's 1840 Pomme de Terre Expeditions

R. Bruce McMillan

Of the many curious and inexplicable phenomena European settlers discovered in the New World, perhaps none—excluding the aboriginal peoples themselves—had more profound impact on and appeal to the immigrant imagination than the giant fossil bones that seemed to erode from almost every stream bank or bog. Fossils of periods long past were plentiful because of the unspoiled nature of the continent. By contrast, many European fossil localities had been destroyed or denuded of their remains centuries prior to the discovery of America.

One of the pioneers of nineteenth-century fossil collecting in North America was Albert C. Koch (1804–1867), a German immigrant born in Roitzsch in Saxony, who moved to the United States when he was 22. In order to understand Koch's role in the development of studies related to the Quaternary, his activities must be evaluated within the intellectual milieu of the late eighteenth and early nineteenth centuries. During this period of history, science was languishing under the tutelage of scriptural authority, for answers to all unexplained phenomena were unquestionably revealed through biblical revelation (Harris 1968:109). Eiseley (1945a:85) excellently characterized the period as follows:

> the eighteenth century and the beginning years of the nineteenth marked
> the rise of intense zoological interest among the intelligentsia of the New

and Old Worlds. The great eighteenth century forerunners of Darwin—
Buffon, Cuvier, and others—were beginning to approach, with much hesi-
tancy and many misgivings, the problem of specific change. . . . America,
with its strange animals, its mysterious bones, and a human race un-
accounted for in Biblical terms, had contributed to those uneasy stirrings.
A science was being born.

By the late eighteenth century some geologists (e.g., Hutton 1788)
were beginning to postulate what were then heretical theories, for example, the theory that geomorphic change might simply be based on the
cumulative effects of nature. Furthermore, discoveries in Europe of artifacts and human bones associated with extinct animals were helping
muddy the scriptural waters (Daniel 1950). Man-made stone tools had
been recognized with the bones of extinct megafauna in England as early
as 1690 (Oakley 1959:6), but at that time the possibility of man's having
had an unrecorded history was unthinkable; it was another 150 years before the intellectual climate would allow consideration of this possibility.

To accommodate the mounting paleontological and geomorphic evidence, and yet rationalize and faithfully adhere to biblical tenets, *catastrophism* was born. The proponents of catastrophism or "Diluvialists,"
such as Baron Georges Cuvier in Paris and William Buckland at Oxford,
held that a series of violent revolutions had swept the earth's surface, and
that these were recorded as profound changes in geologic strata and their
attendant fossils. Fossils were believed to be the remains of former living
organisms annihilated during a catastrophe; new creatures were thought
to have been created after each diluvium (Berry 1968:43). The Genesis
narrative of the Noachian Flood was obviously a historical account of the
most recent catastrophe (Daniel 1950:36).

By the 1830s some of the first accounts of the European "bone caverns"
were published; these presented almost irrefutable evidence of man in
association with extinct animals (Tournal 1833; reprinted in Heizer
1962:71). During the same decade, Boucher de Perthes, on the basis of his
archaeological discoveries in France on the Somme near Abbeville,
argued that man was a contemporary of extinct animals (Lowie 1937:7).
Even so, continued opposition by influential creationists such as Cuvier
and others delayed general acceptance of these discoveries for another 20
years. It was 1859, the same year that Darwin shocked the Christian
world with his *On the Origin of Species*, that the British geologist Charles
Lyell and other Victorian scholars finally accepted Boucher de Perthes'
claims publicly.

THE ST. LOUIS MUSEUM

It was into this intellectual climate of early nineteenth-century Europe
that Koch was born and educated. During his formative years in Germany he had been exposed to his father's penchant for collecting what
were then little-understood natural history "curiosities," including a collection kept in their home (Stadler 1972: xvii–xix). When Koch later

emigrated to North America he carried this interest with him. He settled in St. Louis, Missouri soon after arriving in this country, and opened a private museum, which operated between the years 1836 and 1841 when museums were often nothing more than cabinets of curiosities (e.g., Anderson 1973).

Albert Koch's St. Louis museum advertised such random exotica as a live grizzly bear and five alligators; a two-headed, six-legged lamb; an Egyptian mummy; a great bustard mount; and a 14½-pound oyster shell (McDermott 1948:233; Stadler 1972: xxi). Theatrical entertainment was also very much a part of his museum, where a parade of magicians, vocalists, actors, mimics, and ventriloquists performed during the evening. Some of the more exotic talents he advertised were the "Great Persian Koulah" and "Miss Zelina-Kha-Nourhina, the Peri of the Caspian"—who performed, among other things, the "Feast of Miracles" and a "Kafez Oracle and Sacred Fire [McDermott 1948:235–237]." It was no exaggeration when Mehl (1962:29) compared Koch's showmanship skills with those of the celebrated and immortal P.T. Barnum.

Shortly after Koch opened his museum, stories of fossil vertebrate discoveries west of the city reached St. Louis. These must have captured his interest and imagination for by 1838 Albert Koch had become one of the most tireless and indefatigable fossil collectors in North America, amassing in just 2 years a collection containing more than 300 mastodon teeth, with numerous jaws, tusks, and postcranial parts, besides remains of "ox [probably bison], deer, elk, megatherium, and mylodon [Harlan 1843:69; Hay 1924:27]." Koch (1857:61) later claimed his collection contained more than 600 mastodon teeth, 73 mandibles, nearly as many maxillae, a large collection of tusks of all sizes, as well as five complete skulls and a skeleton.

KOCH'S FOSSIL DISCOVERIES

The major part of Koch's fossil vertebrate collection came from three localities, all in the state of Missouri. In October 1838 he excavated a spring deposit on the Bourbeuse River, 130 km southwest of St. Louis, from which he disinterred parts of a mastodon(s) that he contended had been stoned and burned by Indians. He based this on his impression that many of the blackened bones appeared to have been burned, and on the fact that among the bones there were a large number of rocks of varying sizes. He believed that the latter had been transported there by man (Koch 1839a, 1841:22–24, 1857). To clinch his case, Koch pointed out that both the landowner and he had recovered "several arrowheads, a stone spearhead, and some stone axes" along with the bones (Koch 1857:63). Gross (1951:107) recently illustrated four artifacts, now in the Berlin Museum for Natural History, which are catalogued as specimens from the Bourbeuse River discovery; presumably these represent some of those described by Koch. Prehistorians have debated the authenticity of this reputed association over the years, although alternative hypotheses positing a fortuitous association were published as early as 1860 (Wis-lizenus 1860).

In May 1839 Koch traveled to what he termed "Sulphur Springs," a few kilometers south of St. Louis—the locality, in Jefferson County, Missouri, known today as the Kimmswick bone bed (Hay 1924:262; Adams 1953; Mehl 1962:31). There he excavated a number of bones. Paramount among them was a large skull that he decided "until now was a perfectly unknown animal [quoted in Buckingham 1842:134]." Although in later years he found it to be a mastodon, Koch (1839b), believing then that it was a new type of animal, referred to it as the "*Missourium*," or later, "*Missourium Kochii*" (Osborn 1936:1389). It was from this Kimmswick discovery that Koch's lively imagination created a creature similar to but larger than an elephant that he thought must have inhabited the western parts of America, an animal he would find again in the Osage country. His descriptions of the first example of the "*Missourium*" were quoted by Buckingham (1842:136):

> In the head of this huge monster we observed particularly that while the tusks of an elephant go downward, and those of the mastodon upward, these of the new animal go out *horizontally* in curves, bending backward towards the ear, like horns of some kinds of oxen, or of the buffalo, and that they are solid ivory tusks, proceeding from the upper parts of the mouth, instead of hollow horns proceeding from the temples or sides of the head.

Leaving St. Louis the following spring on March 25, 1840, Koch journeyed to the "Osage Country" where he excavated enough fossil bones from a spring on the Pomme de Terre River to enable him to construct a spectacular mounted skeleton that he claimed was the animal he had first unearthed at Kimmswick, the "*Missourium*" (Figures 5.1, 5.2, and 5.3). With a full mount now at hand, Koch revised his taxonomic designation for the "*Missourium Kochii*" to "*Missourium Theristocaulodon* (Koch)" or "*Leviathan Missouriensis*" (Koch 1842a; Osborn 1936:1389). Later, after its purchase by the British Museum, the skeleton was reassembled by Owen (1842) into its proper anatomical position and, from that time, has been displayed there as one of the more renowned examples of the American mastodon, *Mammut americanum*.

In his Pomme de Terre discovery Koch once again believed he had found evidence for the contemporaneity of man with "diluvial beast." Even during his later years, when he accepted the fact that his "*Leviathan*" was indeed a mastodon, he continued to maintain that he had positive evidence for an association between man-made artifacts and the bones. Koch asserted emphatically that two arrowheads were found with the bones in such a position as to "furnish conclusive evidence, perhaps more than in any other case, that they were of equal, if not older, date than the bones themselves." He went on to insist that "one of the arrowheads lay underneath the thigh bone of the skeleton, the bone actually resting in contact upon it, so that it could not have been brought

Figure 5.1 "Missouri Leviathan," a lithograph produced in London in 1842 during the time the *"Missourium"* was exhibited in the Egyptian Hall, Piccadilly (drawn by G. Tytler and printed by Lefrevre). (Courtesy of the Missouri Historical Society, St. Louis.)

Figure 5.2 "The Missouri Leviathan," a sketch reproduced from Koch's (1842c) article in *The Farmers' Cabinet and American Herd-Book*, Philadelphia.

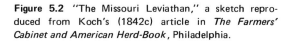

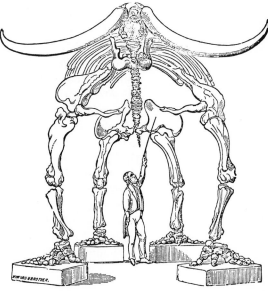

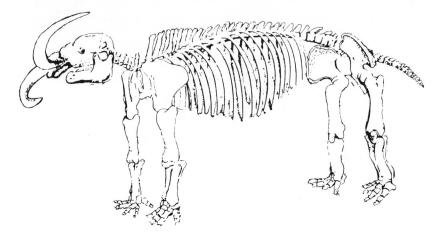

Figure 5.3 *"Missourium Theristocaulodon* Koch (Sichel-zahn),"* an illustration adapted from Koch's (1845) *Die Riesenthiere der Urwelt*, published in Berlin.

thither after the deposit of the bone . . . [Koch 1857:63] ." Rau (1873:396) later illustrated this specimen (Figure 6.8) after seeing it in St. Louis at the home of Koch's widow.

THE OSAGE COUNTRY

Fame of the Osage country as a fossil locality had reached the attention of systematists as early as the beginning of the nineteenth century, several decades before Koch's time. Benjamin S. Barton, an American naturalist and professor of natural history at the college of Philadelphia (now The University of Pennsylvania), wrote to Cuvier in France in 1806 telling of travelers' tales of thousands of mastodon bones in this region (Cuvier 1834:270, cited in Mehl 1962:30). Barton stated "that an intelligent traveler had seen in a particular locality near the river of the Osage Indians thousands of the bones of this animal and that the traveler had collected there among other things 17 tusks [Hay 1924:25] ." Barton had in his possession a molar from there that he later sent Cuvier.

Today paleonotologists recognize two major vertebrate fossil localities in this general area of Missouri. One is within the area of this study, along the lower Pomme de Terre River, and the second is 20 km to the north on the Osage River, near the hamlet of Tackner (Hay 1924:28). Mehl (1962:31) called this latter site the "Warsaw swamp." Although fossils were reaching the east coast from the Tackner locality during Koch's time (e.g., Whipple 1847), available evidence suggests that Koch's work was confined to the Pomme de Terre locality.

Though the lower Pomme de Terre River valley has been famous as a fossil locality for nearly two centuries, there has been a serious question during the past several decades as to the exact place Koch worked. Mehl (1962:30), when attempting to locate Koch's Benton County excavation, noted that Koch had erred in his published location; that "40° latitude, 18° longitude identified a point in the middle of the Atlantic Ocean." Mehl failed to realize, however, that Greenwich, England was not established as the prime meridian until 1884. Koch probably used Philadelphia as his prime meridian, for if one uses this early capitol, his location is correct. In his European editions, he gave the longitudinal location at 95°W, thus switching to Paris for his prime meridian.

Mehl (1962:30) selected a site known today as the Kirby Spring in the SW ¼ NW ¼ NE ¼ NW ¼ of Section 9, T33N, R22W as the location of Koch's original excavation (Figure 3:1). This was also the location given by Hay (1924:26). The informants of both these authors were undoubtedly influenced by a strong oral tradition shared by local residents that maintains that Kirby Spring was the site from which the mastodon now in the British Museum was exhumed.

Apparently local tradition has confused Koch's original work with later excavations. Our research indicates instead that the Koch site is upstream from the Breshears Valley and from the location of Kirby Spring (see Figure 3.1). This location is supported by Shumard's (1867) early map of mineral lands in Benton and Hickory counties, because he located a "mastodon spring" on the left bank of the Pomme de Terre in the approximate location of the spring we have named for Koch. Further corroborating data are found in Lay's (1876:14) history of Benton County, where he notes that Koch worked on the land of Alexander Breshears. Of several springs in the vicinity, only the Koch Spring was on land once claimed by this early pioneer. The best evidence is Koch's own published description of his Pomme de Terre expedition. He writes that:

> The bones were found by me near the shores of the river *La Pomme de Terre*, a tributary of the Osage River, in Benton country [sic], in the state of Missouri, latitude 40° and longitude 95°. In the center of the above mentioned deposit, was a large spring which appeared to rise from the very bowels of the earth. . . . About 200 yards from the said deposit, stands a singular rock, . . . [which] has the appearance of a pillar, on whose top rests a table rock far projecting on every side [Koch 1842a:8–9].

The site we have named Koch Spring is in Section 15 in Hickory County (Figure 3.1). This does not conflict with Koch's location in Benton County since Hickory County was created from lands of the former county 5 years after his work there. The spring location fits Koch's description perfectly, including the table rock located 200 yards (182.8 m) away (Figure 5.4). There are people living along the lower Pomme de Terre River who still refer to the landmark as the "table rock" or the "anvil rock."

According to Koch, settlers had opened the spring and discovered bones prior to his work in 1840, but his was the first major excavation there. During the next couple of decades, however, there was further digging at the site. Hoy (1871:147) noted that upon traveling to the Pomme de Terre valley he hired a laborer who dug in the spring for him

Figure 5.4 The "table rock," a landmark mentioned by Koch in several of his descriptions, located approximately 180m southwest of Koch Spring.

and recovered a molar and tusk fragments, as well as several other mastodon elements. Probably because of Koch's fame for selling his collection, two brothers from Boone County, Missouri undertook a commercial excavation in the Pomme de Terre area, presumably at Koch Spring. They "kept from 15 to 20 hands at work for several months, and took out a large quantity of bones. But the spring at the place so filled the diggings with water that they had to employ a pump to keep the water out, and worked at great expense; and the bones they secured were so badly decomposed that . . . they generally fell to pieces, and the Bradleys were broken by the venture [Lay 1876:14]."

Many contemporary residents argue that Kirby Spring was the site of Koch's work, but we cannot justify this claim. There is proof that Kirby Spring was excavated during Koch's era, prior to the Civil War; this excavation was probably stimulated by Koch's earlier success. It is documented in the original Federal Land Survey notes that work was being carried out there at an early date, because James (1845:368) recorded a "Big Bone Diggings" 10 chains southeast of the corner of Sections 4, 5, 8, and 9 in T38N, R22W, the location of Kirby Spring. The excavators remain unknown, however, since other than the Federal Land Surveys, there is no published description of a location that can be construed as the Kirby Spring. It is possible, perhaps likely, that the commercial venture carried out by the Bradley brothers may have been at Kirby Spring instead of Koch Spring, but this is speculation at best.

There is even the possibility that Koch dug at Kirby Spring during his second expedition to the Pomme de Terre in late 1840, and thus began the local legend. Unfortunately, we can find no account describing the details of his second trip. The evidence for a 2-month return trip to the Pomme de Terre in late August 1840 comes from St. Louis newspapers, which announced both his departure and return. A notice in the *Bulletin* in mid-November 1840 stated that Koch had been successful in finding more bones and that "now for the first time, the *Missourium* could be exhibited" in a perfect state, for several parts that were formerly wanting had recently been obtained (McDermott 1948:248).

Active interest in the Pomme de Terre area seems to have waned with the Civil War, and we have been unable to document any actual digging there during the remainder of the nineteenth century. There was a revival of interest in Koch's claims for the contemporaneity of man and extinct fauna in the 1870s, during a period of renewed debate over man's potential antiquity. Papers published during that time reviewed (and several disputed) Koch's contention that he had found associations between man and mastodon (e.g., Hoy 1871; Dana 1871, 1875; Foster 1873; Rau 1873; Andrews 1875).

THE MISSOURI LEVIATHAN

Koch's frequent absences from St. Louis apparently led to declining attendance at his St. Louis museum. He placed the Kimmswick collection on display 2 weeks after returning from his first Pomme de Terre expedition, but was dissatisfied with the public's response. A month later he announced the exhibition of the antiquities from the Osage country, but became even more impatient with the museum's patronage when European travelers assured him the collections would draw literally thousands of people if exhibited in either London or Paris (McDermott 1948:248).

It was then that Koch decided to advertise his museum for sale. At the same time, after holding a benefit day to raise funds, he returned to the Pomme de Terre in an attempt to find enough bones to complete a skeleton of the *"Missourium."* As indicated earlier, he made the second trip that fall (1840) and, when he returned, had the additional elements needed to complete a mount.

Koch still had not sold his museum upon completion of a full mount of the *"Missourium"* (Figure 5.1). He thus exhibited it in St. Louis using all of his showmanship skills to attract large crowds by having a three-piece band play in the rib cage of the mounted monster. The trick apparently paid off because Koch exhibited it in St. Louis for longer than he had planned, but in January 1841 he sold the museum and left St. Louis to take the *"Missourium"* and other parts of the collection to Europe (McDermott 1948:249). On the way he planned to stop and exhibit the collection in several cities south and east of St. Louis.

Koch took the *"Missourium"* on tour first to New Orleans and then to Louisville. By fall he had reached the East Coast, where he exhibited the collection in the Masonic Hall in Philadelphia. Although travelers had seen and described some of the fossils in St. Louis (e.g., Horner 1840a, b), Koch's collection probably received its first major exposure to the scientific world when it reached Philadelphia. There, several nineteenth-century scientists involved in systematics research had an opportunity to examine and study the collection as well as to comment on Koch's imaginative but abortive attempt at mounting a mastodon (Goddard 1841). Harlan (1843), after having studied the collection, noted that the aggregate contained at least six genera, one a new species that, after some taxonomic debate, became known as *Mylodon harlani* (Owen 1843).

Near the close of 1841 Koch shipped his collection to London (Koch 1841). The *"Missourium"* was exhibited for several months in the Egyptian Hall, Piccadilly, and, as had been anticipated, drew thousands of visitors. During its display, Sir Richard Owen, the famous British anatomist, read a paper before the Geological Society of London pointing out again many of the anatomical mistakes Koch had made. He too disagreed with Koch on the taxonomic classification of *"Missourium,"* since he was certain the beast was composed of nothing more than the elements from several different individual mastodons (Owen 1842). Koch (1842b) answered Owen on the point of classification, but in later years obviously conceded the argument (i.e., Koch 1857).

In 1843 Koch exhibited the collection in Dublin for a few months before returning it to London, where he sold the mounted skeleton and parts of his collection to the British Museum for £1300 (Stadler 1972:xxvii). Soon afterward, Koch traveled to Germany with what remained of his fossils and sold them to the Royal Museum in Berlin. While there, Koch wrote what was perhaps the most detailed account of his early fossil researches in North America (Koch 1845).

Stadler (1972) has detailed Koch's subsequent activities upon his return to North America until the time of his death in 1867.

AN EVALUATION

Some writers, when considering Early Man studies in eastern North America, have virtually dismissed Koch's work because of the way he circused his finds around the country, playing on the curiosity and imagination of the public (e.g., Wilmsen 1965:176). This is justified criticism, as we have seen, but one should not underestimate Koch's role in stimulating nineteenth-century interest in paleonotology and prehistory. Public display and published accounts of his vertebrate fossil collection helped generate considerable interest in paleontological systematics during the mid-nineteenth century. His claims for associations between extinct fauna and man initiated a polemic that began in the 1850s but did not reach a crescendo until two decades later when American science was finally recovering from the Civil War (Hoy 1871; Dana 1871, 1875; Andrews 1875; Rau 1873).

Interest in the Koch finds waned after the late nineteenth century, and were not revived until the rash of finds of fluted points with extinct fauna in North America, beginning with the Folsom discovery in 1927 (Figgins 1927). These discoveries, especially during the 1930s, again brought to focus the question of man's antiquity in the New World and, thereafter, several authors reexamined Koch's accounts with the new knowledge that man had slaughtered megafauna in the West. The debate over the authenticity of Koch's finds began anew (Montagu and Peterson 1944, Eiseley 1945b, 1946; Chapman 1948; Gross 1951; Williams 1957).

The renewed speculation of the 1940s and 1950s over Koch's claims for association between man and mastodon came no closer to answering the question than had the debate of the century before. For, as Stadler (1972:xxxiii) pointed out, until our recent work no one had reexamined one of Koch's original sites.

Our excavations at Koch Spring and other similar springs in southwestern Missouri have produced two sets of data that help in evaluating Koch's original Pomme de Terre work. These are: (1) the geological nature of the springs, and (2) the tangible evidence found in Koch's original excavation (Chapter 6).

In order to interpret Koch's work in light of our new evidence, we need to recall that the nineteenth century was a time of gradual but dramatic change in scientific thought. Explanations for phenomenological change during this period were shifting from the scriptures to a process of scientific reasoning that culminated with Darwin. During the decades before Darwin's (1859) historic treatise, there were many who were accepting the empirical fact of biological and geological change, but who were still attempting to rationalize these processes in biblical terms. Koch was one of these, and to understand his interpretations of his discoveries, or his view of the world in general, we must consider him within this intellectual milieu.

It is evident from Koch's writing that he was a catastrophist in addition to being aware of man's potential antiquity based on European finds such as those of Boucher de Perthes. He was thus ready to accept an "antediluvial race," since pre-Noachian populations could clearly be accounted for. His propensity for seeking literal explanations for empirical evidence in the pages of the Old Testament colored most of his interpretations and, in essence, provided him with an a priori set of answers for all the phenomena he was to find (Koch 1852). This is a crucial point, since his biased interpretations often affected even his basic descriptions.

Koch believed that a holocaust (Noachian Flood) had destroyed the last creation, and that this was recorded throughout the many fossil deposits he was examining in North America. Existing prior to the last catastrophe, he conceptualized a "tropical paradise." His view of this Garden of Eden was no better exemplified than in one of his accounts of the Pomme de Terre (Koch 1843:4–5):

> Geological research shews [sic] us, that . . . the earth presented a surface well watered and abounding with springs, streams and rivulets, uninterrupted by any of the rough broken, rugged deformities which now present themselves on every side; Its surface, was delightfully varied, Its soil, enriched by the dew of heaven, and impregnated with the spirit of animal and vegetable life, poured forth a luxuriant growth, not of noxious weeds,

thorns, and thistles; but of gigantic fruit trees and herbs; and useful for the food of man or animal, fowl or creeping things. The climate also, was free from the noxious vapours and melting heats of the torrid zone, and the chilling blasts of the polar regions. . . . Here every species of animal was richly supported, from the mighty Missourium to the ponderous Mastodon, down to the smallest creeping things. . . .

But Koch saw this utopian state have its end with the Noachian catastrophe:

and the whole of the earth was deluged with a flood of the agitated waters, and unnumbered millions of living things, swept at once from the stage of action, and mingled in the common ruin [Koch 1843:5].

Koch obviously believed that the remains he found constituted evidence for the holocaust he described because, when describing plant macrofossils from the peat deposits at Koch Spring, he wrote:

they had been torn by force from their parent stem before they had arrived at perfection, and were involved in one common ruin with the trees which bore them, these having been torn up by the roots, and twisted and split into a thousand pieces, apparently by lightning, combined with a tremendous tempest or tornado [Koch 1843:14].

It is important to dichotomize Koch's interpretations and his basic descriptions. Recognizing his biases, we believe that Koch actually found what he claimed—artifacts associated with mastodon bones. There is no evidence that Koch, being the showman that he was, attempted to perpetrate a scientific hoax as some have accused.

The evidence we now have from archaeological excavations demonstrates that an aboriginal settlement once surrounded Koch Spring (Chapter 6). Two backhoe trenches, excavated to the center of the spring feeder to cross-section Koch's original excavation, revealed a buried platform, probably placed there by his excavators, and in the debris above the layer of rails and lumber was a considerable amount of scrap mastodon bone and tusk. Mixed with the bone scrap were several chert flakes. Although no finished artifacts were recovered (Chapter 6), the debitage in the feeder was in the original matrix that Koch's men had dug through.

The situation at Koch Spring is analogous to that at Boney Spring where, in an undisturbed stratigraphic context outside the feeder, cultural materials were confined to the upper meter of the terrace, some distance above the bone bed. But within the fluid-like deposits of the feeder, cultural materials had worked their way down to the level of the earlier Pleistocene-age materials; thus, artifacts and mastodon bones co-occurred.

Koch described the bones he recovered from the Koch Spring as located on, or partially mixed in, a "quicksand" and extending into a surrounding deposit of "brown alluvium," which contained a great quantity of vegetal matter (Koch 1841:12). It is helpful to use Trolinger Spring as a model when attempting to understand the gross geological structure that Koch was attempting to describe. The relationship of the feeder sands and peat deposit to the bone bed at Koch Spring was probably similar to the situation shown for Trolinger Spring (e.g., Figure 3.4).

Part of the peat deposit that remained intact and just outside of the original bone bed dug by Koch yielded a radiocarbon date of 31,880± 1340 (Tx1412). Humates extracted from the sample dated slightly younger, 30,880± 1320 (Tx1445), and Haynes (Chapter 3) has suggested that there may be some humate contamination of the peat. The peat layer may actually be older by a few thousand years. At any rate, the bone bed and Koch's American mastodon, displayed in the British Museum today, date from the Mid-Wisconsinan, probably sometime >30,000 years ago. By way of contrast, the earliest evidence for man in connection with the spring, based on the archaeological work surrounding the feeder, is from the early Archaic period, probably no older than 8000 B.P.

In summary, we believe Koch actually found the projectile points mingled with the mastodon bones as he described them, as his men "dug out the muck and earth, often working up to their waists in the water, and groping with their hands at the bottom to find the bones [Andrews 1875:3]." But, because of the complex nature of the spring's feeder, Koch's general lack of geological training, and his a priori notions, we conclude that he misinterpreted the nature and significance of the association.

REFERENCES

Adams, R.M.
  1953 The Kimmswick bone bed. *The Missouri Archaeologist* **15:**40–56.
Anderson, F.J.
  1973 Cabinets of curiosities. *Natural History* **82:**104–109.
Andrews, E.
  1875 Dr. Koch and the Missouri mastodon. *The American Journal of Science and Arts* (3rd series) **10:**32–34.
Berry, W.
  1968 *Growth of a prehistoric time scale.* San Francisco, California: W.H. Freeman and Co.
Buckingham, J.S.
  1842 *Eastern and western states of America*, Vol. 3. London.
Chapman, C.H.
  1948 A preliminary survey of Missouri archaeology, Part IV: Ancient cultures and sequence. *The Missouri Archaelogist* **10:** Bulletin No. 23.
Cuvier, G.
  1834 *Recherches sur les ossements fossiles de quadrupedes* Vol. 2, 4th ed. Paris.

Dana, J.D.

1871 *Manual of geology*, revised ed. New York: Ivison, Blakeman, Taylor and Co.

1875 On Dr. Koch's evidence with regard to the contemporaneity of man and the mastodon in Missouri. *The American Journal of Science and Arts* (3rd series) **9**:335–346.

Daniel, G.E.

1950 *A hundred years of archaeology*. London: G. Duckworth and Co.

Darwin, C.

1859 *On the origin of species*. London: John Murray.

Eiseley, L.C.

1945a Myth and mammoth in archaeology. *American Antiquity* **11**:84–87.

1945b Indian mythology and extinct fossil vertebrates. *American Anthropologist* (new series) **47**:318–320.

1946 Men, mastodons, and myth. *The Scientific Monthly* **62**:517–524.

Figgins, J.D.

1927 The antiquity of man in America. *Natural History* **27**:229–239.

Foster, J.W.

1873 *Pre-historic races of the United States of America*. Chicago, Illinois: Griggs and Co.

Goddard, P.B.

1841 Missourium kochii. *Proceedings of the Academy of Natural Science of Philadelphia* **1**:115–116.

Gross, H.

1951 Mastodon, mammoth, and man in North America. *Bulletin of the Texas Archaeological and Paleontological Society* **22**:101–131.

Harlan, R.

1843 Description of the bones of a new fossil animal of the order Edentata. *The American Journal of Science and Arts* (1st series) **44**:69–80.

Harris, M.

1968 *The rise of anthropological theory*. New York: T.Y. Crowell.

Hay, O.P.

1924 *The Pleistocene of the middle region of North America and its vertebrated animals*. Washington, D.C.: Carnegie Institution.

Heizer, R.F. (Editor)

1962 *Man's discovery of his past: Literary landmarks in archaeology*. Englewood Cliffs, New Jersey: Prentice-Hall.

Horner, W.E.

1840a Note on the remains of the mastodon, and some other extinct animals collected together in St. Louis, Missouri. *Proceedings of American Philosophical Society* **1**:279–282.

1840b Remarks on the dental system of the mastodon, with an account of some lower jaws in Mr. Koch's collection at St. Louis, Missouri, where there is a solitary tusk on the right side. *Proceedings of American Philosophical Society* **1**:306–308.

Hoy, P.R.

1871 Dr. Koch's Missourium. *The American Naturalist* **5**:147–148.

Hutton, J.

1788 *Theory of the earth or an investigation of the laws observable in the composition, dissolution, and restoration of land upon the globe*. Edinburgh: Royal Society of Edinburgh.

James, E.

1845 Surveyors field notes (T38N, R22W). *United States Federal Land Surveys*. Jefferson City, Missouri: Missouri State Archives.

Koch, A.C.

1839a The mammoth [mastodon? Eds.]. *The American Journal of Science and Arts* (1st series) **36**:198–200.

1839b Remains of the mastodon in Missouri. *The American Journal of Science and Arts* (1st series) **37**:191–192.

1841 *Description of the Missourium, or Missouri Leviathan, and a catalogue of the whole fossil collection*, 3rd ed., enlarged. London: E. Fisher.

1842a *Description of the Missourium Theristocaulodon (Koch), or Missouri Leviathan (Leviathan Missouriensis), together with its supposed habits and Indian traditions . . .*, 4th ed. London: E. Fisher.

1842b On the genus Tetracaulodon. *Proceedings of the Geological Society of London* **3**:714–716.

1842c Description of the Missouri Leviathan. *The Farmers' Cabinet and American Herd-Book . . .* **6**:122–124.

1843 *Description of the Missourium Theristocaulodon (Koch), or Missouri Leviathan (Leviathan Missouriensis), together with its supposed habits and Indian traditions . . .*, 5th ed., enlarged. Dublin: C. Crookes.

1845 *Die Riesenthiere der Urwelt oder das neventdeckte Missourium Theristocaulodon (Sichelzahn aus Missouri) und die Mastodontoiden im Allgemeinen und Besondern. . . .* Berlin: A. Duncker.

1852 *Die sechs Schoepfungstage oder die Mosaische Schoepfungsgeschichte in vollem Einklange mit der Geognoise, nebst einer kurz gefassten Naturgeschichte der merkwuerdigsten Geschoepfe der Urwelt.* Vienna: Mechitharisten-Buchdruckerei.

1857 Mastodon remains, in the state of Missouri, together with evidences of the existence of man contemparaneously with the mastodon. *Transactions of the Academy of Science*, St. Louis **1**:61–64.

Lay, J.H.

1876 *A sketch of the history of Benton County, Missouri.* Hannibal, Missouri: Winchell and Ebert Printing and Lithograph Co.

Lowie, R.H.

1937 *The history of ethnological theory.* New York: Holt.

McDermott, J.F.

1948 Dr. Koch's wonderful fossils. *Bulletin of the Missouri Historical Society* **4**:233–256.

Mehl, M.G.

1962 *Missouri's Ice Age animals.* Rolla, Missouri: Missouri Geological Survey and Water Resources.

Montagu, M.F., and C.B. Peterson

1944 The earliest account of the association of human artifacts with fossil mammals in North America. *Proceedings of the American Philosophical Society* **87**:407–419.

Oakley, K.P.

1959 *Man the tool-maker.* Chicago, Illinois: Univ. of Chicago Press.

Osborn, H.F.

1936 *Proboscidea, a monograph of the discovery, evolution, migration and extinction of the mastodonts and elephants of the world*, Vol. 1. New York: American Museum Press.

Owen, R.

1842 Report on the Missourium now exhibiting at the Egyptian Hall, with an inquiry into the claims of the Tetracaulodon to generic distinction. *Proceedings of the Geological Society of London* **3**(2-87):689–695.

1843 Letter from Richard Owen . . . on Dr. Harlan's notice of new fossil Mammalia. . . . *American Journal of Science* **44**:341–345.

Rau, C.
1873 North American stone implements. *Annual Report of the Smithsonian Institution for 1872*, 395–408.

Shumard, B.F.
1867 *A geological report on the mineral lands belonging to R.H. Melton, Esq., Benton and Hickory counties, Missouri.* St. Louis, Missouri: P. Studley and Co.

Stadler, E.A. (Editor) (translated)
1972 *Journey through a part of the United States of North America in the years 1844–1846 by Albert C. Koch.* Carbondale, Illinois: Southern Illinois Univ. Press.

Tournal, M.
1833 General considerations on the phenomenon of bone caverns. *Annales de Chimie et de Physique* 25:161–181. Translated and reprinted in *Man's discovery of his past: Literary landmarks in archaeology*, edited by R.F. Heizer, 1962. Englewood Cliffs, New Jersey: Prentice Hall.

Whipple, S.H.
1847 Notice of mastodon bones. *Proceedings of the American Philosophical Society* 4:35–36.

Williams, S.
1957 The Island 35 mastodon: Its bearing on the age of Archaic cultures in the East. *American Antiquity* 22:359–372.

Wilmsen, E.N.
1965 An outline of early man studies in the United States. *American Antiquity* 31:172–192.

Wislizenus, A.
1860 Was man contemporaneous with the mastodon? *Transactions of the Academy of Science*, St. Louis 1:168–171.

6

Archaeological Investigations at the Pomme de Terre Springs

W. Raymond Wood

Two considerations led us to the investigation of spring bogs in the lower Pomme de Terre River valley. First, we were seeking a vegetational record to correlate with the cultural record contained in the deposits at Rodgers Shelter. Second, Albert Koch's 1840 expedition to the locality (Chapter 5) had raised the possibility, hitherto unresolved, that man and mastodon may have been contemporaneous in the American Midwest. We therefore sought evidence in the springs to support or reject this possibility.

Archaeological remains were recovered in three of the five spring bogs investigated: the Trolinger, Boney, and Koch springs. To anticipate a conclusion: In each case, the tools associated with fossil mammals that we recovered were restricted to the spring conduit or feeder. The association of man and mastodon in these cases is therefore presumably spurious. A synopsis of the evidence in each spring follows to support this assertion; the vegetational record in the springs has already been reviewed (Chapter 4).

TROLINGER SPRING

This spring was investigated in 1967 and 1968, when deposits in and around the conduit were extensively excavated. The only object of undoubted human manufacture found during either season was a small

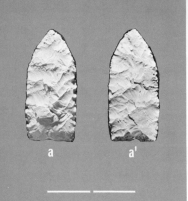

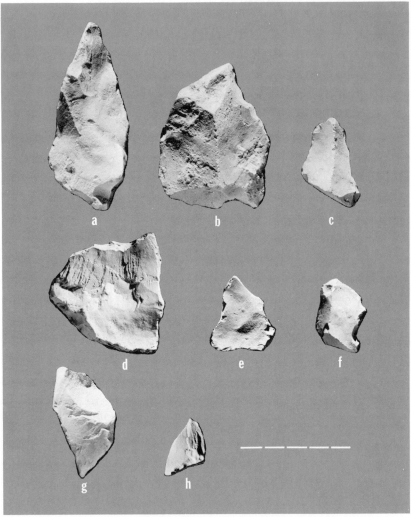

Figure 6.1 Miniature projectile point from Trolinger Spring, unit d_3, obverse and reverse sides (scale in centimeters).

Figure 6.2 Geofacts from Trolinger Spring (a–c), Jones Spring (d-f), and Boney Spring (g-h) (scale in centimeters).

lanceolate-shaped biface (Figure 6.1). It was in unit d_3 near the eye of the spring, and lay about 15 cm above the proximal end of a large mastodon tusk.

The specimen is 26 mm long, 12 mm wide, and 2.5 mm thick, made from a local, mottled white chert. The form and flaking can be readily discerned from the illustration. The base is thinned but is not ground, nor is there any sign of use or wear on any of the margins or on the tip. Its form is suggestive of Paleo–Indian points, although no strictly comparable specimen of this size is known. The very small size, in fact, argues for its identification as an arrowpoint of post-Christian era date, although the specimen cannot now be duplicated among local late complexes. In any case, the dates of 29,000 to 14,000 B.P. for unit d_3 (Chapter 3) are inconsistent with present interpretations of Midwestern prehistory for projectile points of this size and shape. The point is therefore best interpreted as a late intrusion in the spring deposits.

The base of the conduit, unit b, was filled with sand, pebbles, and gravel, and there were a few small chert stones in the fill around the mastodon bones. A sample of them from among and below the bones, studied by University of Missouri Old World archaeologist Ralph Rowlett, shows little evidence of human workmanship, although some of them had small flakes detached along the margins. However, there are no recurrent or commonly recognized forms. Most of the "retouched" edges are heavily rolled and are smooth (Figure 6.2). Rowlett feels that all of them are natural stones with margins battered by rolling in a vigorous spring flow or, perhaps, by trampling of the large mammals that stood on the basal sands and gravel before their deaths.

In sum, the stones among and below the bone bed at Trolinger Spring are *geofacts*, or natural stones battered by spring flow or by trampling of megafauna; and the single artifact recovered above the bone bed is best interpreted as intrusive, from a late prehistoric complex.

BONEY SPRING

The research team first attempted to excavate Boney Spring (Figure 6.3) in 1967, when efforts were made to drain it. A number of chipped stone tools were recovered at that time, when the vegetation mat overlying the spring was removed, and others were found in the spring conduit or feeder as work continued in 1968. A human burial was also discovered in 1968 in the peat about a meter north of the conduit (Bass and McMillan 1973). The spring flow was successfully diverted in 1971, and the spring deposits were excavated to a depth of 3.75 m, completely removing the bone bed of unit E. Tests were also made at this time in the marshy area just north of the spring conduit.

Survey members found chipped stone tools near the spring as well as at several locations on the river terrace nearby. Because surrounding fields were no longer in pasture or cultivation, vegetation was too rank to determine the extent of the site or sites involved. Our work at the spring, however, revealed a major prehistoric occupation around its margin.

Our excavations, two 5-x-5-m squares, were in the marshy area about 10 m north of the spring conduit. The units were dug to a depth of 1.3 m, penetrating a layer of peat averaging about 80 cm thick, and extending into an underlying dark brown clay. Limestone nodules and slabs were

Figure 6.3 Low oblique aerial photograph of Boney Spring before excavation; the view is southwest.

scattered throughout the unit, from top to bottom. Many of them were large and flat, and would have provided firm footing in the boggy deposits.

There were two surface hearths, both of them in the brown clay layer. Both were small, less than 70 cm in diameter, and contained burned earth and flecks of charcoal. One of them was near the edge of a large, basin-shaped pit (Feature 206). This feature, irregularly circular in outline, was 1.28 x 1.48 m in diameter, and at least 40 cm deep. Its depth could not be determined exactly since the pit orifice was not visible in the overlying dark peat. A broken Woodland pottery vessel (Figure 6.4) was scattered in the upper part of the pit fill.

The pit was dug partly into the peat, but vegetal remains from within it contrasted markedly with the composition of the peat. The pit fill contained several times as many hickory nuts and acorns as did the peat, most of them occurring in concentrations. Eight species of seeds were also found in the pit but not in the adjoining peat: domestic squash, dogwood, elderberry, cocklebur, giant ragweed, pokeberry, wild plum, and black haw. Under these circumstances, the feature is probably best regarded as a storage pit (King and McMillan 1975).

The materials from these tests, and those from earlier work near the conduit, appear to represent occupations near the spring margin by Woodland groups, although there are a few earlier, Archaic tools from the conduit and from the surrounding fields.

The most diagnostic Woodland material is the pottery. The broken pottery vessel from the basin-shaped pit was entirely cord roughened, the impressions being vertical or nearly so at the rim, but less regular lower on the body (Figure 6.4). The base is smoothed. The lip is rounded, and the rim is outflaring. Body form is probably a bowl—a round-bottomed vessel with outflaring walls and a gently outflaring rim. There is no decoration. Maximum body thickness, near the base, is 14 mm, decreasing to 10 or 12 mm at the lip. Most of the finely crushed limestone temper near the vessel surfaces is leached away, leaving the sherds friable, probably due to long immersion in the wet bog deposits. Hardness is therefore probably less now than it was originally: 2 to 2.5 (Moh's scale). Vessel exteriors are brown (Munsell 10 YR 5/3) with a black interior (10 YR 2/1). Two holes are drilled into the rim just below the lip, and two similar holes occur on the vessel lower on the body.

There are a few other sherds from the excavations, all of them small cord-roughened body sherds. There are no rim sherds, and no clue to vessel form. In contrast to the limestone-tempered vessel just described, all of them are tempered with fine sand.

Lithic artifacts from the excavation include a large number of cores of a local, mottled gray chert. These were scattered throughout the deposits, as well as numerous decortication and secondary flakes of the same material. Most of the flakes are large, averaging well over 50 mm long. The cores and debitage alike are of very poor quality chert. Retouch and other small flakes are conspicuous by their absence, and many of those present are of different and high quality chert.

Figure 6.4 Woodland pottery rim sherd from Boney Spring (scale in centimeters).

Most of the bifaces, which probably served as dart points, are contracting stemmed varieties (Figure 6.5a–e) with straight bases. There is one corner-notched point from the surface (Figure 6.6a). The contracting stemmed points are common varieties in late Archaic and in Woodland levels at Rodgers Shelter and elsewhere in the Ozarks. Radiocarbon dates of 1900±80, 1910±80, and 1920±50 B.P. (Tx-1471, 1470, and 1472), together with the associated pottery, however, identify all or most of these specimens as Woodland. There are a variety of large bifaces (Figure 6.5f, g, i) and scrapers (Figure 6.5e, h) associated with the Wood-

Figure 6.5 Chipped stone artifacts from the surficial peat bed at Boney Spring (scale in centimeters).

Figure 6.6 Chipped stone artifacts from Boney Spring. Surface finds (a–b), and specimens from the spring conduit (c–e) (scale in centimeters)

land remains. One of the scrapers (Figure 6.5e) has a contracting stem, presumably for hafting.

A partial human skeleton was discovered in 1968 on the north edge of the conduit. The burial, a secondary Woodland interment, was 76 cm below the surface, in the surficial brown peat. No grave outline was visible, and no grave goods accompanied this individual, identified (Bass and McMillan 1973) as a male between 21 and 25 years of age.

Excavations in the spring conduit, prior to removing the bone bed, yielded a number of cores, flakes, and part of a basally notched point (Figure 6.6d). The latter specimen, the only distinctively Archaic artifact from the spring, resembles specimens from Rodgers Shelter dating from about 3500 B.P. All recognizable artifacts from the work in the spring itself were confined to the conduit funnel. A single flake was found just above the bone bed, but there were no tools of any sort among the bones themselves. A few natural chert pebbles, some of them with battered edges, were among the bones (Figure 6.2), but none of them are identifiable artifacts, resembling, instead, the geofacts from the Trolinger and the Jones springs.

In summary, there is an early Woodland site and grave adjoining Boney Spring, dating about 1900 B.P., with cord-roughened pottery and associated contracting stemmed points. Cultural material from this occupation undoubtedly found its way into the spring conduit, joining an earlier basally notched Archaic point in spurious association with the mastodon and other bones.

KOCH SPRING

Historic documentation and internal evidence at this spring (Figure 6.7) combine to identify it as the one that Albert Koch investigated in 1840 (Chapter 5). This was the spring in which he claimed to have found a projectile point associated with mastodon remains. Since the discharge at Boney Spring had attracted prehistoric peoples to its margin (and led to the accidental deposition of chipped stone tools in its conduit), we felt the same circumstances may have obtained at Koch Spring. Accordingly, test excavations were made at different points on the terrace near the spring: Each of them yielded cultural remains.

Excavations in the spring bog itself yielded a number of chert flakes in the area disturbed by prior excavations, principally in the vicinity of the conduit, but no stone tools of distinctive form were recovered. The projectile point that Koch said came from the spring is now lost, but it is presumed to have been a corner-notched variety (Figure 6.8, from Rau 1873: Fig. 1). This variety of point is a common one in the lower Pomme de Terre River valley, especially in the vicinity of the springs (Wood 1961: 100), and a few corner-notched specimens were found in tests around Koch Spring itself.

Figure 6.7 View of the Koch Spring before excavation; the view is southwest.

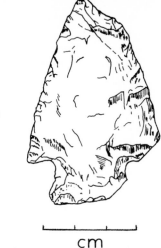

Figure 6.8 Outline drawing of the point recovered at the Koch Spring in 1840. (From Rau 1873: Fig. 1.)

cm

The principal human activities detected in the spring deposits relate to the work of Koch and his possible successors. A cribbed mat of oak and walnut rails was exposed at the base of the disturbed area in the conduit, a platform probably laid down by Koch's workers to provide firm footing in the slippery bog deposits. A few pieces of scrap iron were in the churned deposits above this platform, but no modern tools that could be ascribed to previous excavators were found. There were, however, two sherds of a coarse, utilitarian, stoneware vessel above the platform. They were identified by Robert T. Bray, historical archaeologist at the University of Missouri–Columbia, as being from a wheel-thrown, straight-sided crock made between about 1850 and 1920—which clearly postdates Koch's work at the spring.

Ten 2-x-2-m test pits were dug in 1971 on the terrace around the spring and on the lower slopes of the adjoining hillside. Material was present from the surface to depths of 40 to 50 cm, in surficial deposits of overlying alluvial and colluvial clays and gravels. The tests contained occasional chipped and ground stone tools—projectile points, bifaces, scrapers, and manos—but only two features were exposed in the 10 units.

One of these features, in a test 10 m west of the spring, was an oval, rock-lined hearth, 45 x 65 cm. The only artifacts associated with it were a few flakes. The other feature, in a test 50 m west of the spring, was a very poorly preserved burial with an associated cache of artifacts (Figure 6.9). The interment was covered with about a dozen limestone rocks, none of them exceeding 6 kg in weight. The bone was so poorly preserved that only a trace of it remained, and it was impossible to determine whether the burial was a primary or secondary interment. The attendant artifact cache contained two corner-notched points, 10 bifaces, a core, two flakes with retouch along one margin, a fragmentary beaver *(Castor canadensis)* incisor, and eight pieces of hematite—four of which were ground, presumably to obtain pigment for a paint base. There was no ocher on the burial itself.

The two points from the cache (Figure 6.9f, g) are both corner-notched although varying in size, shape, and flaking. The base of the smaller, basally thinned specimen is lightly ground, and blade edges on both specimens exhibit heavy wear of the sort one might expect on knives (Ahler 1971). The bifaces, too, show evidence of use, especially the elongated, beveled one (Figure 6.9j).

Figure 6.9 Chipped stone artifacts from the Koch Spring locality. Specimens from various tests near the spring (a–b, d–e), from the surface (c), and selected specimens from the cache accompanying the burial (f–j) (scale in centimeters).

The excavated material and the surface specimens alike suggest a long history of occupation near the spring. The base of a lanceolate point (Figure 6.9e) suggests, on the basis of similar specimens from Rodgers Shelter, an early Archaic complex dating between 8000 and 5500 B.P.; a base-notched specimen (Figure 6.9a) probably dates between about 3500 and 2000 B.P.; and three specimens probably date from the Christian era: a corner-notched and a shallow side-notched specimen (Figure 6.9b–c), and a stemmed arrowpoint (Figure 6.9d). The latter three tools are probably of Woodland origin.

No great antiquity is suggested by any of the objects recovered in any of these investigations around the spring. The rarity of material, considering the very long time span represented by it, supports the assertion that there were only transient occupations near the spring from early Archaic times on. No artifacts were recovered from the spring itself, except for a few flakes in disturbed areas near the conduit. Since the point reputedly found in the spring by Koch is so much like forms common to other sites in the vicinity, the chances seem very good that it was an accidental intrusion into the spring deposits. It is, in any event, an unlikely association with either the dates of 840 ± 60 or 640 ± 60 B.P. (Tx-1454 and 1453) from shallow clays and peats at the spring or with the dates of $33,550 \pm 3210$ or $30,880 \pm 1320$ B.P. (Tx-1458 and 1455) from deeper in the spring deposits.

Consequently, there is no reliable evidence from Koch Spring—nor from any of the other springs we have investigated—documenting the contemporaneity of man and mastodon in the lower Pomme de Terre River valley.

REFERENCES

Ahler, S.A.
   1971 Projectile point form and function at Rodgers shelter, Missouri, *Missouri Archaeological Society, Research Series 8*. Columbia, Missouri.
Bass, W.M., III, and R.B. McMillan
   1973 A Woodland burial from Boney Spring, Missouri. *Plains Anthropologist* 18:313–315.
King, F.B., and R.B. McMillan
   1975 Plant remains from a Woodland storage pit, Boney Spring, Missouri. *Plains Anthropologist* 20 (68):111–115.
Rau, C.
   1873 North American stone implements. *Annual Report of the Board of Regents of the Smithsonian Institution for 1872*, pp. 395–408. Washington, D.C.
Wood, W.R.
   1961 The Pomme de Terre Reservoir in western Missouri prehistory. *Missouri Archaeologist* 23:1–131.

IV
Man and His Environment

7

Rodgers Shelter: A Record of Cultural and Environmental Change

R. Bruce McMillan

A focal point of the archaeological excavations in the Pomme de Terre basin was at Rodgers Shelter, where an overhanging dolomite bluff protects an area of just over 100 m² at the base of the Holocene terrace (T1-b). The site was located in the spring of 1962 by Rolland E. Pangborn of the University of Missouri–Columbia and, subsequently, was designated 23BE125 by the Missouri Archaeological Survey. The shelter was named for its owner, Jack Rodgers, although local residents indicated that they previously referred to it as Rash Bluff or Cedar Bluff. During the late 1960s the area was purchased by the United States Government in preparation for the Harry S. Truman Reservoir. Soon afterward the site was added to the National Register of Historic Places.

At least five owners have had deed to the land since it was settled, and most of them used the area beneath the overhang for storage and shelter. One informant, a long-time resident and nephew of a previous owner, related that for many years the area was fenced. Each year, hay and corn were stored there and, during periods of inclement weather, livestock were fed under the shelter. When archaeologists first located the site it was still enclosed with a pole and barbed wire fence, and hay and manure littered the floor (Figure 7.1).

The area in front of the shelter was forested in premodern times, according to the original land surveys, but was cleared for agriculture during the nineteenth century. The excavations attested to the presence of this former forest when several stains containing carbonized material that were the remains of taproots of large trees were discovered. During the 1960s the bottomland was in pasture and the hillslope above was forested in second growth timber.

Fieldwork was begun in 1963 and continued for five summers. In all, 13 months were spent excavating Rodgers Shelter. The first excavations were conducted by William E. Sudderth and Sidney Denny, graduate students at the University of Missouri–Columbia. They dug a 35-x-5-ft (10.7 x 1.5m) test trench that penetrated what was later found to be only the uppermost cultural stratum, Stratum 4 (Chapter 8); this was later backfilled. Although these investigators had tested only the upper cultural layer, it was agreed that Rodgers Shelter had the potential depth for working out certain chronological problems that had plagued archaeologists at other shallow, multicomponent sites in western Missouri. Thus, further excavations were recommended and then planned, based on this 1963 work.

The excavations of the following year established that the culture-bearing deposits were much deeper than had previously been thought, but it was 1965 before the earliest cultural horizon was found, 9 m below the surface near the base of the terrace. McMillan had assumed charge of the fieldwork in 1964 and continued to supervise the project throughout its duration. The overall direction of the research in the reservoir area was first under the charge of Carl H. Chapman; this responsibility was assumed by W. Raymond Wood in 1965. For 3 years the project was funded through contracts between the University of Missouri and the National Park Service; but after 1965, when it was realized that massive excavations would be needed to reach the lower horizons, funds were supplied by three successive National Science Foundation research grants (GS-1185, GS-1604, GS-2112) awarded to Wood (Table 7.1).

TABLE 7.1   Record of Excavations at Rodgers Shelter, Missouri

Date	Field supervisor	Director	Sponsoring agency
June 1963	Sudderth and Denny	Chapman	N.P.S.[a]
August 1964	McMillan	Chapman	N.P.S.
July–August 1965	McMillan	Wood	N.P.S.
June–August 1966	McMillan	Wood	N.S.F.[b]
June–August 1967	McMillan	Wood	N.S.F.
June–August 1968	McMillan	Wood	N.S.F.

[a]N.P.S. = National Park Service.
[b]N.S.F. = National Science Foundation.

PHYSICAL DESCRIPTION

Rodgers Shelter is formed by a projecting portion of a small, 6 m high, dolomite bluff that parallels the Pomme de Terre River for approximately 400 m along the base of the bordering hills (Figures 7.1, 7.2, 7.3, and 7.4). Far more of this lower Ordovician formation is exposed a kilometer upstream where, at Buzzard Bluff, high precipitous cliffs tower over the river.

Shelter is afforded by the overhang for 24.5 m along the bluff. Near the center of this span the greatest distance between the back wall and the dripline is reached—some 8 m. The floor space that is normally protected from precipitation encompasses about 102 m².

The surface beneath the overhang is usually dry and dusty, especially where manure is mixed with the ashy surface deposits. Visiting the site at most times, one might conclude that perishable materials could survive in the deposits. During extremely wet periods, however, a number of drips are activated in the overlying, permeable dolomite, and the floor grows damp until the water ceases to percolate through the rock.

A narrow floodplain (T-0) and terrace (T-1b), together measuring about 90 m in width, separate the shelter from the river's edge (Figure 7.4).

Figure 7.1 Rodgers Shelter, prior to excavation. 1963.

Figure 7.2 Looking across Terrace 1b prior to excavation of Rodgers Shelter, 1963.

Figure 7.3 Telephoto view of shelter from hilltop across Pomme de Terre River, looking northwest.

Figure 7.4 Aerial view of excavation following 1965 field season.

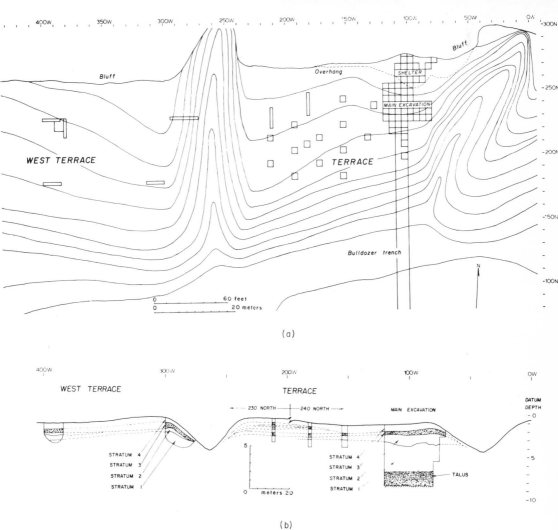

(a)

(b)

Figure 7.5 (a) Map of the site. Contour interval equals 2 ft. (b) East–west cross-section of Terrace 1b at Rodgers Shelter along 230N and 240N.

T-1b, containing all of the site's cultural deposits, was once larger but was truncated during the stream's down-cutting to its present level. It can first be defined at the base of the bluff 45 m upstream from the shelter, and continues for 225 m downstream, where it is again cut by an abandoned channel of the modern stream. The surface of the terrace rests about 3.5 m above T-0.

Two short but steep hollows enter the valley on either side of the shelter. One, to the east, emerges just beside the shelter and contributed significantly to the depositional history of the terrace (Chapter 8). The other enters the valley 45 m west of the overhang. Both form deep ravines where they are entrenched into T-1b (Figure 7.5).

Other than where the ravines cross it, the terrace in front of Rodgers Shelter forms a gently southward-sloping platform that provided far more living space for aboriginal occupants than would have been possible using the shelter alone (Figure 7.2). Debris scattered across the terrace at differing depths demonstrate that some activities were indeed performed in the open in front of the shelter.

EXCAVATION STRATEGIES

A horizontal grid system was employed by establishing base lines to the east (n–s) and south (e–w) of the site (Figure 7.5a). The points of intersection along the grid were designated by the distance north and west of the base lines. Excavation units were staked in 5-ft intervals and referenced from the southeast corner. So, for example, a square 230 ft north of the east–west base line, and 100 ft west of the north–south base line, would be designated 230NW100. [1]

Sudderth and Denny's 35-x-5-ft original test trench was placed at the point of maximum overhang and basically cross-sectioned the shelter's deposits. It was on the basis of this work that we returned in 1964 prepared to excavate completely the areas both in front of and beneath the overhang. With total excavation planned, sampling was not considered a problem.

The 1964 excavation was started on the terrace in front of the overhang (Figure 7.6). The test pits were designed to form four trenches, placed at right angles so they would leave standing a central 10-ft-square block. This was done to permit mapping of the stratigraphy on all sides of the

---

[1] During the excavation of Rodgers Shelter all vertical and horizontal measurements were recorded using the English system. Per contra, other members of the research team working at the springs were employing the metric system. Subsequently, all members of this Ozarks research team have switched to the use of metric measurements.

Measurements throughout this volume are given in metric designations except in some cases where it is impractical to convert English measurements to metric equivalents, such as the grid system at Rodgers Shelter. Even there, a metric scale is included with the English scale when depicting the grid in Figure 7.5.

Figure 7.6   View of excavation at beginning of 1969 field season.

block, and thus give a better idea of the nature of the terrace stratigraphy before proceeding with further excavation. This was accomplished.

During the same summer, one test pit (230NW100) was excavated for depth in an attempt to reach bedrock (Figure 7.7). It was in this pit that the earlier horizons that had not come to light in 1963 were discovered. Upon learning that parts of the site were at least 9 m deep it became obvious that it would be impossible to excavate Rodgers Shelter totally,

Figure 7.7 Crew member standing at the 7m level in deep test pit (230NW100).

Figure 7.8 View of main excavation, 1966.

Figure 7.9 Crew working in large excavation block along 100W line.

within the constraints of time and resources—as well as good judgment. Two problems arose then, that of sampling and the complex logistics of deep site excavation. To accommodate both sampling and excavation it was believed that the best strategy would be that of large block excavation (Figures 7.8 and 7.9).

The large 25-x-30-ft² block excavation was centered in the midden immediately in front of the overhang. This excavation was later extended beneath the shelter back to the bluff wall. During the final season the upper strata at the east end of the shelter (which had been badly disturbed by groundhogs) and along the east edge of the main excavation block were removed with a backhoe in order to reach the lower units and allow an increase in sampling from there. That summer the effort was focused on Strata 1 and 2 beneath the overhang and Stratum 1 in the main excavation area in front of the shelter.

To the west of the major block a checkerboard pattern of test pits was dug to determine if there were occupations that extended across the terrace to the ravine to the west. One large test pit (10 x 10 ft) was also dug west of the ravine over 100 m west of the shelter. Figure 7.5 delimits the area of the total excavation.

Due to the size of the area dealt with and the difficulty in correlating strata across long distances it has been advantageous to divide the terrace into four areas. These are as follows:

the *shelter:*   the protected area beneath the overhang.
the *main excavation:* that portion of the terrace immediately in front of the overhang.
the *terrace:*   the area west of the main excavation extending to the ravine.
the *west terrace:*   that portion of T-lb west of the ravine.

These areas are all labeled in Figure 7.5.

The principal means for separating cultural components was the use of natural stratigraphy. Within a geologic stratum, arbitrary 6-inch (15.2 cm) levels provided a means for further vertical subdivision. Care was taken not to crosscut contacts between natural layers.

Excavators attempted to locate artifacts in situ. When an object was found, its horizontal coordinates were plotted by using the distances north and west of the square's south and east grid lines. During the first two summers, before the depth of the site was known, vertical measurements were taken from the surface. Later, a farmer's level and stadia rod were used to record depths.

As the deposits were excavated, they were normally passed through one-quarter-inch screens to recover cultural items not found by the excavators. Some of the moister sediments from the lower strata were sifted through larger, half-inch mesh screens. In parts of Stratum 3 and Stratum 1, where there was little evidence of occupation, the sediments were not screened.

Figure 7.10 Water-screening technique for recovery of small-scale remains.

Beginning in 1965, during the excavation of Strata 1 and 2, a small block (1 ft^2) was saved in each level to enhance recovery of small-scale cultural remains. This was accomplished by washing the matrix through a tub screened with eighth-inch hardware cloth (Figure 7.10).

Two types of mechanical excavation were employed at the site's margins and on the nearby floodplain to create exposures for the geological investigations. A bulldozer trench extending from the south edge of the excavation to the edge of T-1b was opened in 1965. Two years later this trench was deepened and extended across the floodplain to the river bank.

During the final season, seven strata trenches about 4.5 m deep and 3 m in length were opened with a backhoe to trace terrace stratigraphy outside the area of occupation. Two of these were on the terrace west of the main excavation, and the others were on the west terrace.

CORRELATION OF LEVELS

In order to evaluate the proper stratigraphic relationships among materials recovered from across the site, some means had to be devised to compensate for the varying thickness and inclination of geologic strata from different points beneath the overhang and on the terrace. Strata were usually thicker nearer the shelter than they were farther out on the terrace, and one of the lower units followed the slope of the underlying bedrock. These problems are clearly revealed in the next chapter.

To compensate for these problems, a numerical scale was devised to accommodate each of the site's four major areas. We have called these *correlative levels* (Table 7.2). These correlative units lump together a series of arbitrary excavation levels from different squares that are judged to be stratigraphically contemporaneous, based on their relative

TABLE 7.2 Relation of Correlative Levels to Natural Stratigraphy

Stratum	Shelter	Main excavation	Terrace	West terrace
4	1	1	1	1
	2	2	2	2
	3	3	3	3
	4	4		
	5	5		
	6	6		
	7			
	8			
3	9	7	4	4
	10	8	5	5
		9	6	
		10		
2	11	11	7	6
	12	12	8	7
	13	13	9	8
	14	14	10	9
	15	15	11	
	16	16	12	
	17		13	
	18		14	
	19		15	
1	20	17	16	
	21	18	17	
	22	19	18	
	23	20	19	
	24	21	20	
	25	22	21	
		23	22	
		24	23	
		25	24	
		26	25	
		27	26	
		28	27	
		29	28	
		30	29	
		31	30	
		32		
		33		
		34		
		35		
		36		
		37		
		38		
		39		
		40		
		41		
		42		

vertical position within a geologic stratum. Although they provide a more general stratigraphic picture than that derived from the superposition within an individual excavation unit, the correlative levels, numbered from the surface downward, are presently the only means for evaluating internal superposition across broader areas.

In the following chapters, vertical distributions are shown by correlative level, and attention is focused on the main excavation and shelter areas where there were adequate samples with which to work. In Chapter 12 it is desirable to move to an even higher level of abstraction in order to clarify chronological trends in the geologic, faunal, and artifactual record. Using radiocarbon dates, correlative levels are combined into 12 culture/time stratigraphic units that transcend the bias introduced by differing sedimentation rates. This is discussed in greater detail in Chapter 12.

8

Sedimentary Processes at Rodgers Shelter

Stanley A. Ahler

The focus of investigations at Rodgers Shelter is on the cultural record contained within a remnant of Terrace 1b of the Pomme de Terre River. By the fourth season of fieldwork, excavations to bedrock in the heart of the site in front of the overhang (Figure 8.1) had shown that the T-1b deposits consisted of four major natural stratigraphic units, designated Strata 1 through 4 from the base upwards (Figure 8.2). In the final season of work, backhoe trenches and hand-excavated test pits across the terrace and west terrace revealed that these four strata could generally be followed throughout Terrace 1b (Figure 7.5b). However, it was clear very early in the field program that several minor stratigraphic subunits existed within the four major strata, and this situation was reflected in the early field notes and stratigraphic descriptions referring to as many as eight natural layers at the site (McMillan 1965:341).

What follows in this chapter is largely a discussion of laboratory analyses providing both explicit descriptive information on the deposits at the site and a more refined picture of stratigraphic units and the depositional processes than was attainable from field observations alone. This work was initiated after the completion of excavations. Perhaps the discussion here will suggest hypotheses to be investigated while future work is in progress, although it was obviously of no aid in structuring the field research design at Rodgers Shelter.

Figure 8.1 Rodgers Shelter east profile along 100W line at the end of the 1966 field season. (After McMillan 1971: Fig. 13.)

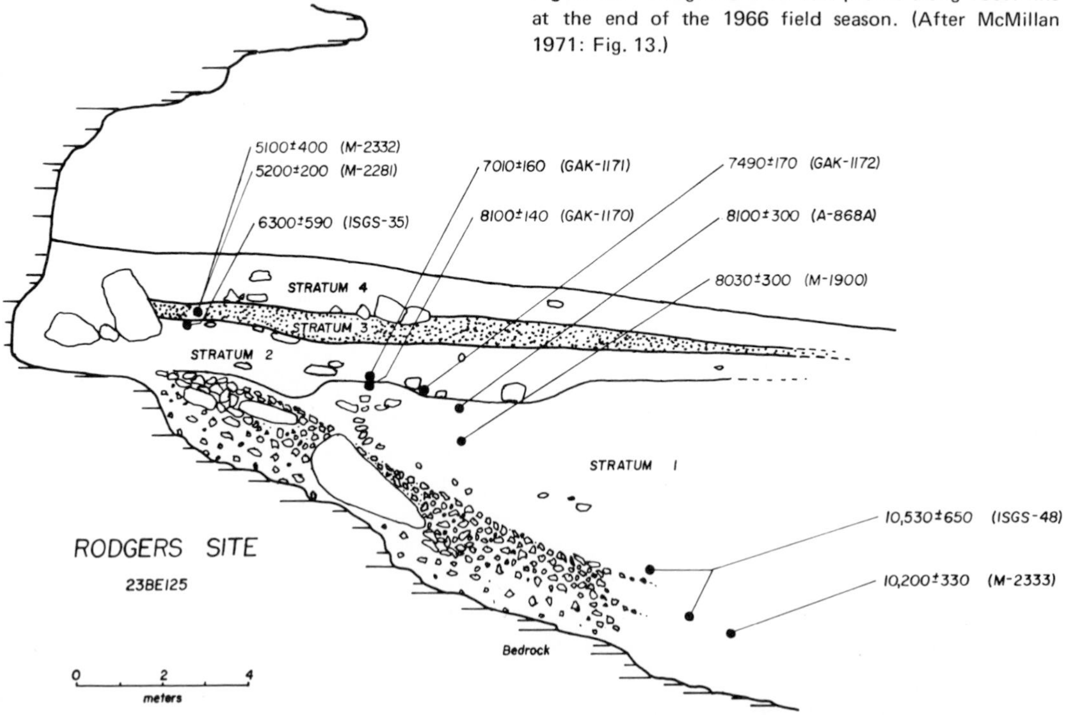

5100±400 (M-2332)
5200±200 (M-2281)
6300±590 (ISGS-35)
7010±160 (GAK-1171)
8100±140 (GAK-1170)
7490±170 (GAK-1172)
8100±300 (A-868A)
8030±300 (M-1900)

STRATUM 4
STRATUM 3
STRATUM 2
STRATUM 1

10,530±650 (ISGS-48)
10,200±330 (M-2333)

RODGERS SITE
23BE125

Bedrock

0   2   4
meters

Figure 8.2 East profile along the 100W line, showing the four major strata and projected locations of dated Carbon 14 samples.

ANALYTICAL PROCEDURES AND RESULTS

Both chemical and physical properties of the sediments were examined in some detail, and descriptions of this work as well as many of the raw data can be found elsewhere (Ahler 1973a, b). The focus of analysis was on 25 samples from the main excavation area. Samples 1–20 represent a continuous stratigraphic sequence from the surface to just above bedrock; sample 21 is from a Dalton hearth in Stratum 1; and samples 22–25 represent a sequence through the talus unit at the base of Stratum 1. Sediment samples were consistently collected in the field from near the center of each arbitrary excavation level and from the walls of backhoe trenches. Those analyzed were selected to represent all four major strata with emphasis on transitional zones between strata. Chemical determinations alone were made on an additional 45 samples from the main excavation area and from test pits on the terrace. These analyses were oriented toward evaluating the utility of various chemical tests (Ahler 1973b); the results are largely of secondary importance in this discussion.

Physical analysis generated data on both particle size and composition. Particle angularity was only generally observed since the secondary origin of much of the deposits negated the use of angularity as a direct measure of frost activity and environmental change (Cornwall 1958:30–34; Butzer 1964: 160–164; Shackley 1972). Size distribution was determined for particles larger than clay (0.002 mm) by a combination of the hydrometer method for the silt range (0.002–0.06 mm) and wet sieving of sands and gravels (greater than 0.06 mm) (Ahler 1973a: 7; Klippel 1971: 178–180). Relative percentages of standard textural classes are shown graphically with respect to datum depth in Figure 8.3. These data give a general picture of change from somewhat coarse sediments at the base of the deposit to very fine-grained materials at the top of Stratum 1, then increasingly coarser deposits again in Strata 2 and 4. Stratum 3 stands out as being highly sorted toward the gravel fraction, suggesting alluvial rather than colluvial processes in operation. It is clear that the bulk of the deposits represent rather fine-grained alluvial materials and that no pure loess exists at the site. However, there is strong suggestion that the middle part of Stratum 1 may be derived in part from windblown silt mixed with alluvial clay, or from the erosion and redeposition of Wisconsinan loess, which thinly mantles the flatter upland areas around the site.

Composition analysis was based on the macroscopic and microscopic examination of particles greater than 0.35 mm in diameter, with reference to their mineral and rock composition. Categories recognized included unpatinated chert, patinated chert, quartz, dolomite, metallic concretions, and quartz siltstone. Fragments of culturally derived chert flakes, bone, mollusk shells, hematite, and charcoal were set aside and dealt with in the chemical analysis. Chert occurs naturally in abundance in the site area, weathering from the Jefferson City dolomite bedrock

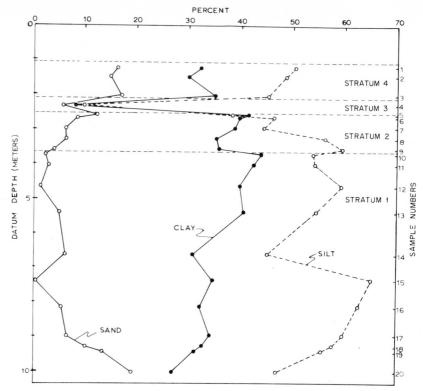

Figure 8.3 Percentage of clay, silt, and sand versus datum depth, samples 1–20, Rodgers Shelter. Percentage of gravel not plotted, but equals 100 minus the sum of all other textural classes. (After Ahler 1973a: Fig. 4.)

(Branson 1944: 50-61). The distinction made between patinated versus unpatinated chert was thought to be of some significance in reference to the origin of the deposits, since yellow to brown patinated chert gravels occur commonly in the bed of the Pomme de Terre River today and are thought to be indicative of weathering in a stream-bed environment. Dolomite sand particles were consistently crystalline and angular in shape, indicating that they were of quite local origin and had undergone little mechanical or chemical weathering. Quartz siltstone and metallic concretions were consistently rounded in shape and appeared to have survived considerable mechanical and chemical weathering. Taken together, these observations suggest that deposits containing large quantities of dolomite sands are more locally derived than deposits containing high percentages of patinated chert, concretions, and quartz siltstones. Percentages of various selected grades and components are shown according to datum depth (Figure 8.4). Obviously, great variation exists in the composition of the deposits. However, patterned relationships are apparent, such as in the frequency of occurrence of concretions, quartz siltstone, and unpatinated chert. Their co-occurrence suggests that these materials were simultaneously eroded, transported, and deposited, deriving from a common source.

An R mode principal components factor analysis (program FACTOR, Veldman 1967: 206–236) was applied to the raw data behind the graphs in Figures 8.3 and 8.4 in an effort to reduce the original variation in the data to a small number of patterned relationships, and to discover a small number of basic independently operating dimensions or factors responsible for the accumulation of deposits at the site. Such factors are directly interpretable in terms of depositional processes and environmental conditions by observing the combined depositional and environmental significance of the variables that load highly on each. Three factors occur, and the varimax rotated factor loading matrix is presented in Table 8.1.

The first factor points out the dichotomous occurrence of materials highly resistant to weathering (those with high positive loadings) versus materials poorly resistant to weathering (negative loadings). This factor

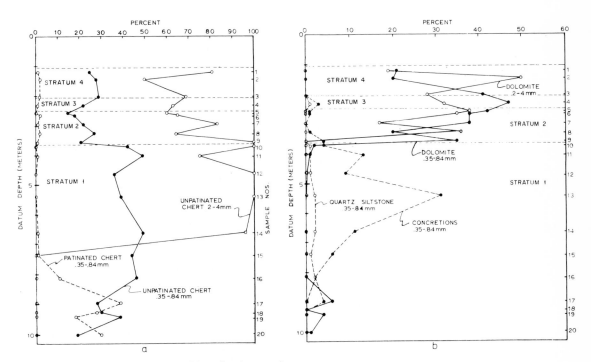

Figure 8.4 Mineral and rock composition of various sand and gravel classes according to datum depth, samples 1–20, Rodgers Shelter. (After Ahler 1973a: Fig. 6.)

TABLE 8.1 Varimax Rotated Factor Loading Matrix from Principal Components Analysis of Samples 1-25 (Eigenvalues greater than 1.0)[a][b]

Variable	Factor 1	Factor 2	Factor 3	Percentage of communality
Quartz siltstone S2	**.86**	.23	.06	79.2
Unpatinated chert S2	**.75**	—.01	.38	70.1
Concretions S2	**.69**	.43	.11	67.7
Dolomite G2	**—.67**	.08	—.15	47.9
Dolomite S2	**—.60**	.29	**—.64**	85.2
Patinated chert S2	.03	**—.90**	.01	82.0
Unpatinated chert G2	.13	**.87**	—.01	77.6
Percentage of silt	.24	—.12	**.89**	86.8
Percentage of clay	.04	.30	**.84**	79.2
Percentage of sand	—.49	—.43	—.29	50.2
Percentage of variance, unrotated factors	39.0	21.3	12.3	Total = 72.6%

[a]After Ahler 1973a: Table 4.
[b]Figures in boldface type indicate loadings greater than .60; G2 = gravel 2.0-4.0 mm, S2 = sand 0.35-0.84 mm.

is interpreted as representing the erosion and redeposition of highly weathered upland soils on the one hand, as opposed to the erosion and redeposition of locally derived parent materials. Factor scores indicate graphically (Figure 8.5) the shift in the sources for the deposits, with positive scores indicating where the upland source is dominant, and negative scores indicating where local bedrock sources play an important role. It is suggested that the shift in sources seen between Strata 1 and 2 is causally linked with changing environmental conditions and concomitant changing hillslope vegetation cover, with local depositional materials being more easily transported as hillslope denudation progressed.

Assuming that patinated chert is indicative of weathering in a stream-bed environment, Factor 2 represents a shift in the location of the Pomme de Terre River channel in relation to the site. Factor scores (Figure 8.5) indicate that patinated chert is most common in the lowest portion of the deposit, with unpatinated chert becoming dominant above the middle part of Stratum 1. This in turn can be interpreted to mean that the lowest deposits are derived from channel or lateral accretion deposits from the river, and that later in time the river channel shifted away from the bluff, allowing the accumulation on the floodplain of unpatinated chert derived from mass wastage of upland materials.

Factor 3 points out a dichotomous situation, with the occurrence of fine-grained materials (clay and silt) varying inversely with the occurrence of coarser dolomite sands. This factor is interpreted to depict the

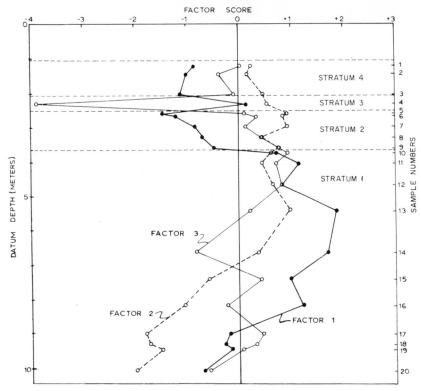

Figure 8.5 Varimax rotated factor scores according to datum depth, samples 1–20, Rodgers Shelter. (After Ahler 1973a: Fig. 7.)

process of overbank alluviation or vertical accretion by the Pomme de Terre River, in opposition to the deposition of materials washed directly from the hillside onto the surface of the aggrading floodplain. Factor scores (Figure 8.5) show vertical accretion to be most important in Strata 1 and 2, and to be least important during Stratum 3 deposition. Thus, there is a strong indication that Stratum 3 is well-sorted alluvial fan material derived from the hillside north of the site.

With a general understanding of the depositional processes in operation at the site in mind, multivariate techniques are again of considerable aid in reaching a better understanding of site stratigraphy and depositional history. Rotated factor scores for each case (sample) in the analysis are a direct measure of the influence of each of the three independently operating depositional processes at any one point in time or place in the stratigraphy. By clustering cases or samples on the basis of similarity in factor scores, groups of samples can be found that represent depositionally distinct stratigraphic units in the site, and that represent periods of time when a relatively constant set of depositional processes were in operation. Weighted average cluster analysis (program BMDP2M, Engleman and Fu 1971) was applied to the factor scores and cases were successively combined on the basis of minimal Euclidean distance in three-dimensional space. Results of the clustering procedure are in the form of a dendrogram (Figure 8.6). The seven-group level is optimal, judging by the large increase in amalgamation distance associated with the move from seven to six groups. These seven groups represent deposits that accumulated under relatively similar depositional conditions. These can be subdivided into 10 stratigraphically contiguous blocks of samples, A[1] through G, each of which represents a major depositional unit of the site. (Units A[1], A[2], B[1], B[2], and B[3] were designated Units A, H, I, B, and J, respectively, in the original report on the deposits; Ahler 1973a: 18–23). The approximate boundaries of these units are shown in Figure 8.7, and mean factor scores provide a method of interpreting the depositional processes responsible for each (Table 8.2).

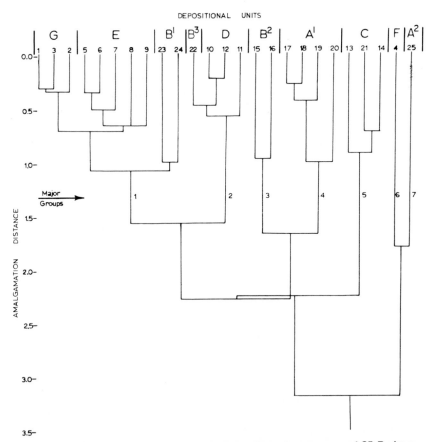

Figure 8.6 BMDP2M clustering sequence of 25 Rodgers Shelter sediment samples on three factor scores. (After Ahler 1973a: Fig. 8.)

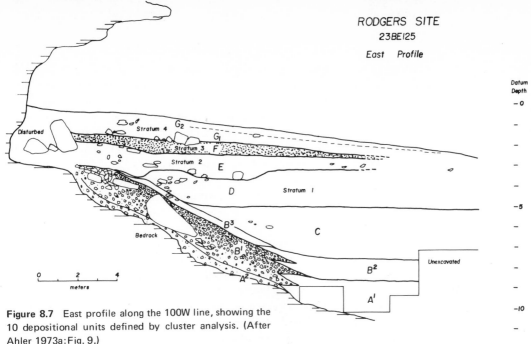

RODGERS SITE
23BE125
East Profile

Figure 8.7 East profile along the 100W line, showing the
10 depositional units defined by cluster analysis. (After
Ahler 1973a: Fig. 9.)

TABLE 8.2 Mean Factor Scores and Interpretative Data on Depositional Units Defined by Cluster Analysis

Depositional unit	Samples combined	Stratum	Cluster group	Mean factor scores		
				Factor 1	Factor 2	Factor 3
Main strata sequence						
A^1	17–20	1	4	0.09	−1.95	0.16
B^2	15,16	1	3	1.01	−0.73	0.48
C	13, 14, 21	1	5	1.83	0.73	−0.22
D	10–12	1	2	0.62	0.81	0.81
E	5–9	2	1	−0.96	0.75	0.18
F	4	3	6	0.55	0.37	−3.51
G	1–3	4	1	−0.89	0.14	−0.14
Talus series						
A^2	25	1	7	−0.94	−0.20	−2.57
B^1	23,24	1	1	−1.02	−0.24	0.82
B^3	22	1	2	0.18	0.77	0.51

Factor Score Interpretation

High positive score	*High negative score*
Factor 1 Erosion and redeposition of weathered topsoils from upland areas as indicated by high frequency of resistant chert, concretions, and siltstone.	Erosion and redeposition of unweathered subsoils and parent material from the immediate site locality as indicated by high frequency of dolomite.
Factor 2 Main channel of Pomme de Terre some distance from the bluff allowing deposition of locally derived unpatinated chert on the surface of aggrading floodplain.	Main channel of Pomme de Terre near the base of the bluff and lateral accretion of channel alluvium as indicated by high frequency of patinated chert gravels.
Factor 3 Pomme de Terre aggrading by vertical accretion as indicated by fine sediments. Some aeolian mixture possible.	Coarse, sorted materials from the hillslopes deposited as alluvial fan debris on the floodplain.

Study of the chemical properties of the deposits provides additional information on the depositional history of the site (Ahler 1973b). Determinations of organic matter, available phosphorus, and total phosphorus were made for samples 1–25 as well as for a number from other site locations. To provide a means of comparing chemical and cultural variation throughout the site, two measures of cultural activity were used as well: lithic debris density and microdebris counts. The former is the number of culturally derived flakes and cores collected from each arbitrary excavation unit from which a sediment sample was analyzed. The latter represents all the cultural material set aside in the compositional analysis of the coarse sands and gravel from each sediment sample.

Several of the results are worthy of elaboration. First is the patterned relationship depicted in Figure 8.8, indicating a generally high degree of correlation between all chemical measures used and the intensity of cultural activity. This picture bears some refinement, however. It can be seen that available phosphorus correlates less well with cultural measures than does total phosphorus, particularly in Stratum 2 (Unit E). Also, available phosphorus was found to show significant subsurface peaks at locations on the terrace that stratigraphically correspond with Stratum 2 at the shelter, but that lack significant peaks in cultural debris or total phosphorus (Ahler 1973b: 128–130). This is interpreted as meaning that available phosphorus is measuring (to a large extent) natural phosphorus build-up on an old ground surface, i.e., peaks on the terrace far removed from the shelter represent incipient soil formation corresponding stratigraphically with the Stratum 2 occupation at the shelter. This implies at least intermittent cessation in aggradation of Terrace 1b, with a stable ground surface being exposed for some time during the Stratum 2 period of occupation.

Another discovery was the increase in total phosphorus and cultural debris from the top to the bottom of Stratum 2 (Unit E) (Figure 8.8), as seen in the main strata series samples. Surprisingly enough, this situation was not paralleled in a similar series of samples from a square only 3 m to the south (Ahler 1973b: 127). It is known that an erosional uncomformity separates Stratum 2 (Unit E) from Stratum 1 (Unit D), and the location of the two series with respect to this erosional feature provides a possible explanation for the discrepancy. The major strata series lies directly over an irregularly shaped erosional depression in the surface of Stratum 1, while the more southern series was from an area where erosional contact was more than 30 cm higher. Since the uppermost part of Stratum 1 is known to contain considerable cultural debris, it follows that the unusually high concentration of cultural debris and total phosphates in the low-lying parts of Stratum 2 may be a result of erosional deflation of the uppermost Stratum 1 deposits. If this is a reasonable explanation, it brings up the highly probable situation that the cultural debris found in the low-lying parts of Stratum 2 actually represents a mixture of material from the two units, rather than pure Stratum 2

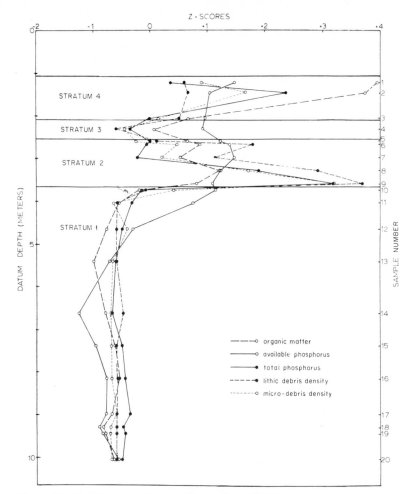

Figure 8.8 Chemical and cultural concentrations according to datum depth, samples 1–20, Rodgers Shelter.
Z – scores derived from all analyzed samples. (After Ahler
1973b: Fig. 4.)

materials, regardless of how well defined this contact may have appeared
in the field. This possibility is posed as an hypothesis to be further investigated by careful study of diagnostic artifact distributions in this part of
the site.

RODGERS SHELTER STRATIGRAPHY

By drawing on the results of the physical analysis, chemical analysis,
and field observations of site stratigraphy, the depositional history of the
site and Terrace 1b can be summarized by depositional unit and stratum.
Suggestions of absolute dating for each unit are based on the series of

radiocarbon age determinations from the site (Figure 8.2) and from nearby Blackwell Cave (Falk 1969; McMillan 1971:183).

Unit A[1] rests directly on bedrock at the base of Stratum 1 (Figure 8.7), beneath a depth of about 8.7 m below datum. This unit, an alluvial sand–silt–clay grading upwards to a clayey silt, contains scattered patinated chert stream gravels, and was deposited by lateral accretion by the Pomme de Terre River at some time prior to 10,500 B.P. At this time the river channel was adjacent to or very near the bluff face on the north side of the valley. Color grades upwards from gray to pale brown, indicating considerable chemical reduction of the lowermost deposits that are below the modern water table. Little cultural material exists in this layer.

Unit B[2] is a light yellowish brown clayey silt directly overlying Unit A[1] and laterally adjacent to and contemporaneous with Units B[1] and B[3] (Figure 8.7). Unit B[2] extends from about 7.3 to 8.7 m below datum and is suggested to have been deposited between 10,500 and 10,000 years B.P. By the time this unit was deposited the river channel had shifted some distance from the bluff and Terrace 1b had begun to aggrade under the influence of overbank flooding or vertical accretion by the Pomme de Terre. Sediments are derived in part from erosion of weathered upland surfaces surrounding the site area. High silt content indicates some aeolian admixture may have occurred. Only a color change separates Units A[1] and B[2], and no visual distinction exists between Unit B[2] and the overlying Unit C. Seasonally moderate to high precipitation patterns can be suggested to account for the relatively rapid aggradation occurring at this time.

Units A[2], B[1], and B[3] represent subdivisions of a talus unit that accumulated beneath the overhang and on the southward-sloping surface of exposed bedrock (Figure 8.7). Unit A[2] is a light yellowish–brown silty gravel derived in large part by in situ weathering of the dolomite bedrock. Unit B[1] is a light yellowish–brown clayey silt, probably of alluvial origin (and similar to Unit B[2]), interspersed with angular dolomite cobbles derived by frost and gravity from the bluff face above the site. Dolomite cobbles are more dense toward the upper boundary of this layer, and several distinct cobble lenses interfinger with alluvial Unit B[2] at the base of the talus slope (Figure 8.9). This indicates partial contemporaneity of Units B[1] and B[2] with several periods of alluvial inactivity accompanied by continued talus slope accumulation. Talus formation apparently began sometime prior to 10,500 B.P. during the formation of Unit A[1], and ceased by or slightly before 10,000 B.P. Unit B[3] is somewhat hypothetical in nature, being defined by only one analyzed sample. It can be described as a light yellowish–brown clayey silt, perhaps representing the weathered surface of the exposed talus slope, following cessation of talus accumulation. High silt content suggests aeolian deposition on the exposed talus surface. This layer is contemporaneous with the upper part of Unit B[2] and the lowest part of Unit C. Both Units B[1] and B[3] contain

Figure 8.9 Terminus of the talus slope, showing the interlaying of talus and alluvium. (After McMillan 1971:Fig. 14b.)

evidence of Dalton occupations thought to be lateral extensions of cultural activities exposed in Unit B^2 (Chapter 10).

Units A^1, A^2, B^1, B^2, and B^3 are all overlain by the 2.4 m thick Unit C (Figure 8.7), which is a light yellowish–brown clayey silt derived almost exclusively from vertical accretion by the Pomme de Terre River. This unit represents a period of maximum aggradation of Terrace 1b, with materials being derived from erosion and redeposition of weathered upland soils in the area. Seasonally high precipitation rates are inferred from the high aggradation rate, while local hillslope vegetation remained stable. This unit is highly interspersed with horizontal or slightly southward-sloping lenses and bands of unpatinated chert gravels and coarse sands. The coarser materials are thought to have washed from hillside ravines onto the aggrading surface of T-1b. Except for scattered Dalton materials at the very base, cultural activity was extremely scarce in this unit, which is suggested to have formed between 10,100 and 8,800 years B.P.

Unit D varies from 1.4 to about 1.8 m in thickness and consists of a clayey silt, grading from light yellowish brown at the base to yellowish brown near the top (Figure 8.7). No visible boundary separated this unit from the underlying Unit C. This layer is the uppermost subdivision of Stratum 1, and was formed by a combination of vertical accretion by the Pomme de Terre River and minor addition of slope wash materials in the form of gravel lenses as in the unit below. High clay content indicates that the velocity of flood waters has decreased. The increasing occurrence of dolomite sands in the upper part of this unit indicates that hillslope vegetation patterns are changing, with bedrock being exposed, eroded, and redeposited on the floodplain. A period from 8800 to 8000 years B.P. is suggested for the accumulation of this unit, during which time the site was frequented by Middle Archaic I peoples (Chapter 10).

An erosional unconformity marks the upper boundary of Unit D, and variations in elevation indicate that at least 46 cm of this layer were removed in some places near the overhang. Test units on the terrace did not reveal evidence of major erosion of that part of the terrace surface, and it appears that the erosional depression seen in front of the shelter is the result of beginning entrenchment into the surface of T-1b of a meandering water-course emitting from the hillside just east of the shelter. This erosion represents a minor interruption in the aggradation cycle of T-1b, and a hiatus in Carbon 14 dates between Unit D and overlying Unit E indicates that this erosion took place sometime between 8000 and 7500 B.P. As discussed earlier, this erosional activity is of considerable importance to the interpretation of the cultural remains, since cultural debris appears to have been dropped by deflation from the upper part of Unit D (Stratum 1) and subsequently mixed with materials in the lower parts of Unit E (Stratum 2). The erosional contact between Units D and E was detectable at two locations on the west terrace.

The overlying Unit E corresponds with Stratum 2 as designated in the field (Figure 8.7). At the shelter this layer is a homogeneous, 1.8-m-thick, brown to dark brown clayey silt with interspersed fall rocks and dolomite cobbles. In test pits on the terrace some distance from the shelter this unit is composed of two or more bands of brown to dark brown clayey silt separated by thin bands of dolomite gravel and cobbles. Similar layering may have existed under the shelter had cultural activities not mixed the deposits soon after successive layers formed. Thus, high negative scores on Factor 1 and knowledge of the original structure of this layer indicate that Unit E is a mixture of materials deposited by two separate processes: bands of clayey silt laid down by vertical accretion by the Pomme de Terre River, alternating with bands of coarse alluvial fan debris eroded from the adjacent hillside. The high occurrence of dolomite in this unit indicates that vegetation and soil cover on the hillside north of the site had changed drastically from conditions throughout Stratum 1, with bedrock being widely exposed to erosion. Peaks in available phosphorus for units on the terrace indicate that some soil development began to take place during the accumulation of this layer (Ahler 1973b: 129). The apparent slowdown in terrace aggradation by the Pomme de Terre River suggests a lower volume of water moving through the valley and, considering all evidence, we can hypothesize this to have been a period of decreased precipitation. A temporal span from 7500 to 6300 years B.P. is given for this unit, and density of cultural debris indicates intense occupation by Middle Archaic II populations (Chapter 10). A transverse profile in the bank of the larger erosional gulley indicates that the intermittent streams flowing from the hillside ravines probably became firmly entrenched into the T-1b surface during the deposition of Unit E. Unit E was detectable across the west terrace as a 30-cm-thick band of brown clayey silt, containing quantities of cultural debris near the central bluff face.

Unit F (equivalent to Stratum 3) conformably overlies Unit E (Figure 8.7) and consists of chert and dolomite gravels and cobbles mixed with minor amounts of brown clayey silt. This is a major layer of coarse alluvial fan debris that is spread from the mouth of hillside ravines and over the bank of the gulley crossing the terrace east of the shelter. Maximum thickness is at the edge of the gulley and near the bluff face, with the layer thinning in all directions from this point. A corresponding alluvial fan of similar material exists for the western gulley (Figure 7.5b) spreading across the west terrace and parts of the terrace proper. Actually, several discrete episodes of alluvial fan deposition are represented, as some interlayering is detectable along the east bank of the western gulley, and since a band of cultural material was detected within the middle of Unit F beneath the overhang. This layer is significant in that it represents both a cessation in overbank alluviation by the Pomme de Terre River and a maximum in local hillslope erosion. We can hypothesize minimal vegetation cover on the hillside above the site, and minimal precipitation, coming perhaps in the form of intense seasonal thunderstorms. This unit is culturally significant since it represents a hiatus in human activity at the site lasting from about 6300 to 3000 years B.P. (McMillan 1971: 84).

Unit G corresponds to Stratum 4 (Figure 8.7) and is a very dark gray clayey silt, a maximum of 76 cm thick on the west terrace and 1.2 m thick beneath the overhang. Two subdivisions of this unit (G_1, G_2) were not detected by the laboratory analysis of the sediment samples. The lower one-third to two-thirds contains numerous scattered dolomite cobbles, which are absent in the upper part of this layer (Figure 8.10). These cobbles are thought to have been incorporated in the basic matrix of Unit G as a result of frost action on the bluff face adjoining the terrace. A cultural origin for the cobbles is ruled out since the cobble-bearing zone exists in areas containing little evidence of cultural activity, and since almost none of the cobbles show evidence of burning. Particle size analysis failed to distinguish the two layers since field sampling procedures

UNIT G$_2$

UNIT G$_1$

UNIT F

1 m

Figure 8.10 Units F and G, showing the transition from cobble-filled zone (G$_1$) to cobble-free zone (G$_2$).

tended to exclude isolated cobbles from sample collection. Unit G is thought to be composed largely of colluvium transported by gravity from the hill overlooking the site, with alluvial fan debris or minor amounts of overbank alluvium from the Pomme de Terre possibly being present. Hillside vegetation cover is assumed to have been denser than during the accumulation of Unit F, and precipitation rates are inferred to have been similar to those of the present. Based on the presence of frost-derived cobbles, the lower subdivision of this unit (G$_1$) is thought to represent a period when temperatures were lower than those of today. A temporal span of 3000 to 1750 B.P. is suggested for this layer (McMillan 1971: 183), and abundant evidence of Late Archaic occupation is found in this sub-unit.

The upper cobble-free part of Stratum 4 (G$_2$) represents a cessation in frost-weathering and amelioration in temperatures. This subunit formed between about 1750 and 500 years B.P. (McMillan 1971: 183), and contains evidence of Woodland occupation in association. After about 500 B.P., deposition on T-1b ceased, thus ending a 10,500-year-long record of environmental and cultural interaction at Rodgers Shelter.

REFERENCES

Ahler, S.A.
  1973a Post-Pleistocene depositional change at Rodgers shelter, Missouri. *Plains Anthropologist* 18(59):1–26.
  1973b Chemical analysis of deposits at Rodgers Shelter, Missouri. *Plains Anthropologist* 18(60):116–131.
Branson, E.B.
  1944 The geology of Missouri. *University of Missouri Studies* Vol. 19, No. 3. Columbia, Missouri.
Butzer, K.W.
  1964 *Environment and archaeology: An introduction to Pleistocene geography.* Chicago, Illinois: Aldine.
Cornwall, I.W.
  1958 *Soils for the archaeologist.* London: Phoenix House, Ltd.
Engleman, L., and S. Fu
  1971 BMDP2M. Cluster analysis by cases. Health Sciences Computing Facility, University of California, Los Angeles. Xeroxed.
Falk, C.R.
  1969 Archeological salvage in the Kaysinger Bluff Reservoir, Missouri: 1966. Region Two, National Park Service, Omaha. Unpublished manuscript.
Klippel, W.E.
  1971 Prehistory and environmental change along the southern border of the Prairie Peninsula during the Archaic period. Ph.D. dissertation, Department of Anthropology, University of Missouri–Columbia.
McMillan, R.B.
  1965 The Rodgers shelter, 23BE125: A preliminary report. In *Part II. Preliminary archaeological investigations in the Kaysinger Bluff Reservoir area*, edited by C.H. Chapman. Report to the National Park Service, Region Two, Omaha. Pp. 330–403.
  1971 Biophysical change and cultural adaptation at Rodgers shelter, Missouri. Ph.D. dissertation, Department of Anthropology, University of Colorado, Boulder.
Shackley, M.L.
  1972 The use of textural parameters in the analysis of cave sediments. *Archeometry* 14:133–145.
Veldman, D.J.
  1967 *Fortran programming for the behavioral sciences.* New York: Holt.

9

Changing Subsistence Patterns at Rodgers Shelter

Paul W. Parmalee, R. Bruce McMillan, and Frances B. King

Some portions of the archaeological record are unequally represented due to the differential preservation of various kinds of materials. This is especially true for food residues since the bones of vertebrates and the shells of mollusks are normally preserved far better than the remains of vegetal foods. The only direct evidence for the vegetal diet at Rodgers Shelter is a relatively small number of carbonized seeds and nut hulls. By contrast, large numbers of bone and shell fragments make it possible to gain better insights into that part of the subsistence system attending the procurement and consumption of animal flesh.

Data from past subsistence systems provide a body of information on both the cultural practices and the environmental milieu in which they were conducted.

PLANT FOODS

Service (1966:10) has reminded us of the almost universal importance that vegetal resources play in the diets of hunting and gathering peoples. This was probably the case for the prehistoric inhabitants of Rodgers Shelter, although it is difficult to assess the relative importance of plant resources in their diets. There is no doubt that the potential for plants to supply much of the diet was great during the past, since in Historic times there were more than 200 different species of edible plants growing in or near the study area (Appendix A).

The small-scale debris from the water-screened samples produced 964 identifiable fragments of nuts and seeds that provide some insight into a portion of the plants exploited for food. By far the most common remains were small carbonized fragments of hickory nuts and black walnuts, and the fragmented seeds of hackberries. Other plant species identified were oak (acorns), grape, persimmon, and black cherry (Table 9.1).

TABLE 9.1 Carbonized Plant Remains from Rodgers Shelter [a]

Shelter area correlative level	Hickory nut (*Carya* spp.)	Black walnut (*Juglans nigra*)	Acorn (oak) (*Quercus* spp.)	Hackberry (*Celtis occidentalis*)	Grape (*Vitis* spp.)	Persimmon (*Diospyros virginiana*)	Black cherry (*Prunus* cf. *serotina*)	Total
1	1	11		186				198
5	2	6		96				104
11	12	1		7				20
12	15	7		22	1			45
13	27	6		21				54
14	8	9		22				39
15	37	5	1	20		1		64
16	33	6		37	1			77
17	30	8	1	61				100
18	21	11		61			1	94
19	79	14		42				135
20	3			2				5
22	24	4		1				29
Totals	292	88	2	578	2	1	1	964

[a] Counts are numbers of hull fragments or seeds, except for *Celtis* fragments which have been converted to the equivalent number of whole *Celtis* seeds. Average *Celtis* seed = .070 gm.

Several factors preclude making more than casual observations on the significance of the botanical remains to the overall subsistence system. Thick-hulled nuts such as hickory and walnut are more conducive to being charred than thin-walled seeds or nuts that would more likely be burned to ash. Another problem is that the sampling and water-screening techniques employed to recover small-scale remains in the early to mid-1960s did not meet standards employed today, and many fragile remains were no doubt lost. The most serious interpretive problem is the inadequate sample size, which obviates any serious quantitative statements.

Realizing these limitations, it is still important to note the apparent importance of hickory nuts throughout the Archaic levels; this has been recorded elsewhere for an Archaic sequence in the central Mississippi River valley (Asch *et al.* 1972). King has demonstrated (Appendix B) that, at the time of settlement, the oak–hickory and bottomland forests within a 10-km radius of Rodgers Shelter had the potential to produce several thousand bushels of hickory nuts each year, even during years of minimal yield.

The abundance of hackberry remains, especially in the upper two levels, may have been introduced in part by small rodents; most of the remains throughout the sequence were charred and fragmented, however, and are interpreted as part of the subsistence base.

FAUNA

The shifting emphasis in archaeology during the past few years from problems concerned with chronology building to attempts to answer questions related to culture process is also reflected in faunal studies. In the past, zoologists were often approached with a poorly formulated set of questions and, more often than not, were merely asked to provide a list of identifications. Today, we realize that an archaeological faunal assemblage contains data relevant to certain zoological problems, in spite of having passed through a "cultural filter" (e.g., Reed 1963:210).

Perhaps the most striking change in faunal studies during the past few years has been the attempt by archaeologists to treat faunal data as an integral part of the cultural record, and to seek to establish points of articulation between the faunal chronology and other parts of the past cultural and environmental system. Several questions relating to past environments can be answered, in part, by the analysis and interpretation of the distribution and frequency of faunal remains in time and space. Faunal studies contribute data that can be used for studying past distributional patterns of animal species whose ranges may have changed, past faunal associations, and past climate and flora (Parmalee 1957:45; Reed 1963:205; Cleland 1966:40; Chaplin 1971:143–159).

The implications faunal remains have for cultural interpretations are as numerous and important as they are for those of an environmental nature. The range of these studies was recently reviewed by Daly (1969) and Read (1971).

The Vertebrate Fauna

Approximately 46,230 fragments of bone were recovered by passing the excavated deposits through one-quarter-inch mesh screens and, in the case of a selected number of samples, by water-screening. A large portion of this bone (38,945 = 84%) could be identified only as to class; however, unidentified mammal bone generally could be separated into two groups representing large and small species. In the sample of 7285 identifiable bones, 44 species of terrestrial vertebrates and aquatic turtles were identified, and 14 others were determined as to genus. Thirteen additional groups were assigned to higher taxonomic levels. There were nine varieties of fish, but only three could be positively identified as to species. Complete lists of the identified elements for each species are given in Table 9.2 (main excavation) and Table 9.3 (shelter).

A problem arose in attempting to separate that part of the faunal sample resulting from past human activities from the remains of animals that may have occurred there naturally. Species whose presence are the most difficult to interpret are the small animals such as mice, voles, rats, insectivores, snakes, lizards, salamanders, and frogs. Many of these small animals inhabit areas along bluffs where they den or hibernate in cavities in the rock exposures or in the surface litter along the bluff base. Guilday and Tanner (1952:136), admitting that most of the faunal debris in an open village is the result of human activities, argue that many smaller species are often intrusive in rock shelters. They assert that:

> In a rock shelter . . . occupation is often intermittent or seasonal, and when the humans leave, other animals move in. Carnivores often den in such areas; rodents live there normally; snakes hibernate in such spots. The result is a collection of bones, not all of which are associated with aboriginal occupation.

Realizing the problem of natural inclusion of faunal remains, care should be taken not to exclude fauna as inedible because of our own cultural bias. Ethnographic evidence for North American hunters and gatherers, as well as analyses of prehistoric Indian paleofeces (Watson 1969:55), have proved that some nonhorticultural American Indians ate a wide range of small vertebrate and invertebrate fauna. This gastronomic diversity is aptly portrayed in Baegert's (1864:364) account of the California Peninsular Indians:

> The chase of game, such as deer and rabbits, furnishes only a small portion of [the] provisions. The hunting of snakes, lizards, mice, and field-rats, which they practice with great diligence, is by far more profitable and supplies them with a much greater quantity of articles for consumption. Snakes, especially, are a favorite sort of small game, and thousands of them find annually their way into the stomachs of the Californians.

Since smaller animals such as amphibians, reptiles, and small rodents were probably seldom dismembered by butchering before cooking, their bones would exhibit little or no evidence of alteration.

TABLE 9.2 Distribution of Faunal Elements from the Shelter Area, Rodgers Shelter[a]

Correlative level	PELECYPODA (Bivalve mollusks) — Naiads: Freshwater mussels	OSTEICHTHYES (Fishes) Aplodinotus grunniens, Freshwater drum	Cyprinidae: Minnow	Catostomidae: Sucker	Moxostoma spp., Redhorse	Micropterus spp., Bass	Ictalurus spp., Bullhead	Ictalurus spp., Catfish	Ictalurus cf. punctatus, Channel catfish	Lepisosteus spp., Gar	Osteichthyes: Unidentified fish
1	150										8
2	313			**1** *1*							
3	173										
4	192										
5	346										8
6	221										
7	134										
8	319										
9	468										
10						**1** *1*					
11	315			8 *1*				3 *1*			60
12	106	1 *1*	1 *1*	5 *1*				6 *1*		2 *1*	26
13	82		1 *1*	6 *1*				4 *1*	2 *1*	2 *1*	**1** 72
14	93	1 *1*		**1** 4 *1*				**2** 2 *1*		2 *1*	**3** 114
15	92	1 *1*		23 *1*	**1** *1*		3 *1*	**1** 3 *2*		9 *1*	**4** 188
16	49			17 *2*			**1** *1*	5 *1*		7 *1*	**4** 225
17	25	1 *1*	1 *1*	**1** 46 *2*	2 *1*		2 *1*	11 *2*		6 *1*	400
18	30			28 *2*			**6** *1*	10 *2*		**1** 4 *1*	**3** 329
19	30	**3** *1*	**1** *1*	11 *3*	1 *1*			**2** 11 *2*	**1** *1*		268
20	8			2 *1*							**1** 6
21	1										
22	25			1 *1*							**2** 2
23											
24	1										
25											
Totals	3173	**3** 4 *5*	**1** 3 *4*	**3** 151 *17*	**1** 3 *3*	**1** *1*	**7** 5 *4*	**5** 55 *13*	**3** *2*	**1** 32 *7*	**18** 1706

[a] Figures in boldface type are elements recovered from one-fourth-inch dry screening; figures in standard type are elements recovered from one-eighth-inch water screening; and figures in italics represent the minimum number of individuals of major subsistence species recovered from both dry and water screening.

TABLE 9.2 (continued)

Correlative level	AMPHIBIA (Amphibians)					REPTILIA (Reptiles)													
	Rana spp., Frog	Bufo spp., Toad	Salientia: Frog/toad	Caudata: Salamander	Amphibia: Unidentified amphibian	Terrapene spp., Box turtle			Chrysemys/Graptemys/Pseudemys spp., Turtle			Sternothaerus cf. odoratus, Musk turtle		Trionyx spp., Softshell turtle			Testudines: Turtle		Serpentes: Snake
1																			
2							2	*1*											2
3									**1**		*1*						2		
4						**2**		*2*											
5						**2**		*1*											
6						**1**	3	*1*	**1**		*1*								6
7						**1**		*1*											
8						**1**		*1*	**1**		*1*								
9																	1		
10																			
11	3	4				**4**	10	*2*		1	*1*						2	2	6
12			1			**2**	5	*1*	**1**		*1*			**1**		*1*	1	8	13
13		1	1			**13**	5	*2*	**1**		*1*							9	19
14		1	1			**16**	13	*2*	**1**		*1*							3	25
15	2	2	9	1		**18**	7	*2*	**5**	2	*1*	**2**	*1*				4	10	34
16		1	6	1		**7**	5	*1*	**1**		*1*						1	7	48
17		3	17			**6**	16	*3*	**2**	1	*1*			**1**		*1*		12	34
18	1	2	7	1		**6**	19	*2*	**1**	1	*1*						1	18	48
19	1	4	1		1	**4**	18	*1*									1	13	59
20			8												1	*1*			1
21						**4**		*1*									1		
22						**2**		*1*									2	3	4
23																			
24																			
25																			
Totals	7	18	51	3	1	**89**	103	*25*	**15**	5	*11*	**2**	*1*	**2**	1	*3*	16	85	299

TABLE 9.2 (continued)

Correlative level	Anatinae/Aythyinae: Duck	Anserinae: Goose	Tympanuchus cupido, Prairie chicken	Colinus virginianus, Bobwhite	Meleagris gallopavo, Turkey	Ectopistes migratorius, Passenger pigeon	Corvus brachyrhynchos, Crow	Buteo spp., Hawk	Strix varia, Barred owl	Otus asio Screech owl	Passeriformes: Perching bird	Gallus gallus, Domestic chicken	Aves: Unidentified bird
AVES (Birds)													
1											1	1	4 4
2					1 1								17
3		1 1			3 2								2
4													8
5					1 1								3 1
6					4 2							3	5
7			1 1										4
8													
9													4
10													
11					1 1						3		21 5
12			1 1	1 1	2 1						1		22 5
13					1 1						1		21 14
14		1 1		2 1	3 2						2		48 13
15		1 1	1 1	1 1	4 2	1 1			1 1		11		68 16
16	1 1	1 1	2 1	1 1	6 2	1 1		1 1		1 1	2		68 21
17					4 2	4 1 1					1 10		32 34
18				1 1	5 2						11		50 56
19	1 1			1 1	9 2	1 1	1 1				11		56 45
20											1		22 2
21	1 1				3 2								35
22					1 1								25 3
23													2
24							1 1						1
25													
Totals	3 3	4 4	5 4	2 5 4	48 24	6 2 4	2 2	1 1	1 1	1 1	1 54	4	518 219

TABLE 9.2 (continued)

MAMMALIA (Mammals)

Correlative level	*Didelphis marsupialis*, Oposum	Vespertilionidae: Bat	*Eptesicus fuscus*, Big brown bat	*Blarina brevicauda*, Short-tailed shrew	*Crytotis parva*, Least shrew	*Scalopus aquaticus*, Eastern mole	*Synaptomys cooperi*, Southern bog lemming	*Peromyscus* spp., Deer mouse	*Perognathus* sp., Pocket mouse	*Microtus* spp., Vole	*Microtus pennsylvanicus*, Meadow vole	*Sciurus niger*, Fox squirrel
1	**1** *1*											
2												
3												
4												
5	**1** *1*											
6						**1**						
7												
8												
9												
10												
11				2	2	**3** 8		4		9		
12		2		1		**1** 12		1		3		
13		1		1		7	1	4	1	12		
14			1	1		10		2		12	1	
15		3				6	**1**	2		24	1	**1** *1*
16		1				**1** 1		4		19	1	
17		1		5		6	1	3		20		
18		**1** 1			1	8	3	8	1	33	4	
19		3	3	1	1	10	4	3		28	2	
20							**1**			1	**1**	
21						**3**	**1**			**1**	**1**	
22						**5**				1		
23												
24												
25												
Totals	**2** *2*	**1** 12	4	11	4	**14** 68	**3** 9	31	2	**1** 162	**3** 8	**1** *1*

TABLE 9.2 (continued)

	MAMMALIA (Mammals)																									
Correlative level	*Sciurus carolinensis*, Gray squirrel			*Sciurus* supp., Fox squirrel/Gray squirrel			*Tamias striatus*, Eastern chipmunk		*Neotoma floridana*, Eastern wood rat			*Geomys bursarius*, Plains pocket gopher			*Marmota monax*, Woodchuck			*Ondatra zibethicus*, Muskrat			*Castor canadensis*, Beaver			Rodentia: Unidentified rodents	
1									1		*1*				1		*1*								5	
2				1		*1*						1		*1*	1		*1*				3		*1*			
3																										
4												1		*1*	6		*2*									
5				1	1	*1*									6		*2*				1		*1*		2	
6															1		*1*							1		
7															1		*1*				1		*1*			
8																										
9																										
10																										
11	1		*1*		21	*1*				5	*1*	1	11	*2*	2		*1*				2	1	*2*		31	
12					15	*1*			3	4	*1*	3	4	*1*							1		*1*		18	
13				4	21	*2*			2	6	*1*	3	12	*2*	3		*1*							1	36	
14				18	27	*3*			1	9	*1*	6	8	*2*	2		*1*				2		*1*	1	41	
15	1		*1*	20	64	*4*				3	*1*	4	15	*3*	1		*1*	1		*1*				1	36	
16	1	1	*1*	15	42	*3*			1	10	*2*	3	12	*5*										3	43	
17	4	3	*1*	15	81	*6*	2	*1*	2	11	*2*	1	42	*2*	2		*1*				2		*1*		63	
18	1	3	*1*	18	93	*6*			1	12	*1*	2	37	*3*	6		*1*	1	1	*1*	1	2	*1*		87	
19	6	1	*1*	34	123	*7*			1	6	*2*	1	15	*3*	20	1	*2*	1	1	*1*	3	1	*1*		69	
20				21	4	*3*			1		*1*	1		*1*										1	5	
21				9		*1*			3		*1*				2		*1*				1		*1*			
22	1		*1*	4	8	*1*			2	4	*1*		3	*1*							1		*1*	1	5	
23																										
24									1		*1*															
25																										
Totals	15	8	*7*	160	500	*40*	2	*1*	15	71	*17*	27	159	*27*	50	5	*17*	2	2	*3*	18	4	*12*	9	441	

TABLE 9.2 (continued)

MAMMALIA (Mammals)

Correlative levels	*Sylvilagus floridanus*, Eastern cottontail			*Lepus* sp., Jack rabbit		*Canis* spp., Dog/Coyote			*Urocyon cinereoargenteus*, Gray fox			*Procyon lotor*, Raccoon			*Taxidea taxus*, Badger			*Mustela vison*, Mink		
1	**3**		*2*																	
2	**3**		*1*									**1**		*1*						
3	**1**		*1*									**1**		*1*						
4	**5**		*2*			**1**		*1*				**1**		*1*	**1**		*1*			
5	**2**	4	*1*																	
6																				
7						**5**		*1*												
8												**1**		*1*						
9														*1*						
10														*1*						
11	**7**	43	*3*									**3**		*2*						
12	**14**	34	*3*			**2**		*1*				**1**		*1*				**1**		*1*
13	**13**	56	*3*			**1**		*1*				**2**		*2*	**1**		*1*			
14	**40**	67	*4*			**3**		*1*	**1**		*1*	**7**		*2*		**1**	*1*			
15	**68**	90	*9*										1	*1*	**1**		*1*			
16	**60**	106	*11*			**2**		*1*	**2**		*1*	**1**	2	*2*	**1**		*1*			
17	**27**	157	*5*	**1**	*1*	**3**		*1*		1	*1*	**4**		*1*						
18	**57**	225	*7*			**3**	1	*1*				**1**		*1*	**3**		*1*	**1**		*1*
19	**81**	196	*8*			**3**		*1*		1	*1*	**2**		*1*						
20	**11**	3	*3*			**1**		*1*				**1**								
21	**14**		*3*			**1**		*1*				**2**		*1*						
22	**11**	12	*2*									**4**								
23																				
24												**1**								
25																				
Totals	**417**	993	*68*	**1**	*1*	**25**	1	*11*	**3**	2	*4*	**33**	5	*21*	**7**	1	*6*	**1**	1	*2*

150

TABLE 9.2 (continued)

MAMMALIA (Mammals)

Correlative Level	*Mephitis mephitis*, Striped skunk		*Spilogale putorius*, Spotted skunk			Carnivora: Unidentified carnivore	Mammalia: Unidentified small mammals		*Odocoileus virginianus*, White-tailed deer			*Cervus canadensis*, Elk		*Bison bison*, Bison		Mammalia: Unidentified large mammals	
1	1	*1*						250	5	3	*1*					37	38
2	1	*1*							9		*1*					97	
3									3		*1*					17	
4	2	*1*							17		*2*					38	
5	2	*1*						100	10	1	*1*					40	12
6									4		*1*					38	
7							1		2		*1*					23	
8							1		1		*1*					20	
9							14		2		*1*					7	
10																	
11							11	900	5	1	*1*					86	39
12							13	925	10	3	*1*					78	37
13							28	1,225	9	1	*1*					133	57
14			1		*1*		99	1,500	16	16	*1*					176	56
15			3		*1*		109	1,768	24	2	*2*					189	78
16			1		*1*	1	84	2,150	11	10	*2*					185	74
17							40	3,400						1	*1*	116	113
18							52	4,300	13	7	*2*					169	175
19			1	1	*1*		105	5,925	33	8	*2*			2	*1*	211	149
20							26	1,500	4		*1*					90	12
21	1	*1*					51		16		*1*					135	
22						1	35	250	8		*1*	1	*1*			167	16
23							1		2		*1*					13	
24							6		2		*1*					19	
25									2		*1*					2	
Totals	7	*5*	6	1	*4*	2	676	24,193	208	52	*28*	1	*1*	3	*2*	2086	856

TABLE 9.3 Distribution of Faunal Elements from the Main Excavation Area, Rodgers Shelter[a]

Correlative level	PELECYPODA (Bivalve mollusks) Naiads: Freshwater mussels	OSTEICHTHYES (Fishes) Aplodinotus grunniens, Freshwater drum	Cyprinidae: Minnow	Catostomidae: Sucker	Moxostoma spp., Redhorse	Ictalurus spp., Bullhead	Ictalurus spp., Catfish	Osteichthyes: Unidentified fish	AMPHIBIA (Amphibians) Rana sp., Frog
1	**156**						**1** *1*	**2**	
2	**363**								
3	**320**								
4	**652**								
5	**334**				1 *1*				
6	**202**								
7	**6**								
8									
9									
10									
11	**20**								
12	**7**						**2** 1 *1*	1	
13	**4**								
14	**6**	**1** *1*				**1** *1*		**1** 6	
15	**7**		1 *1*			**1** *1*	1 *1*	**1** 5	
16	**15**	1 *1*		1 *1*		**1** *1*	**3** *1*	9	2
17	**2**						1 *1*	2	
18		**1** 1 *1*						3	
19		**1** *1*						**2**	
20	**1**								
21									
22									
23									
24									
25									
26									
27									
28									
29									
30									
31									
32									
33									
34									
35									
36									
37									
38									
39								**1**	
40									
41									
42								**1**	
Totals	**2095**	**3** 2 *4*	1 *1*	1 *1*	1 *1*	**3** *3*	**8** 1 *5*	**8** 26	2

[a]Figures in boldface type are elements recovered from one-fourth-inch dry screening; figures in standard type are elements recovered from one-eighth-inch in water screening; and figures in italics represent the minimum number of individuals of major subsistence species recovered from both dry and water screening.

152

TABLE 9.3 (continued)

	REPTILIA (Reptiles)						AVES (Birds)								
Correlative levels	*Terrapene* spp., Box turtle	*Chrysemys/Graptemys/Pseudemys* spp., Turtle	*Chrysemys/Graptemys/Pseudemys* spp., Turtle	*Trionyx* spp., Softshell turtle	Testudines: Turtle	Serpentes: Snake	Podicipedidae: Grebe	Anatinae/Aythyinae: Duck	*Branta canadensis,* Canada goose	*Olor buccinator,* Trumpeter swan	*Tympanuchus cupido,* Prairie chicken	*Meleagris gallopavo,* Turkey	*Ectopistes migratorius,* Passenger pigeon	Strigidae: Owl	Aves: Unidentified birds
1												2 *1*			2
2	2	*1*													8
3	7	*1*		1 *1*	1							2 *1*			12
4	6	*1*	2 *1*	1 *1*	4							1 *1*			27
5	3	*2*			3							1 *1*			16
6					1							1 *1*			11
7												1 *1*			
8															
9															
10															
11	3 *1*	*1*			3 *3*								1 *1*		24 *3*
12	12 *3*	*2*	1 *1*		6 *3*	1						3 *1*			47 *2*
13	18	*1*	1 *1*		5 *2*				1 *1*			3 *2*			48 *1*
14	38 *6*	*2*	3 *1*		6	1						4 *1*			81 *2*
15	41 *3*	*2*	9 *1*		7 *4*				1 *1*		2 *1*	14 *2*			102 *4*
16	25 *6*	*2*	7 *1*		5 *2*						1 *1*	6 *3*			103 *9*
17	16	*2*	2 *1*		9 *2*	2			1 *1*		1 *1*	6 *2*			66 *3*
18	28 *1*	*2*			4			1 *1*				1 *1*			34 *1*
19	8	*1*			3							6 *1*			25
20	8	*1*			1							2 *1*			13
21	8	*1*			1							1 *1*			14
22															9
23	1	*1*					1 *1*								11
24												1 *1*			11
25															7
26															3
27														1 *1*	2
28															1
29															
30															
31															
32															
33															
34															
35															
36															
37															
38															
39					1					9 *1*		1 *1*			5
40												1 *1*			3
41															4
42	1	*1*													5
Totals	225 *20*	*24*	25 *7*	2 *2*	60 *16*	4	1 *1*	1 *1*	3 *3*	9 *1*	4 *3*	57 *24*	1 *1*	1 *1*	694 *25*

TABLE 9.3 (continued)

MAMMALIA (Mammals)

Correlative level	*Didelphis marsupialis*, Opossum	Vespertilionidae: Bat	*Eptesicus fuscus*, Big brown bat	*Blarina brevicauda*, Short-tailed shrew	*Scalopus aquaticus*, Eastern mole	*Synaptomys cooperi*, Southern bog lemming	*Peromyscus* spp., Deer mouse	*Microtus* spp., Vole	*Microtus pennsylvanicus*, Meadow vole	*Sciurus carolinensis*, Gray squirrel	*Sciurus* spp., Fox squirrel/Gray squirrel	*Tamias striatus*, Eastern chipmunk	*Neotoma floridana*, Eastern wood rat	*Geomys bursarius*, Plains pocket gopher	*Marmota monax*, Woodchuck	*Ondatra zibethicus*, Muskrat	*Castor canadensis*, Beaver
1					1												
2	1 *1*									1 *1*							
3					1									2 *1*			2 *1*
4														2 *1*			2 *1*
5														2 *1*			2 *1*
6																	
7	1 *1*																
8																	
9																	
10																	
11											1 *1*		1 *1*				1 *1*
12											5 4 *2*	1 *1*	1 *1*				1 *1*
13					1						9 4 *2*			2 1 *3*			2 *1*
14			1		2						11 7 *3*			2 *1*	2 *2*	2 *1*	4 *1*
15				1	2			1		1 *1*	36 5 *5*	1 *1*	2 2 *1*	4 1 *3*	1 *1*		4 *1*
16		1			2						41 20 *6*		1 *1*	2 *1*	1 *1*	1 *1*	6 *1*
17	1 *1*				1 *1*					2 *1*	23 13 *4*		1 *1*				1 *1*
18										1 *1*	13 8 *2*			1 *1*			4 *1*
19					4						28 2 *3*		1 1 *1*				3 *1*
20					5			1			9 *3*					1 *1*	1 *1*
21					7						8 *2*			1 *1*		1 *1*	
22											1 *1*						
23	2 *1*				10						4 *1*		1 *1*				
24					3	1					3 *1*		2 *1*				
25					4	1			1		3 *1*						
26					5	1					3 *1*						
27					1		1				1 *1*						
28																	
29																	
30																	
31																	
32																	
33																	
34																	
35																	
36																	
37																	
38																	
39					6	1					5 *1*			2 *1*			
40						1					2 *1*						
41											1 *1*			1 *1*	1 *1*	1 *1*	1 *1*
42					1								1 *1*		1 *1*		
Totals	5 *4*	1	1	1	49 *8*	5	1	2	1	5 *4*	207 63 *42*	2 *2*	8 6 *9*	21 2 *15*	6 *6*	6 1 *6*	30 *12*

TABLE 9.3 (continued)

MAMMALIA (Mammals)

Correlative level	Rodentia: Unidentified rodents		Sylvilagus floridanus, Eastern cottontail			Lepus sp., Jack rabbit		Canis familiaris, Domestic dog		Canis latrans, Coyote		Canis spp., Dog/Coyote		Urocyon cinereoargenteus, Gray fox		Procyon lotor, Raccoon		Taxidea taxus, Badger		Lynx rufus, Bobcat		Mustela vison, Mink		Mephitis mephitis, Striped skunk		Spilogale putorius, Spotted skunk		Carnivora, Unidentified carnivora
1			3		2																								
2			1		1																								
3																													1
4												1	1			1	1							1	1			
5												1	1															
6			1		1																								
7																													
8																													
9																													
10																													
11			16	5	3							1	1			2	1											
12	1		32	15	6							2	1	1	1	2	2											
13			30	21	8							2	1			4	1											
14	1		73	21	13	2	1			1	1	2	1			6	3	1	1					1	1	2	1	
15	2		120	47	13							6	1	1	1	14	4			1	1							
16	1	3	121	79	14			7	1			7	2	3	2	15	4	3	1			1	1	1	1	1	1	
17	1	3	58	41	11			1	1			2	1			4	2											
18	1	2	50	21	8							4	1			3	1			3	1							
19	1		66	8	6							3	1			3	2			1	1							
20			24		3							2	1	1	1	7	2											
21			10		3							1	1			6	2											
22			2		1							3	1			2	1											
23	4		13		1							8	1			2	1											
24	1		3		1											2	1											
25			7		2											2	1											
26	1		1		1																							
27	2																											
28			1		1																							
29																													
30			1		1																							
31																													
32																													
33																													
34																													
35																													
36			1		1																							
37			1		1																							
38																													
39	6		8		1					1	1					4	1											
40	1	1	4		1											1	1											
41	1															1	1											
42	2		1		1																							
Totals	21	14	648	258	105	2	1	8	2	2	2	45	16	6	5	81	32	4	2	5	3	1	1	3	3	3	2	1

TABLE 9.3 (continued)

Correlative level	MAMMALIA (Mammals)															
	Mammalia: Unidentified small mammal		Ursus americanus, Black bear		Odocoileus virginianus, White-tailed deer			Antilocapra americana, Pronghorn		Cervus canadensis, Elk		Bison bison, Bison		Platygonus compressus, Peccary		Mammalia: Unidentified large mammals	
1					6		1							1^{b1}		38	
2	2				3		2									102	
3	1				13		2									147	
4					21		1									228	
5	1				13		1	1	1							126	
6	1				3		1									32	
7																1	
8																	
9																*	
10																	
11	7	57			11	1	1									150	10
12		274	1	1	23	1	1									396	10
13	6	267			28		4									267	24
14	5	339			42		2	1	1							534	22
15	2	488			105	8	4									744	39
16	10	719			105	4	4									650	58
17		423			47		2	1	1	1	1	3	1			316	17
18	1	169			44		2			2	1	1	1			202	4
19	12	63			19		2					5	1			142	2
20					20		1			1	1	3	1			107	
21	20				8		1					1	1			64	
22	3				1		1									17	
23	86				3		1									6	
24	31				2		1									2	
25	36				3		1									13	
26	5				1		1									2	
27	1																
28	4																
29	1																
30																	
31																	
32																	
33	1															2	
34																	
35	1															1	
36																	
37																1	
38	1																
39	33				13		1									95	
40	34	50			25	2	2									91	6
41	14				3		1									31	
42	18				4		1									14	
Totals	337	2849	1	1	566	16	42	3	3	4	3	13	5	1	1	4521	192

[b] See text.

Fish

All of the identified fish from the shelter are varieties that inhabit the waters of the Pomme de Terre River today. According to descriptions of habitat requirements (Pflieger 1971), the fish from all strata were probably taken from the stream not far from the site. The preferred habitats for all of the principal species—channel catfish, bullhead, freshwater drum, gar, and suckers—are deep pools and eddys that characterize the Pomme de Terre River along its lower reaches.

There appears to be a preference for species of two families—Ictaluridae (catfishes) and Catostomidae (suckers). It is impossible to say whether this bias is a result of selectivity by the shelter's occupants, a reflection of greater availability of these fishes, or the result of procurement systems to which these species were especially vulnerable.

Amphibians and Reptiles

The water-screened residues produced quantities of frog, toad, salamander, lizard, and snake bones. As discussed earlier, the remains of these vertebrates may be either natural or cultural or, more likely, both.

There is little doubt that a variety of terrestrial and aquatic turtles was eaten. Both the eastern box turtle, *Terrapene carolina,* and the ornate box turtle, *T. ornata,* probably occur in the sample, but it is difficult to distinguish between them on the basis of fragmentary remains. The terrestrial forms were not only used for food, but their carapaces were sometimes modified for use as containers or bowls (Chapter 10).

Although aquatic turtles were not as numerous as their terrestrial counterparts, their bones indicate that the Indians did obtain them from the river along with fish and mussels. Most of the aquatic forms were map turtles *(Graptemys),* painted turtles *(Chrysemys),* and pond terrapins *(Pseudemys).* Representatives of these genera, as well as the other aquatic forms identified, inhabit the Pomme de Terre River today.

Birds

Bird remains constituted less than 4% of the total faunal sample. The majority of bones were from wild turkey and small perching birds (Passeriformes). There were a few elements of waterfowl, other gallinaceous species, and raptorial birds. None of the ducks could be identified to species, but a few elements of the Canada goose were recognizable. A femoral section from a grebe and nine trumpeter swan bones, representing a single individual, came from the lower part of Stratum 1. The trumpeter swan is no longer part of Missouri's avifauna. Waterfowl were apparently of only minimal economic importance; their remains represent only 0.2% of the bone in the total identified sample.

Gallinaceous birds from a variety of habitats were recorded. The small number of bones of prairie chicken and bobwhite indicated that these species were not commonly procured. Those elements found were clustered in Stratum 2. Prairie chickens were probably taken from grassland areas near the shelter, while the bobwhite should have occurred locally in almost any of the edge areas. The most common of the gallinaceous species represented was the wild turkey, which could have been taken from nearby forested areas. Turkey bones constituted 1.4% of the total identified sample, and the majority of the larger unidentified bird bone fragments were probably from turkey.

Nine elements of the passenger pigeon suggest that this extinct species played only a minor role in the subsistence system. Raptorial birds and the common crow are represented by only a few elements.

The second largest group of identified bird bones was from small perching birds, although these could only be distinguished to family level. Four domestic chicken bones were obviously intrusive and came from a disturbed area in Stratum 4 beneath the overhang.

Mammals

Nearly 90% of all identified vertebrate remains from Rodgers Shelter were mammals. From this sample, 31 species were identified, while 6 others were determined to genus, and 3 groups were recognized at the family level. Six of these species no longer have ranges that include the study locality, and several others are marginal to the area.

Bones of bats, shrews, moles, mice, and voles were recovered during the water-screening process. As discussed earlier, it is problematical as to what part of this sample represents the remains of foods eaten by the human inhabitants. Two species of rodents identified from the faunal sample have ranges that no longer include this part of Missouri. The pocket mouse *(Perognathus)*, reported by Schwartz and Schwartz (1959:335) as only rarely occurring in western Missouri, today normally ranges only as near as eastern Kansas. The contemporary range of the meadow vole *(Microtus pennsylvanicus)*, a species presently having a more northerly distribution, may reach the northern border of Missouri (Schwartz and Schwartz 1959:336).

Some of the larger native rodents were apparently important as meat supplements during most periods of occupation. Numerous elements of tree squirrels *(Sciurus)*, and lesser numbers of bones of wood rats and pocket gophers, had a relatively wide temporal and horizontal distribution. The distal ends of ulnae and tibiae of several squirrels bore cuts indicating they were butchered; the tibia of one wood rat bore similar marks.

Woodchuck bones were distributed throughout the deposit. Although this large rodent may have occupied the shelter during some periods, most of the remains were probably subsistence debris. The presence of only one individual could definitely be attributed to a natural death, based on an articulated skeleton found just above bedrock outside the overhang.

Bones of mammals from aquatic environments were scarce, but a few elements of mink, beaver, and muskrat indicate that the stream habitat was exploited for mammals as well as turtles, fish, and mussels.

The large number of cottontail remains recovered suggest this small brush and forest-edge species was one of the most important of all the food animals. A few jack rabbit bones probably represent animals taken from nearby grasslands, possibly in local prairie areas that also supported populations of the prairie chicken.

Except for the very earliest levels, canid remains were distributed through most of the deposit. The majority of these can probably be referred to dog, although three skull and jaw elements were determined as probably being coyote. It is uncertain as to whether the dogs were eaten, but at least one was not; rather, the animal had been buried with care under a stone tumulus (McMillan 1970).

Elements of several species of medium-sized carnivores or omnivores, including gray fox, raccoon, badger, bobcat, striped skunk, spotted skunk, and opossum, were found in varying numbers. Of these mammals the raccoon was selected most often, judging from the greater abundance of bones. The badger no longer occurs in the study locality (Schwartz and Schwartz 1959:291).

Remains of white-tailed deer were the most numerous of the larger animals, and deer meat was apparently the staple throughout much of the site's history. However, its importance was greater during some periods than others; an evaluation of this animal's significance through time will be discussed later (Chapter 12).

Only a few elements of bison and elk were recovered. These animals were obviously never an important part of the total food economy, although the quantity of meat realized from one bison or one elk would obviously have been more significant than that from other animals. Three pronghorn teeth (three individuals) represent one of the first valid records for the occurrence of this plains herbivore in Missouri. The absence of bear remains in the sequence seems noteworthy; only a single tarsal could be tentatively attributed to this woodland omnivore.

A tusk from the extinct Pleistocene peccary *(Platygomus compressus)* was recovered in the fill of a former channel of the ravine east of the site, where it crossed Terrace 0 in front of the shelter. There is no doubt that it was redeposited there. Mehl (1966:73) reports the Pleistocene peccary became extinct in Missouri sometime near the end of the Wisconsinan stage.

Several observations on butchering were recorded for four of the species described earlier. They are:

Deer: distal end of humerus—severing the forelimb at the "elbow"
Squirrel: cuts on the neck of the femur head—removal of the "thigh" (upper hind leg) from the pelvis

Raccoon: cuts on the ramus of the jaw—possibly from skinning or from severing the lower jaw from the skull
Beaver: cuts on the shaft of a tibia—possibly from skinning, removal of flesh, or an attempt at severing the foot at the point of articulation with the leg; cuts on the ramus of a jaw—possibly from skinning or from severing the lower jaw from the skull

The Invertebrate Fauna

A study of the large sample of terrestrial gastropods and freshwater mussels from Rodgers Shelter, started several years ago, is still incomplete. Fortunately, raw counts of the numbers of mussels from each level were made prior to the time they were submitted to the specialist who agreed to conduct the study, so some measure of the potential importance of mussels within the subsistence system for each of the components can be made. The numbers of valves for each correlative level are given in Tables 9.2 and 9.3.

The descriptive data in this chapter are interpreted in Chapter 12.

REFERENCES

Asch, N.B., R.I. Ford, and D.L. Asch
  1972 Paleoethnobotany of the Koster Site: The Archaic horizons. *Illinois State Museum, Reports of Investigations* No. 24, Springfield. (Research Papers 6, Illinois Valley Archaeological Program.)
Baegert, J.
  1864 An account of the aboriginal inhabitants of the California Peninsula, translated by Charles Rau. *Annual Report of the Board of Regents of the Smithsonian Institution, 1863*, Washington, D.C. Pp. 352–369.
Chaplin, R.E.
  1971 *The study of animal bones from archaeological sites.* New York: Seminar Press.
Cleland, C.E.
  1966 The prehistoric animal ecology and ethnozoology of the Upper Great Lakes Region. *Anthropological Papers* No. 29, Museum of Anthropology, University of Michigan, Ann Arbor.
Daly, P.
  1969 Approaches to faunal analysis in archaeology. *American Antiquity* 34:146–153.
Guilday, J.E., and D.P. Tanner
  1962 Animal remains from the Quaker State Rockshelter (36Ve27), Venango County, Pennsylvania. *Pennsylvania Archaeologist* 31:131–137.
McMillan, R.B.
  1970 Early canid burial from the Western Ozark Highland. *Science* 167:1246–1247.

Mehl, M.G.
   1966 Notes on Missouri Pleistocene peccaries. *Missouri Speleology* 8:54–74.
Parmalee, P.W.
   1957 Zoology. In *The identification of non-artifactual materials*, edited by W.W. Taylor, Pub. 565:45–46. National Academy of Science—National Research Council, Washington, D.C.
Pflieger, W.L.
   1971 A distributional study of Missouri fishes. *University of Kansas Publications, Museum of Natural History* 20:225–570.
Read, C.E.
   1971 Animal bones and human behavior: Approaches to faunal analysis in archeology. Ph.D. dissertation, Department of Anthropology, University of California, Los Angeles.
Reed, C.A.
   1963 Osteo-archaeology. In *Science in archaeology*, edited by D. Brothwell, and E.S. Higgs. New York: Basic Books, Inc. Pp. 204–216.
Schwartz, C.W., and E.R. Schwartz
   1959 *The wild mammals of Missouri*. Columbia, Missouri: University of Missouri Press.
Service, E.R.
   1966 *The hunters*. Englewood Cliffs, New Jersey: Prentice-Hall, Inc.
Watson, P.J.
   1969 The prehistory of Salts Cave, Kentucky. *Illinois State Museum, Reports of Investigations* No. 16, Springfield.

10

Material Culture at Rodgers Shelter: A Reflection of Past Human Activities

Stanley A. Ahler and R. Bruce McMillan

One of the major research objectives at Rodgers Shelter is to explicate the changing relationships between the prehistoric inhabitants and their natural environment. Analysis of the material culture here is along lines that maximize the available information on the nature of this cultural–environmental intersystemic articulation. Such an approach is by definition functional, since an understanding of the function of the archaeological remains is in itself an explication of the role that these manifestations, be they artifacts or contextual remains such as features, once played in the interface between man and his surroundings.

Two analytical procedures are followed here, each providing a different form of information. The first entails an essentially traditional functional classification of the artifacts. Through a consideration of artifact morphology, technology, and, in some cases, wear patterns, the nonperishable material from the site is divided into a number of functional artifact categories. With a few refinements, this functional classification is based on the functional typology proposed by McMillan (1971) in his preliminary analysis of the Rodgers cultural remains. These classes are defined to convey maximum information specifically related to artifact use and function, with little or no consideration of stylistic variation. The stylistic dimension is best dealt with through the study of varying morphology and technology within discrete functional artifact classes, and such variation will be considered in detail in a future report. The only treatment of style in this report is the visual portrayal of the extremes of formal variation through the use of extensive artifact illustrations (Figures 10.1 to 10.15).

While specific functional artifact categories defined at Rodgers are occasionally unique, the approach followed here is little different from that used by Winters (1969) and Fowler (1959) in their analyses of other large Midwestern archaeological collections. However, a departure is made from Winters's (1969:30) practice of combining several artifact categories into more general, higher-level functional groupings. Such an approach is not followed here since it is thought more productive to allow the option of investigating the relationships among the lower-level functional categories, rather than merging them on a priori grounds into groups with undemonstrated explanatory superiority.

The second phase of the analysis, indeed, the heart of the analytical procedure, is the presentation of data on cultural remains in terms of specific prehistoric *activities* as documented by *activity indicators*, rather than in terms of functional artifact types. An activity indicator is any observable unit of analysis that documents in unambiguous terms a single type of activity performed by members of a prehistoric human society. An indicator may be in the form of an artifact, a single attribute or configuration of morphological attributes of an artifact, or a contextual relationship among various cultural or noncultural remains (or "features," in field terminology). Such postulated activities may vary from those whose primary purpose is to reinforce social boundaries and enhance the continuation of stylistic traditions (such as parallel oblique flaking of projectile points) to those that tend to guarantee group survival through successful manipulation of available natural resources. With the ecological problem orientation of the Rodgers research in mind, the emphasis here is on the latter activities: We will concentrate on activity indicators that best provide direct evidence of cultural–natural intersystemic articulation.

The shift from the artifact to the activity indicator as the basis for functional analysis allows us to quantify human behavior in the simplest, most unambiguous terms. Consider, for example, the functional artifact category *mano*. The definition used here is not exceptionally broad and refers to manos as rounded cobbles, small enough to be held comfortably in one hand, that exhibit at least one ground, convex surface. Actually, many assemblages contain manos with one to four ground surfaces, manos with and without single-pitted and multiple-pitted surfaces, and manos with and without evidence of hammering and pounding on the margins (cf. Winters 1969:61, 62; Greenwood 1969:15–20). It can readily be seen that individual artifacts placed in a single functional category represent varying combinations of attributes derived from more discrete instances of human behavior, i.e., activity indicators. For the purpose of quantifying and demonstrating change in human behavior, it seems more advantageous, then, to deal with the indicators themselves, rather than with the attribute combinations familiar to us as artifacts.

A discussion of field-recognized features, or culturally derived contextual relationships among cultural and noncultural items, is given in the description of activity indicators. Features are logically included here since many are not composed of artifacts but, more accurately, are simple and direct evidence of man's structuring his physical surroundings.

The use of activity indicators as the basis for analysis differs little in concept from procedures advocated by Dunnel (1971), who suggests the use of the "tool" as the basic unit of functional analysis, and by Knudson (1973), who uses the EU or "employable unit" as the basis for comparative functional analysis of Paleo–Indian assemblages. Stated in terms more familiar to some, the second phase of the analysis is essentially an analytic classification (Rouse 1960:313–315), using attributes that signify a number of procedural modes specifically indicative of man's manipulation of his natural surroundings.

FUNCTIONAL ARTIFACT CATEGORIES

Thirty-one functional artifact categories are discussed. Examples of each category are given in Figures 10.1 through 10.15, which are designed to illustrate the maximum formal variation in each functional grouping. Distributional data for 3611 artifacts from the shelter and main excavation areas are given by correlative levels (Chapter 7) in Tables 10.2 and 10.3.

Functional classification of chipped stone artifacts commonly referred to as projectile points is increasingly recognized as a complex problem that has recently received considerable attention in the literature (Hester and Heizer 1973; Morse 1973:25; Nance 1970, 1971; Keeley 1974; Ahler 1971). A number of researchers have claimed, and with some basis, that these ubiquitous artifacts served a number of purposes, only one of which was as the tip of a projectile. This problem is of special interest here.

To avoid unnecessary terminological confusion, in this report the term *point* refers to any bifacially flaked, bilaterally symmetrical, chipped stone artifact exhibiting a point of juncture on one (distal) end and some facility (notching, constriction, lateral grinding) for hafting on the opposite (proximal) end. Thus *point* is a morphologically defined class of chipped stone tools, and the term as used here does not convey any particular functional interpretation.

The previous study of a sample of points from Unit E (Stratum 2) of Rodgers (Ahler 1971) is of particular relevance to the functional classification of these artifacts. Based on this work and other recent studies of material similar to that at Rodgers (Goodyear 1971; Knudson 1973), five main assumptions form the basis for the functional classification of these tools:

1. Multiple functional classes exist within the morphological class *point* as defined earlier. The basis for this assumption is Ahler's (1971:119–120) work, which demonstrated through experiments and wear pattern analysis the functional diversity (cutting, sawing, whittling, scraping) within a sample of Unit E points from Rodgers Shelter. His conclusion from that pilot study is assumed to apply to all of the Rodgers material.

2. Within the morphological class *point*, there remains a close correlation between artifact form and artifact function. Thus, it is assumed that morphological groupings of points are internally functionally homogeneous, while great differences in function may exist between such groups. Most previous research has assumed that the strongest form–function correlation is on the level of point, as defined earlier, equated with projectile usage. Here it is assumed that the form–function relationship is still valid, but at a different level than previously accepted, that is, on the level of morphological subgroups (sometimes equatable with stylistic types) within the basic category *point*. This proposition was demonstrated to be acceptable for a sample of Rodgers material (Ahler 1971:119), and its use here follows directly from that study.

3. Given unrestricted availability of raw material for chipped stone tools, there is a point size below which items are more likely to have been used as projectiles than as hafted cutting tools. It is assumed that extremely small implements would not function as efficiently for hafted cutting, scraping, or prying activities as would large specimens, due to limitations in structural strength and length of usable cutting edge for the smaller tools. Conversely, small size does not limit the efficiency of projectiles, as is illustrated by the documented use of small triangular points as arrowtips in the killing of large game such as bison (Fletcher and La Flesche 1972:282, 451). This basic assumption of size as related to function recalls Fenenga's (1953) study of the weight distribution of points, and suggests an alternate interpretation of his data. Also, this assumption would not necessarily hold true under conditions where raw material limitations or preferences dictate that all points be of relatively small size (Winters 1969:25–27).

4. An impact fracture, or longitudinally oriented flake driven from the distal tip of the point (e.g., Figure 10.2c), is direct evidence of the artifact's having been used as a tip for a projectile. This assumption is based on observations of such fractures on specimens morphologically identical to arrowpoints found hafted in foreshafts (Witthoft 1968); the experimental production by Jim Spears of such fractures through impact of actual projectiles (Ahler 1971:86); and the association of archaeological

impact fractures with microscopic wear patterns such as longitudinally oriented surface striations and distally pronounced edge wear, which are also directly indicative of projectile usage (Ahler 1971:86, 105).

5. Moderate to large size and transverse blade fractures are direct indicators of points that were used for purposes other than as tips for projectiles. This assumption receives support from Ahler's study (1971:58, 79), which indicates a high correlation of transverse fracture and large size with pronounced edge rounding and smoothing, the latter features taken as indicative of a variety of scraping and cutting activities.

The functional classification of the Rodgers points began by grouping the sample into a number of morphologically similar subgroups. Functional classification was then made on the basis of the frequency of functionally important attributes for each group; that is, according to the second assumption listed, the subgroups, rather than individual artifacts, were functionally classified. The Rodgers points were grouped into three major functional categories, largely on the basis of size and the relative frequency of impact fractures and transverse blade fractures.

Projectile points, referred to here as PPs, are interpreted as artifacts used only as tips for spears, darts, or arrows (Figure 10.1a–h). These artifacts are characterized by small size in relation to all other Rodgers points, a relatively high frequency of impact-fractured and complete specimens and relatively few specimens with transverse blade fractures (Table 10.1). These are specialized, single-purpose implements that first occur in Unit E (Stratum 2) (Tables 10.2, 10.3).

Projectile point/hafted cutting tools, referred to here as PP/HCTs, are unspecialized, multipurpose implements that functioned first as tips for lances or darts, and secondarily as some form of hafted cutting, scraping, sawing, or prying tool (Figure 10.1i–q and Figure 10.2). This functional diversity suggests hafting in a removable foreshaft of the type found in Woodland deposits in Research Cave, central Missouri (Shippee 1966:23, 70–71). The points are characterized by medium to large size relative to other Rodgers points, a relatively high frequency of impact fractures, and a low frequency of transverse blade fractures (Table 10.1). It will be noted that virtually all lanceolate and large side-notched forms, including the earliest points from the site (Figure 10.2), are classified as PP/HCTs. The creation of this multipurpose functional category is in agreement with a number of observations: (1) Microscopic wear patterns observed on Rodgers specimens indicate that lanceolates and other typologically early specimens functioned at least occasionally as tools other than projectiles (Ahler 1971:119, 120); (2) Morse (1973:25), based on wear pattern studies by Goodyear (1971), has concluded that Dalton points functioned as cutting tools rather than projectiles; (3) technologically and stylistically distinct artifacts, San Jon points, have been found in primary kill site context confirming their use as projectile points on weapons used to

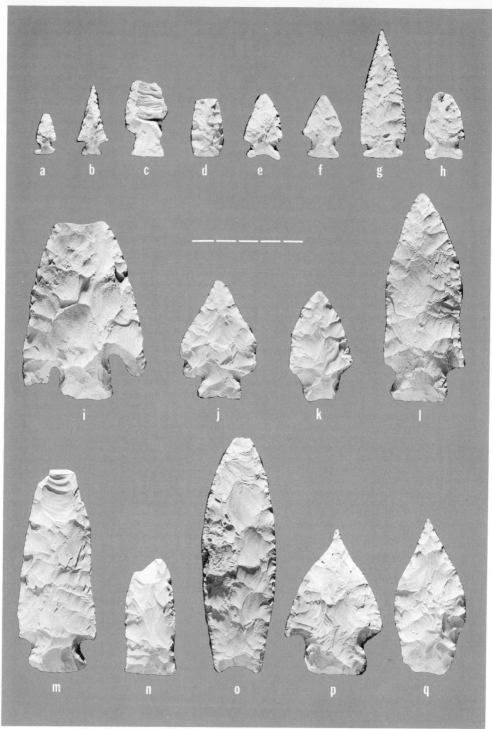

Figure 10.1 Chipped stone artifacts from Rodgers Shelter. Projectile points from Unit G_2 (a–d), Unit G_1 (e,f), and Unit E (g,h). Projectile point/hafted cutting tools from Unit G_2 (i–k) and Unit G_1 (l–q) (scale in centimeters).

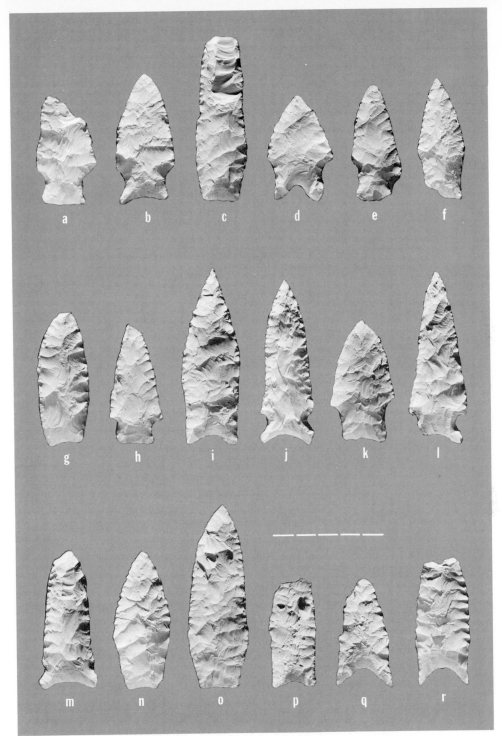

Figure 10.2 Projectile point/hafted cutting tools from
Rodgers Shelter Unit E (a–l), Unit D (m–o) and Unit B
(p–r) (scale in centimeters).

kill large game (Wheat 1972:97), while morphologically identical specimens found in a campsite context exhibit wear patterns indicating use as cutting implements (Knudson 1973:128); and, finally, (4) tools specialized toward hafted cutting tool usage are lacking in the earliest documented cultural assemblages both at Rodgers and throughout the Midwest and Plains, making it highly likely that the earliest points, and later stylistic derivatives of these early forms, were actually multipurpose, generalized implements. The earliest recognizable specialized hafted cutting tool is probably the Hellgap Knife or the Cody Knife (Irwin and Wormington 1970:29), which are both derived from contemporaneous forms interpretable as PP/HCTs.

Hafted cutting tools, or HCTs, are specialized tools that functioned other than as tips for projectiles. They are characterized by medium to large size, a high occurrence of transverse blade fractures, and a near absence of impact fractures (Figure 10.3, Table 10.1). Wear pattern studies of a HCT sample from Rodgers indicate that a variety of uses are involved, ranging from slicing to cleaving, sawing, and scraping. Use-wear observed on these items is distinctly more pronounced than on the less specialized PP/HCTs (Ahler 1971:119, 120). The specialized tools first appear in Unit D (Upper Stratum 1) (Tables 10.2 and 10.3). Since wear pattern studies were not made on the entire Rodgers point sample, further subdivision into more specific use classes was not attempted.

Chipped stone bifaces of every size and shape that lacked features of specialized functional significance and that lacked facility for hafting were placed in the functional category *generalized cutting implements* (Figures 10.4 and 10.5). Microscopic examination of a sample of these tools indicates that a variety of functions is represented, from cutting to scraping and whittling activities. Also, flake patterns, fracture patterns, and intentional edge grinding indicate that a number of these artifacts are unfinished tools broken in manufacture. In general, however, there is little obvious correlation between variation in biface form and variation in wear patterns and inferred function. For that reason, these tools are grouped into a single functional category regardless of formal variation. Frequency distributions (Tables 10.2 and 10.3) do not include segments and distal and edge fragments, since it was not always possible to separate these fragments from similar fragments originally belonging to PPs, PP/HCTs, and HCTs. Tabulations of the latter three categories also exclude such fragments.

TABLE 10.1   Fracture Type Percentages According to Functional Classification of Points at Rodgers Shelter

	Impact fracture	Transverse blade fracture	Unfractured	Total
Projectile points	31%	42%	27%	100%
Projectile point/ hafted cutting tools	26%	43%	31%	100%
Hafted cutting tools	10%	70%	20%	100%

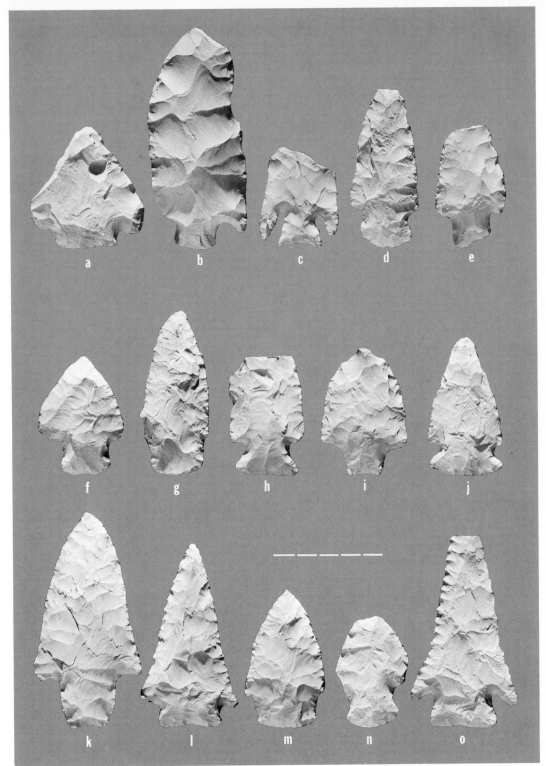

Figure 10.3, Hafted cutting tools from Rodgers Shelter
Unit G (a–e), Unit E (f–m), and Unit D (n–o) (scale in
centimeters).

Figure 10.4 Generalized cutting tools from Rodgers Shelter Unit G (a–c) and Unit E (d–f) (scale in centimeters).

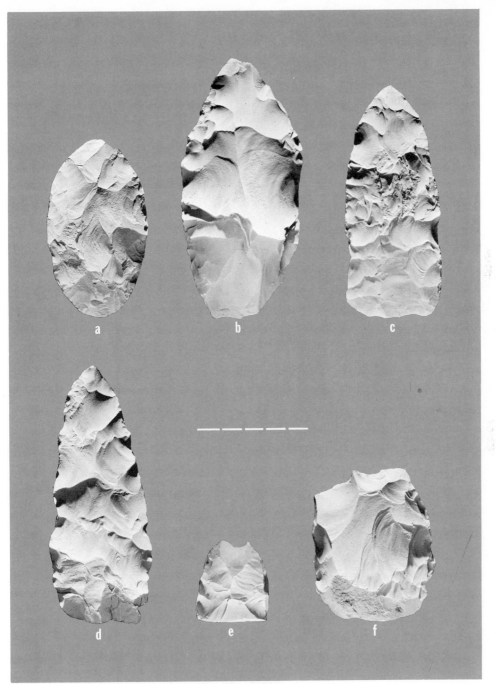

Figure 10.5 Generalized cutting tools from Rodgers Shelter Unit E (a), Unit D (b), Unit C (c), and Unit B (d–f) (scale in centimeters).

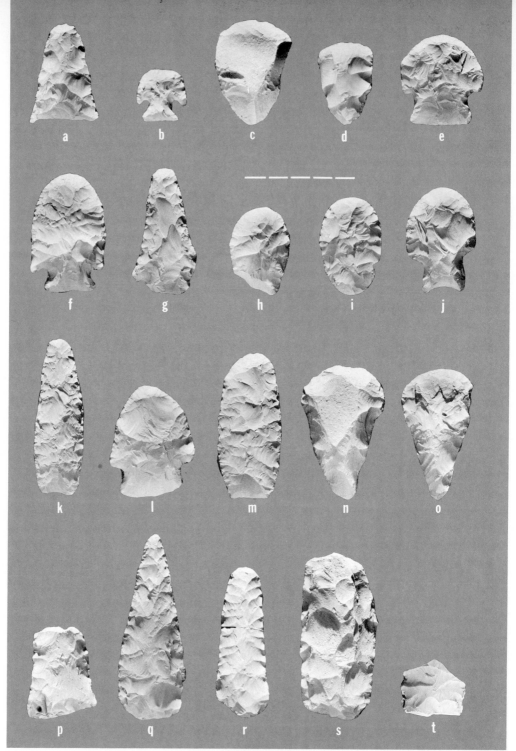

Figure 10.6 Specialized scraping tools from Rodgers Shelter. Hafted scrapers from Unit G (b–e), Unit E (a, f–i, k), Unit D (j, l–n), and Unit B (o). Transverse scraper/grinders, working edge toward bottom of page, from Unit G (p), Unit E (q–s), and Unit D (t) (scale in centimeters).

174

The functional category *hafted scraper* includes tools characterized by bilateral symmetry, a single beveled working edge oriented transverse to the long axis of the tool, and alteration by flaking, grinding, or notching of the lateral margins and end opposite the working edge for the assumed purpose of hafting (Figure 10.6a–o). The presence of a haft facility is assumed to indicate functional specialization within the general realm of activities fulfilled by beveled-edge implements. Hafted scrapers occur throughout the deposits (Table 10.2 and 10.3), but formal configurations vary considerably through time.

Transverse scraper/grinders are relatively long and narrow bifacial tools with a transversely oriented working edge at one or both ends (Figure 10.6p–t). The double beveled or transverse fracture plane working edge is characterized by an extremely steep edge angle (ca. 90°) and pronounced use-wear in the form of faceting, rounding, grinding, and striations (e.g., Ahler 1971:38–39). Striations from grinding are oriented perpendicular to the working edge axis and parallel to the longitudinal tool axis. Wear placement indicates that these blunt-bitted tools were held in much the same position as a modern wood chisel while in use. Wear indicates, however, that these tools are neither adzes nor chisels. Tool motion was in a back-and-forth fashion parallel to the long axis, as the implement was used to scrape, abrade, grind, or knead some hard, abrasive material. Functionally similar implements with similar morphologies and nearly identical wear patterns are recognized by the authors from Extended Coalescent sites (Lehmer 1971:115–120) along the Middle Missouri River in South Dakota (Ahler 1973). The working edges of a large percentage of the Plains Village Tradition specimens are impregnated with traces of an unidentified black (apparently inorganic) substance that was being scraped or ground. The Rodgers specimens retained no microscopic traces of the material being worked. At Rodgers these tools occur almost exclusively in Unit E (Stratum 2) (Tables 10.2 and 10.3), making the functional similarities between these and the South Dakota specimens made some 5000 years later all the more noteworthy.

The category *irregular scrapers* includes all flakes, chert fragments, or bifaces with a unifacially worked, beveled edge, and which lack any obvious provision for hafting (Figure 10.7). The lack of hafting presumably makes these tools functionally distinct from the hafted scrapers described earlier. No further shape or size restrictions are placed on tools in this category. While a number of them exhibit a serrated or denticulate working edge, all are assumed to have been used within the general realm of scraping activities. Cursory wear pattern examinations indicate that this functional interpretation generally holds true, as evidenced by a high frequency of edge rounding, smoothing, and striations perpendicular to the beveled-edge axes (Wilmsen 1968:158–159; Semenov 1964:85–93).

Figure 10.7 Irregular scrapers from Rodgers Shelter Unit G (a,b), Unit E (c–e), Unit D (f, g), and Unit B (h, i) (scale in centimeters).

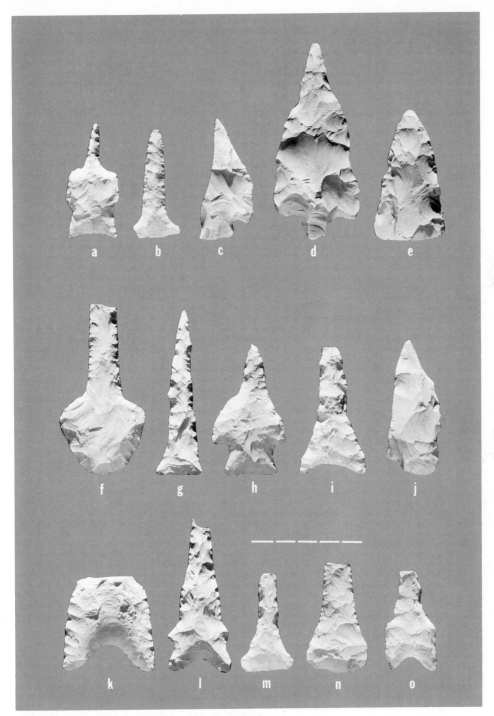

Figure 10.8 Chipped stone perforators from Rodgers Shelter Unit G (a–e), Unit E (f–k), Unit D (l–n), and Unit B (o) (scale in centimeters)

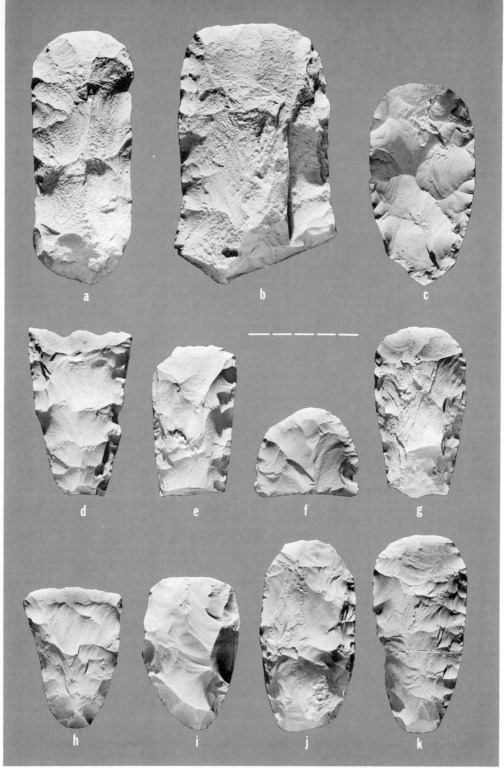

Figure 10.9 Chipped stone axe/adzes from Rodgers Shelter Unit G (a-e), Unit E (f-h), Unit D (i), and Unit B (j, k) (scale in centimeters).

178

Bifacial chipped stone artifacts or artifact fragments with extremely narrow, parallel-sided blades and steep-angled lateral edges are classified as *perforators* (Figure 10.8). These tools are functionally interpreted as piercing, perforating, or boring implements, morphologically equivalent to the "chipped stone drills" commonly referred to in the literature. A variety of haft facilities occur on their proximal ends.

The functional category *chipped stone axe/adze* includes large, thick bifacial tools, shaped by bold percussion flaking, and possessing a single bifacially flaked, transversely oriented working edge on one end (Figure 10.9). Lateral margins are heavily ground, presumably for the purpose of hafting. The steeply angled working edge is almost always unworn, suggesting resharpening. On some specimens there is slight smoothing and polish on one or both faces immediately adjoining the working edge. Several tools have a restricted area of surface polish in the center of one face, presumably the product of haft friction. Specimens from the Dalton Zone, Units B^1, B^2, B^3, and C (lower Stratum 1) (Figure 10.9j–k) are morphologically and technologically equatable with artifacts recently described as "Dalton adzes" (Morse and Goodyear 1973). Some specimens (e.g., Figure 10.9d) in the lower part of Unit G (Stratum 4) are similar to tools called "Clear Fork tools" (Hester *et al.* 1973:93). The Rodgers Shelter "Clear Fork tools" are the only specimens having a clearly unifacially beveled working edge. On the basis of working edge morphology, these items may be adzes or wood scrapers (Hester *et al.* 1973:94–95), with the remainder being wood-chopping tools.

Fully grooved and partially grooved *ground stone axes* were manufactured from dolomite, chert, or hard hematite by flaking or pecking followed by grinding (Figure 10.10). All raw materials are locally available, suggesting that these items were made near the site. These tools have a relatively limited chronological distribution in the site (Tables 10.2 and 10.3). Differences in shape, weight, and hafting techniques indicate that these tools and the chipped stone axes/adzes are of qualitatively different functions.

The functional category *antler flakers* is indicated by the presence of distal scarring and abrasion on detached deer antler tines (Figure 10.11a–b). Microscopic examination of these and antler tines used experimentally for pressure flaking indicates nearly identical wear patterns. Several of the Rodgers specimens were sawed or chopped partly through near the base of the tine, then snapped from the main antler shaft before use. Two of the three specimens from the Dalton Zone are shaped by scraping and have considerably larger tip diameters than other specimens, indicating possible variation in knapping technology.

Deer ulnae and other segments of large mammal long bones with rounded and blunted ends are interpreted as *punches*, which were apparently used for pressure flaking or indirect percussion flaking of stone implements (Figure 10.11c–e).

Figure 10.10 Grooved axes from Rodgers Shelter Unit E
(a, b) and Unit D (c, d) (scale in centimeters).

180

Figure 10.11 Worked bone and ceramics from Rodgers
Shelter. Antler flaking tools from Unit E (a) and Unit B
(b). Punches, Unit E (c–e). Awls, Unit E (f, g). Antler
handle, Unit G(h). Fishhook, Unit E (i). Worked beaver
incisor, Unit E(j). Turtle shell bowl fragment, Unit G (k).
Smoothed cord-marked, incised, and stamped sherds from
Unit G_2 (l–n) (scale in centimeters).

The functional category *bone awl* includes sharply pointed bone implements presumably used to pierce or perforate pliable materials such as leather or fabric (Figure 10.11f–g). Such tools are made of splinters or articular segments of deer or other large mammal long bones. Microscopic examination reveals that nearly all specimens were shaped by scraping or whittling with a sharp-edged flake or other chipped stone artifact, and modification by grinding is minimal.

The functional category *antler handle* is represented by several sections of deer antler that were hollowed longitudinally from one end (Figure 10.11h), forming a socket presumably suitable for hafting a narrow-bladed tool such as a chipped stone perforator.

One complete *fishhook*, one fragment, and one unfinished specimen were in Unit E (Figure 10.11i, Tables 10.2 and 10.3). All are made of dense bone—probably deer long bone—and shaped by incising and scraping.

A single fragmentary *worked beaver incisor* was in Unit E (Stratum 2) (Figure 10.11j). This artifact apparently functioned as a chisel used on wood or bone.

The use of *turtle shell bowls* is indicated by fragments of turtle carapace with scraped and smoothed interior surfaces (Figure 10.11k). The specific function of these bowls is unknown, but their small size (most being *Terrapene* sp.) suggests use as food-serving utensils rather than long-term storage or transportation utensils.

A small piece of deer antler tine was ground to resemble a canine tooth, and then ringed for suspension as a *pendant*.

The functional category *miscellaneous worked bone and antler* includes all functionally unclassified fragments or elements of bone and antler that were modified by whittling, chopping, scraping, sawing, grinding, incising, or smoothing.

Ceramics consist of a number of sherds representing a few pottery vessels from the upper part of Unit G (Stratum 4). The presence of sherds at the base of Unit G in the shelter area is evidence of the extensive mixing of the upper deposits in that part of the site (Table 10.2). Surface decoration is most often plain or cord-marked (Figure 10.11l–n), and tempering material is crushed calcite and limestone, sand, and clay grog. The majority of sherds are from large conoidal vessels interpreted as food storage and cooking containers.

A number of chert cores are battered and pounded along the angular platform margins and are classified as *core hammerstones*. Variation in the intensity of battering is pronounced, resulting in specimens ranging from those with only slight alteration to nearly spherical tools hammered on all surfaces (Figure 10.12a–c). One functional interpretation is that these tools served as mano-hammers, or implements used to pulverize, grind, or otherwise process some form of vegetal material. The presence of considerable faceting, grinding, and smoothing on the chert hammer surface has been noted on some late Archaic specimens and has been cited as supporting evidence for this functional interpretation (Klippel

Figure 10.12 Artifacts from Rodgers Shelters. Core hammerstones from Unit E (a,c) and Unit D (b). Noncore hammerstone, Unit E (d). Anvils from Unit G (e) and surface (f). Mano, Unit G (g) (scale in centimeters).

1969:29). In marked contrast, microscopic examination revealed that only one of the 138 core hammerstones from Rodgers has a smoothed surface, and that none show noticeable evidence of grinding or pronounced faceting.

It has been suggested that these tools were used to peck and shape other and softer stone implements that are usually classified as ground stone tools (Greenwood 1969:55; Bordaz 1970:105). Experiments by Rose Duffield at Northwestern University (personal communication) have demonstrated the usefulness of core hammerstones for this purpose. Two hypotheses–(1) that core hammerstones were used to manufacture other ground stone implements, and (2) that they were mano-like implements used in processing wild plant remains—can be tested by comparing data from Rodgers to data from the late Archaic Booth site in the Prairie Peninsula of Missouri (Klippel 1969) and data from the Browne site, an early milling stone complex site in southern California (Greenwood 1969). All three sites contain numbers of morphologically similar core hammerstones, manos, and milling stones (metates). The latter two sites are inferred to represent stations where plant food processing was of considerable importance (Klippel 1969:28, 29; Greenwood 1969:54). The ratios of manos to metate–milling stones are quite similar, being 155/35, 47/7, and 1525/208 (4.4:1, 6.7:1, and 7.3:1) at Rodgers, Booth, and Browne, respectively. From this we can perhaps infer that manos and milling stones are indeed functionally related, co-occurring in approximately the same relative frequencies across time and space. In contrast, the ratio of total manos and milling stone–metates to core hammerstones, which occur in some frequency at each site, are widely divergent, being 1.4:1, 2.5:1, and 19.7:1 at Rodgers, Booth, and Browne, respectively. Most of the manos, milling stones, and other tools at Browne were shaped by pecking, but the ratio of such milling tools to core hammers is markedly greater than at the Midwestern Booth and Rodgers sites where the milling stone complex is much less prominent. The obvious conclusion is that core hammerstones were probably not universally used to manufacture manos and metates, nor were they functionally tied to such implements in the processing of plant foods. It should be pointed out that all ratios are quite similar at Booth and Rodgers, suggesting that functional similarities may prevail despite their markedly different wear patterns.

Given the depth and complexity of the surficial micro-fractures on core hammerstones, it would seem that if they had been used to pulverize a softer, nonperishable material, some trace of the work would be found adhering to tool surfaces. One likely possibility is hematite, which was common at Rodgers in both rock and powdered form. Microscopic examination of the surfaces revealed one tool with minute hematite stains; one with a yellowish ochre-like substance on the surface; and one with a brown organic (?) impregnation. It is probably safe to conclude that pigment processing was not the primary function of these tools at Rodgers. One remaining alternative is that these tools were used for the often inferred, but rarely implicitly stated function of percussors of chipped stone tools. The vertical distribution of core hammerstones, however, does not correlate very closely with that of bifaces—which are the artifacts most likely directly derived from hard hammer percussion. This final functional hypothesis can best be tested by comparing the distributions of hammerstones with those of cores and flaking debris, but the necessary data are presently unavailable.

Because the chert core hammerstones are so distinctive in their method of manufacture, a second functional grouping was used to include all hammerstones not manufactured on a chert core: *noncore hammerstones*. This category includes chert nodules and dolomite and sandstone cobbles that exhibit one or more areas of marginal battering or pounding (Figure 10.12d). Chert tools are the most common. The distribution of this group parallels that of core hammerstones, except that noncore tools are more frequent in Unit G (Table 10.2 and 10.3).

The functional category *anvil* includes all dolomite, chert, and sandstone cobbles and slabs that lack surface grinding but which exhibit one or more small pits or depressions pecked into a surface (Figure 10.12e–f). Anvils may have functioned as platforms for some pounding or hammering activity.

Dolomite, chert, and sandstone cobbles with one or more ground and abraded convex surface are interpreted as hand-held grinding/crushing implements termed *manos* (Figures 10.12g and 10.13a–b). Some specimens exhibit single or multiple pits on one or more surfaces. A few have battered ends or margins. These tools are assumed to have been used in combination with a lower element such as a stone or wooden metate, a mortar or milling stone, or with another mano as suggested by Winters (1969:62). The function of the pits is unclear. Ethnographic observations (Waugh 1916:59, pl. 14, Figs. c, d) suggest that these depressions probably held unground seeds or grain prior to and during the grinding process. On the contrary, Greenwood (1969:18, 19) contends that meal clogs in the depressions while grinding, thus reducing grinding efficiency. She suggests that the depressions are finger holes to aid in grasping the mano while grinding with one of the lateral mano edges. Neither explanation is wholly acceptable, since a number of pits are found on cobbles with no evidence of grinding (anvils), and, in the Brown site assemblage, Greenwood (1969) gives no figures on the co-occurrence of pitting and edge wear on the same specimen. Thus, there is no reason to assume that the pits are secondarily important to or are necessarily functionally linked to grinding.

The category *mortar/metate* includes large sandstone and dolomite slabs that have large concave depressions ground and/or pecked into one or both flat faces. These are interpreted as the lower halves of a two-part grinding system, being used in combination with hand-held grinding or crushing implements. Two fragments of a single broken metate (Figure 10.13c) were found in Units D and E, respectively, separated by 4 m

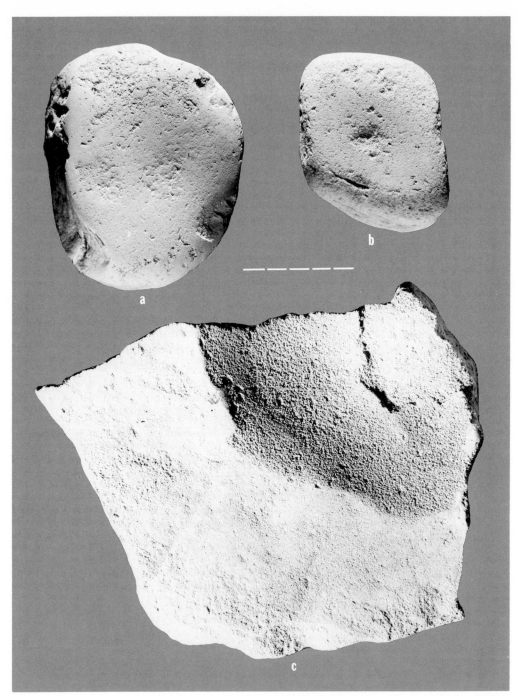

Figure 10.13 Artifacts from Rodgers Shelter. Manos from Unit G (a) and Unit D (b). Mortar/metate fragment, Unit D (c) (scale in centimeters).

Figure 10.14 Artifacts from Rodgers Shelter. Whetstones from Unit E (a) and Unit D (b). Abrader, Unit G (c). Rubbed hematite, Unit E (d). Rubbed galena, Unit E (e). Atlatl weight fragment, Unit G (f) (scale in centimeters).

Figure 10.15 Engraved dolomite plaque from Rodgers Shelter Unit G (scale in centimeters).

horizontally and 30 cm vertically. This graphically illustrates the erosional deflation of Unit D and the subsequent mixing of cultural remains in Unit D and E (see Chapter 8).

Tabular slabs and small flat pieces of fine-grained sandstone with smoothing on one or more faces are termed *whetstones* (Figure 10.14a–b). Margins are angular and the ground surfaces are flat, rather than convex or concave, distinguishing them from hand-held grinding stones and metates. Wear is also less pronounced than that on manos, with the ground surfaces being naturally flat from fracture along a bedding plane. Several are too large to be hand-held, yet lack the intense pecking and grinding localized in the central depression of metate/mortars. It is suggested that they are stationary platforms against which some object was ground. Hematite was impregnated in some of the ground surfaces, suggesting their use in processing hematite into red ochre.

Small cobbles of soft siltstone and dolomite with shallow U-shaped grooves are interpreted as *abraders* used to grind or smooth bone or wood. One specimen, of perhaps more specialized function, exhibits grooves crossing at right angles at one end and pits on opposing faces (Figure 10.14c).

The functional category *rubbed hematite* includes ground and faceted hematite fragments that are the residue from processing larger pieces into red ochre (Figure 10.14d). The specific function of the red ochre is unknown, but the decorative and ceremonial use of red pigments is well documented in aboriginal North America. The abundance of rubbed hematite in certain layers at Rodgers suggests that perhaps a surplus of red ochre was produced there, with the excess used at other localities.

Small crystals of the mineral galena were processed in a manner similar to that for hematite, producing residual fragments of *rubbed galena* (Figure 10.14e). This mineral was probably used to produce black powder for pigment.

A single *atlatl weight* fragment of brown carboniferous siltstone, a material not native to the immediate locality, was at the base of Unit G (Figure 10.14f).

An *engraved dolomite slab* was at the base of Unit G. Both faces were engraved with finely incised geometric figures of unknown symbolic, ritualistic, or artistic importance (Figure 10.15).

No data are presented here for a number of potentially important functional artifact categories. Studies of flake tools and flaking debris are still in progress; hence, distributional data are unavailable for such categories as cores, unmodified flakes, and retouched and utilized flakes, the latter including gravers or spurs (Irwin and Wormington 1970:29, 30) from the Dalton levels.

TABLE 10.2 Distribution of Functional Categories by Correlative Levels for the Shelter Area, Rodgers Shelter

Correlative level	Projectile point	Projectile point/hafted cutting tool	Hafted cutting tool	Generalized cutting tool	Hafted scraper	Transverse scraper/grinder	Irregular scraper	Perforator	Chipped stone axe/adze	Ground stone axe	Antler flaker	Punch	Bone awl	Fishhook	Antler handle	Turtle shell bowl	Worked beaver incisor	Antler pendant	Miscellaneous worked bone and antler	Ceramics	Core hammerstone	Noncore hammerstone	Anvil	Mano	Mortar/metate	Whetstone	Abrader	Rubbed hematite	Rubbed galena	Atlatl weight	Engraved dolomite slab	Total
1	3	9	5	8			2	3								1				15			1					1				41
2	4	13	3	7			1	2								1				54								1				87
3	2	3	1	4			3													13			1									31
4		9		2				2	1											4				1								22
5		10	2	6			2				1								1	9					2			1				32
6	1	5	1	5				1			1									7			1	1				4				26
7		2	1	6			1												1	3								11				24
8	1	3		4									1							3				1				8				25
9			1																									2		1	1	3
10				2																												2
11	2	5	9	14	2	1	5	2	1	1	1		1			1			2		2		1	1	1	4		42	3			98
12	2	4	5	7	1	1	6	1			2		1	1							5			1		1		27	1			69
13	2	6	4	4	3		1	1	1	1	1	1	2			1			2		1		1	2		6		16	2			55
14		3	5	7		2	5	1			1	1	3			2	1		5		3		1	4	1	5		28	1			78
15		7	4	17	1	3	7	1	2				6	1	1				9		4	1		4		10		21	1			102
16	1	7	5	10	4	1	5	4	2	1			4			1			5			2		3		6		19	1			79
17	1	7	9	7	1	2	5	3	1		2		1			2			9				1	1		4		18	1			76
18		7	5	13			3		1		2	1	3			1			3		1	1	1	1				11	1			59
19		12	5	5	1	1	1	1			2	2	3						6		1		2	1	3	5		11	2			62
20		3	1	1	1		2																	2	5			3	2			20
21				1	1		1			1									2									3				8
22		3		2					3		1																					9
23																																2
24																																0
25																																0
Totals	19	118	66	132	15	11	50	22	12	4	14	4	25	2	1	10	1	0	45	108	17	4	10	23	12	41	0	227	15	1	1	1010

190

TABLE 10.3 Distribution of Functional Categories by Correlative Levels for the Main Excavation Area, Rodgers Shelter

Correlative level	Projectile point	Projectile point/hafted cutting tool	Hafted cutting tool	Generalized cutting tool	Hafted scraper	Transverse scraper/grinder	Irregular scraper	Perforator	Chipped stone axe/adze	Ground stone axe	Antler flaker	Punch	Bone awl	Fishhook	Antler handle	Turtle shell bowl	Antler pendant	Miscellaneous worked bone and antler	Ceramics	Core hammerstone	Noncore hammerstone	Anvil	Mano	Mortar/metate	Whetstone	Abrader	Rubbed hematite	Rubbed galena	Total
1	17	37	8	30			11	3											22	1		6	7				5		147
2	13	35	7	28	2		10	1	4				1					1	46		1	8	5		1		11		174
3	18	33	14	44		1	12	3	6		1	1	1					1	36	1		4	10		1	1	8		196
4	13	23	20	70	1		3	8	5				2		1				8		5	4	3		3		17		186
5	3	28	11	45	1		7	3	5		1		1					4	2	3	4	13	13		3		25		172
6		11	1	14	1			1													1	2	1	1	1		6		40
7																													0
8				2																							1		3
9																													0
10																													0
11		6	13	16	3		6	6	3				2			2		3		8	2	5	2		10		55	1	143
12	1	11	11	13	3	3	9	5	2	1		1	3			2		4		12	1	3	1		12		58	1	157
13		10	13	22	4	3	9	8	7		3		3			12		2		5	1	5	5	3	5		63	2	185
14		9	25	42	2		15	7	2	1	1		6		1	22		13		20	4	3	12	1	10	1	43	3	243
15	1	19	34	62	7	1	30	9	3	1	9	2	8	1	1	18	1	10		32	5	8	14	3	23		87	8	397
16		12	15	31	4	2	13	2	1	4			5			12		10	4	16	9	10	30	7	23		42	1	253
17		4	6	14	3		5						3	1	1	7	1			6	1	7	9	1	12	1	13	1	96
18		3	8	12	1	1	8	3	2				1		1	16		3		5		5	3	2	4		5		83
19		2		7			2	2					2			1		2		2	1	4	2	1	6		6		40
20		4	2	4			1			1						2		1				3	2	3			2		25
21			1	4	1																		2	2			2		12
22				1																									1
23		1				1																							2
24				2																									2
25				3					1																				4
26				1																									1
27																													0
28																											1		1
29				1																			1						2
30																													0
31																													0
32																													0
33				1																									1
34																													0
35																											1		1
36																													0
37											1																		1
38																													0
39		3		9	3		1		1	1	1																2		21
40		3		1			1			1													1				1		8
41																													0
42				1			2																1						4
Totals	66	254	189	480	37	11	146	62	41	9	28	6	40	1	4	92	1	48	114	111	35	83	132	23	114	3	454	17	2601

ACTIVITIES

Based on the study and functional classification of the cultural remains and the recognition of a number of features in the field, 23 different activity classes are inferred for the prehistoric inhabitants of the Rodgers site. Each type of activity is thought to be of particular significance to understanding the changing nature of the occupants' involvement with and adaptation to their natural surroundings. Distributional data for the activity indicators are summarized in Chapter 12.

Hunting

The presence of any item used as a tip for a lance, dart, or arrow is taken as evidence of hunting activity. Attributes indicating hunting activity thus include the occurrence of both projectile points and projectile point/hafted cutting tools. The single atlatl weight fragment is also noted as a hunting indicator.

Fishing

The presence of fishhooks and fishhook manufacture are taken as attributes indicating fishing.

Specialized Cutting

The use of hafted cutting implements, either projectile point/hafted cutting tools or hafted cutting tools, is taken to indicate specialized cutting activities. This activity is contrasted with generalized cutting activity performed with unhafted cutting tools or bifaces. Also included here are notched and stemmed hafted scrapers, since lateral margins of these implements exhibit evidence of heavy-duty cutting similar to that performed by hafted cutting tools.

Generalized Cutting

Generalized cutting activity is indicated by the presence of generalized cutting implements or bifaces. The lack of a haft facility on these implements suggests that they represent activities distinct from those performed by hafted cutting implements. Bifaces with a single beveled margin are noted as an indicator of both generalized cutting and generalized scraping.

Specialized Scraping

Specialized scraping activity is indicated by the presence of hafted scraping tools and specialized implements categorized as transverse scraper/grinders.

Generalized Scraping

Generalized scraping activity is indicated by bevel-edged implements functionally categorized as irregular scrapers, and by beveled edges on unhafted bifaces. These tools are morphologically heterogeneous, and their lack of hafting facilities or formal stylization is taken to indicate scraping activity distinct from that performed with hafted scrapers and scraper/grinders.

Perforating

Following Winter's functional analysis (1969:48–52), perforating activity is inferred by the presence of either bone awls or chipped stone perforators. The bone tools were almost certainly used to perforate soft plant or animal materials, and wear patterns on the stone specimens indicate that they were not involved in drilling activities or other functions distinct from those of the bone implements.

Woodworking

While the specific functions of chipped stone axes, adzes, and grooved axes may have been distinct, all are taken as indicators of some type of heavy woodworking activity.

Precision Flaking

Pressure flaking or indirect percussion flaking of chipped stone tools is indicated by antler tine flakers and bone and antler punches. These tools represent activities related to the final shaping or resharpening of chipped stone tools, as opposed to initial stages in manufacture probably carried out with percussion implements.

Bone Working

While functionally interpretable bone or antler artifacts are rare in the Rodgers assemblage, a great number of bone and antler fragments consist of residue from artifact-manufacturing processes. All occurrences of bone or antler modification by scraping, grinding, chopping, smoothing, whittling, sawing, or incising, both on recognizable artifacts and on unidentifiable fragments, are taken to indicate activity involving the working of bone.

Containment

Short-term storage, long-term storage, and containment for transportation are indicated by fragments of pottery vessels and turtle carapace bowls.

Hammering

Since wear pattern analyses and other comparative studies failed to establish that core hammers functioned as vegetal grinding or processing tools at Rodgers, these tools are assumed to be functionally equivalent to noncore hammerstones. The presence of either core or noncore hammerstones is taken to indicate some unspecified hammering, fracturing, or pulverizing activity. Correlation of these activity indicators with other activities at the site remains the major avenue for functional interpretation of core hammerstones.

Stone Pecking

The presence of a stone surface or stone tool fragment modified by means of pecking is noted here as an indicator of stone-pecking activity. Pecked surfaces indicate the use of a specialized stone-working technique. Such modification occurs most frequently on grooved axes and mortar/metates.

Handstone Pitting

Although the functional interpretation of the numerous shallow pits in the faces and edges of manos and anvils is unclear, such pits are assumed to be evidence of a discrete activity worthy of separate investigation. Each occurrence in this activity class is represented by a single pit on the surface of a stone tool small enough to be held in one hand. If there are three pits on a mano, three occurrences are noted for this activity. The size restriction placed on the context of these activity indicators insures that each is indicative of a potential percussor, rather than anvils or pitted platforms, which are recorded in the following class.

Anvil Pitting

Tabulated here are the number of individual pits or hemispherical depressions on the surfaces of stones too large to be grasped comfortably in one hand. This contextual restriction assures that these pits represent activities performed on an anvil, rather than with a percussor. The activity indicators noted here are attributes found on artifacts commonly referred to as "nutting stones."

Complex Grinding/Crushing

This activity class is indicated by all ground and smoothed convex surfaces on cobbles small enough to be held comfortably in one hand. It is assumed that the convex surfaces were produced by moving the handstone over a stationary surface such as a metate. Also included here are all concave ground surfaces, i.e., mortar and metate depressions, that form the complementary part of the two-piece grinding/crushing system consisting of a hand tool and a base. Individual convex and concave surfaces are recorded as activity indicators, regardless of the number of artifacts involved. The use of complementary convex and concave grinding/crushing surfaces is referred to as a complex system, as opposed to a simple grinding system described in the next section. Materials processed in the complex system are actually crushed and only secondarily ground between the resistant handstone–anvil stone surfaces. The presence of elements of the complex grinding/crushing system is traditionally taken to indicate activity involved in the processing of plant foods. The presence of hematite stains on several manos indicates, however, that several activities are involved, and not all are directly tied to subsistence behavior.

Simple Grinding

The presence of a flat or grooved grinding surface is an indication that a simple grinding system was in use. In such activity, the substance being worked was hand held and rubbed directly on the abrasive surface of the grinding tool. Thus, the flat and grooved surfaces are assumed to have been used without the aid of another hand-held tool. Simple and complex grinding activities also differ in the mechanics of destruction of the material being processed: Materials are actually abraded away in the simple system, while the complex system operates primarily by crushing the work material between resistant surfaces. Indicators of simple grinding activity correspond to individual abraded surfaces on whetstones and abraders.

Pigment Processing

The production of mineral pigments is indicated by pieces of rubbed hematite, pieces of rubbed galena, and the presence of hematite stains on whetstones, manos, anvils, metates, and hammerstones. Also noted are two features under the shelter in Unit E (Stratum 2) that are recognized as centers of localized hematite processing. Each feature is composed of a mass of powdered hematite or red ochre about 8 cm thick and 50 cm in diameter, surrounded by a number of hematite-stained sandstone whetstones. Each lump of processed hematite is recorded as a single attribute indicating hematite processing, as is each hematite-stained artifact surface found in the area of the features.

Ornamentation

The single antler tine pendant, ground to resemble a canine tooth, is noted as an occurrence of ornamentation.

Caching

Activity involving the intentional accumulation and long-term storage of tools or raw materials for future use is indicated by a group of five deer antler tines in Unit E under the shelter. The tines are approximately of the same size, and each was detached from the main shaft by sawing a notch and snapping it free at the base. Figure 10.11a illustrates one tine from the cache that was used for flaking; the remainder are unused. The importance of this cache is that it indicates recurrent seasonal or long-term site occupation.

Ceremony or Ritual

Three features and a single artifact indicate the performance of activities concerned with ideological rather than subsistence or technological aspects of life. Their significance lies not in the nature of the activities, but in the fact that the site was used for their performance. The features include two fully flexed burials from the lowest part of Unit G (see Chapter 11). The few artifacts near the interments shed no light on the nature of the burial ceremonies. Except for the Dalton Zone, isolated fragments of human bone are scattered throughout all parts of the deposits, but their association with burial or other ceremonies is not inferred.

Another feature indicating ceremony or ritual is the careful interment of a domestic dog *(Canis familiaris)* beneath a tumulus of dolomite cobbles at the base of Unit E (Stratum 2). This is one of the earliest intentional dog burials documented in the New World (McMillan 1970).

The engraved dolomite tablet (Figure 10.15) at the base of Unit G is also an indication of ideological activities. While the purpose of the plaque is unknown, the engraved designs are assumed to have had symbolic meaning.

Stone Heating

The use of stones as a heat source for the presumed purpose of cooking or heat retention and redistribution is indicated by the discovery of features consisting of heaps or concentrations of fire-cracked and heat-discolored dolomite and sandstone cobbles. The rock concentrations often adjoined hearths, or areas of heat-discolored earth, and were frequently associated with charcoal-stained sediments.

Fire Maintenance

The long-term maintenance of wood fires in a single location is indicated by concentrated areas of highly oxidized orange or reddish sediments. In many cases no charcoal accompanied these fire hearths. In the Dalton Zone several hearths were built on the aggrading floodplain sur-

Figure 10.16 Hearth areas partially destroyed by aboriginal disturbance in Unit E, beneath the overhang, Rodgers
Shelter. Arrows indicate approximate centers of three
highly oxidized and shrinkage-cracked hearth remnants.

face at the base of the talus slope. These features sometimes measured
more than 1 m in diameter and 10 cm thick, and were often surrounded by
dark organic-stained sediments and concentrations of cultural debris including flakes, calcined animal bone, and stone tools.

Bits of orange-fired sediments were scattered throughout Unit E, tes-
tifying to the extensive maintenance of fires and their subsequent disturbance in that zone. One fragment of fired clay from Unit E preserved
the impression of a woven mat or fabric. The cultural disturbance in Unit
E made the fired areas less easily interpretable as the focal points of
specific activities (Figure 10.16). Among other things, heat treatment of
chipped stone bifacial preforms was probably accomplished at these features. Archeomagnetic samples were extracted from three fired areas in
Unit E by Robert L. DuBois, of the University of Oklahoma, for the
purpose of establishing points on his master paleomagnetic curve for the
midwestern United States.

While Unit G sediments contained considerable ash content, particularly under the overhang, no hearths or concentrated areas of fired earth
were found in that zone, suggesting a different use of fire during that
occupational period.

The descriptive data in this chapter are interpreted in Chapter 12.

REFERENCES

Ahler, S.A.
1971 Projectile point form and function at Rodgers shelter, Missouri. Missouri Archaeological Society *Research Series* No. 8. Columbia, Missouri.
1973 Description of the chipped stone artifacts from the Walth Bay site: 1970 excavation. Unpublished ms. submitted to the Midwest Region of the National Park Service. Lincoln, Nebraska.

Bordaz, J.
1970 *Tools of the Old and New Stone Age.* Garden City, New York: Natural History Press.

Dunnel, R.C.
1971 Anthropological and scientific models of function in archaeology. Paper presented at the 70th Annual meeting of the American Anthropological Association, 19 November 1971, New York.

Fenenga, F.
1953 The weights of chipped stone points: A clue to their function. *Southwestern Journal of Anthropology* 9:309–323.

Fletcher, A.C., and F. La Flesche
1972 *The Omaha tribe.* Lincoln, Nebraska: Univ. of Nebraska Press.

Fowler, M.L.
1959 Summary report of the Modoc Rock Shelter, 1952, 1953, 1955, 1956. *Illinois State Museum Reports of Investigations* No. 8. Springfield, Illinois.

Goodyear, A.C.
1971 The Brand site: The Dalton tool kit with an intrasite analysis. M.A. thesis, Department of Anthropology, University of Arkansas, Fayetteville.

Greenwood, R.S.
1969 The Browne site. Society for American Archaeology *Memoir* No. 23. Salt Lake City, Utah.

Hester, T.R., D. Gilbow, and A.D. Albee
1973 A functional analysis of "Clear Fork" artifacts from the Rio Grande Plain, Texas. *American Antiquity* 38:90–96.

Hester, T.R., and R.F. Heizer
1973 Arrowpoints or knives? Comments on the proposed function of "Stockton Points." *American Antiquity* 38:220–221.

Irwin, H.T., and H.M. Wormington
1970 Paleo–Indian tool types in the Great Plains. *American Antiquity* 35:24–34.

Keeley, L.H.
1974 The methodology of microwear analysis: A comment on Nance. *American Antiquity* 39:126–128.

Klippel, W.E.
1969 The Booth site: A late Archaic campsite. Missouri Archaeological Society *Research Series* No. 6. Columbia, Missouri.

Knudson, R.
1973 Organizational variability in late Paleo–Indian assemblages. Ph.D. dissertation, Department of Anthropology, Washington State University, Pullman.

Lehmer, D.J.
1971 Introduction to Middle Missouri archeology. National Park Service *Anthropological Papers* No. 1. Washington, D.C.

McMillan, R.B.
    1970 Early canid burial from the western Ozark Highland. *Science* **167**:1246–1247.
    1971 Biophysical change and cultural adaptation at Rodgers shelter, Missouri. Ph.D. dissertation, Department of Anthropology, University of Colorado, Boulder.

Morse, D.F.
    1973 Dalton culture in northeast Arkansas. *The Florida Anthropologist* **26**:24–38.

Morse, D.F., and A.C. Goodyear
    1973 The significance of the Dalton adze in northeast Arkansas. *Plains Anthropologist* **18**:316–322.

Nance, J.D.
    1970 Lithic analysis: Implications for the prehistory of central California. *Archeological Survey Annual Report* **12**:61–103. (Department of Anthropology, University of California, Los Angeles.)
    1971 Functional interpretations from microscopic analysis. *American Antiquity* **36**:361–366.

Rouse, I.
    1960 The classification of artifacts in archaeology. *American Antiquity* **25**:313–323.

Semenov, S.A.
    1964 *Prehistoric technology*. London: Barnes and Noble.

Shippee, J.M.
    1966 The archaeology of Arnold Research Cave, Callaway County, Missouri. *Missouri Archaeologist* **28**:1–40; 48–107.

Waugh, F.W.
    1916 Iroquois foods and food preparation. *Memoir of the Geological Survey* No. 86. Canada Department of Mines, Ottawa.

Wheat, J.B.
    1972 The Olsen-Chubbuck site: A Paleo-Indian bison kill. Society for American Archaeology *Memoir* No. 26.

Wilmsen, E.N.
    1968 Functional analysis of flaked stone artifacts. *American Antiquity* **33**:156–161.

Winters, H.D.
    1969 The Riverton Culture. *Illinois State Museum Reports of Investigations* No. 13, *Illinois Archaeological Survey Monograph* No. 1. Springfield.

Witthoft, J.
    1968 Flint arrowpoints from the Eskimo of northwestern Alaska. *Expedition* **10**(2):30–37.

11

Human Burials from Rodgers Shelter

William M. Bass III and William L. Rhule II

Two human burials were recovered during the 1966 excavations at Rodgers Shelter. Both came from about a meter below the surface near the wall of the shelter; their stratigraphic position suggests they were members of a late Archaic population who occupied the shelter about 2500 B.P.

BURIAL 1

This inhumation was beneath the overhang, about 2 m from the shelter wall. It was in the loose, gray ashy matrix of Stratum 4, just south of Burial 2. The base of the feature was only a few centimeters above the contact with Stratum 3. The remains are primary and flexed, a burial type arguing for the individual's having been interred in a pit. The loose, ashy texture of the surrounding deposits, coupled with the fact the grave had been disturbed by groundhogs prior to excavation, however, made it impossible to see a grave pit outline. A horizontal profile was cut at the time the bones were first discovered, and a vertical profile was made later; in neither instance was a pit outline visible.

The burial, that of a female, was in a semiflexed position with the head directed to the south. It was removed in a plaster of paris jacket to be excavated in the laboratory. The remains were badly fragmented and none of the postcranial bones could be measured. Several bones in the thoracic area were missing, and neither of the arms was in its proper anatomical position. Several artifacts were near enough to the bones to suggest that they may have been in the grave pit we assume was present: an oval biface, two stemmed projectile points, a scraper, and a modified flake. A small chert core was also found beneath the left parietal when the burial cast was excavated in the laboratory.

Sex was determined by observations on the innominate and femora. The sciatic notch is wide and shallow (Krogman 1962:139), the pubic length is great, there is buildup of bone on the sacroiliac joint, and there is a preauricular sulcus (Brothwell 1963:52). These criteria suggest a female. The pubis exhibits depressions on the dorsal surface (Figure 11.1) suggestive of childbirth (Stewart 1957:9–18). The head of the left femur has a maximum diameter of 40 mm, thus placing it well within the female range (Krogman 1962:143–145). Anthropomorphic measurements are given in Table 11.1.

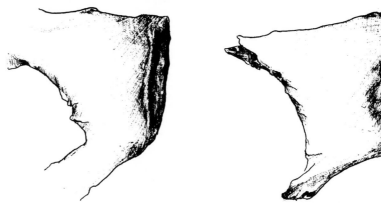

Figure 11.1 The left pubis, dorsal view, showing deep depressions along the edge of the female pubic symphysis from Rodgers Shelter (right) compared with a pubis with no depressions (left).

TABLE 11.1 Comparison of Anthropometric Measurements and Indices

		FEMALE					
	Rodgers Shelter Burial 1	Indian Knoll[a]			Eva[b] (Big Sandy Component)		
Measurement		Number	Range	Mean	Number	Range	Mean
Cranial							
Maximum length	182	209	159–182	172.1	2	179	179.0
Maximum breadth	137	211	120–143	131.5	2	129–131	130.0
Minimum frontal breadth	85	188	78–99	88.2	2	86–88	87.0
Biorbital breadth	95	160	85–101	93.7	—	—	—
Mandible							
Symphysis height	33	138	24–38	31.6	2	—	—
Cranial index	75.3	207	69.1–84.9	76.3	2	72.0–73.2	72.6
Postcranial							
Femur							
Maximum head diameter	40	222	35–44	39.1	—	—	—

[a]Snow 1948: 381–491; Steele 1948: 492–509   [b]Lewis and Lewis 1961: 103–171.

Table 11.1 (continued)

MALE

Measurement	Rodgers Shelter Burial 2	Lansing Man	Indian Knoll			Eva (Big Sandy Component)		
			Number	Range	Mean	Number	Range	Mean
Cranial								
Maximum length	(172)	189	253	166–193	178.8	8	175–185	180.5
Maximum breadth	143	139	258	118–150	135.4	8	132–140	136.2
Minimum frontal breadth	92	94	264	80–104	91.6	8	83–99	90.6
Cranial index	82.7	73.5	252	67.4–86.0	75.8	8	73.6–78.2	75.1
Postcranial								
Humerus								
Maximum head diameter	39	—	297	38–50	44.3	—	—	—
Femur								
Maximum morphological length	415	440(R)	263	386–487	437.1	—	—	—
Physiological length	412	—	263	384–483	434.8	—	—	—
Maximum head diameter	42	—	290	37–48	43.3	—	—	—
Mid-shaft Anterior-posterior	26	27.5(R)	285	22–33	27.8	—	—	—
Mid-shaft transverse	19	27.5(R)	288	20–31	24.2	—	—	—
Subtrochanteric								
Anterior-posterior	23	24.5(R)	295	25–36	31.0	—	—	—
Subtrochanteric transverse	26	24.5(R)	293	19–27	23.0	—	—	—
Tibia								
Maximum morphological length	(355)	357(L)	218	310–409	362.4	—	—	—
Physical length	(341)	—	238	310–400	350.1	—	—	—
Nutrient foramen Anterior-posterior	29	—	272	28–41	33.9	—	—	—
Nutrient foramen transverse	22	—	278	17–26	21.8	—	—	—
Mid-shaft Anterior-posterior	—	31(L)	252	25–37	30.0	—	—	—
Mid-shaft transverse	—	20(L)	253	15–25	19.9	—	—	—
Sacrum								
Maximum length	101	—	146	87–120	106	—	—	—
Stature								
Centimeters	160.5	165.0	—	—	164.0	9	157.4–170.2	167.6
Feet	5.25	5.4	—	—	5.45	9	5.2–5.6	5.5

When the skull was examined for sexual characteristics using Hrdlicka's (1952:127–134) criteria, it was found to have several criteria in the male range (for example, medium supraorbital ridges, blunt edges on the eye orbits, moderate mastoid processes, and heavy muscle marking on the occipital bone).

The age of 35–45 years assigned to this individual is based on observations of the pubic symphysis (McKern and Stewart 1957:71–85). Symphyseal components are 4, 5, 5, suggesting an age of over 29 years, with a mean of 35.8 years. In addition, extensive arthritic lipping on the lumbar vertebrae and the sacrum suggest an older person.

The only upper tooth remaining in place is the right canine. Both central incisors and the left canine had abscessed and were lost before death. Resorption was advanced in the incisal region of the alveolus, but had not begun around the root of the canine. The first and second molars had been lost for some time before death, for there is some resorption of the alveolar process. The second and third molars on the left appear to have been lost after death. The right half of the maxilla was not recovered.

The following teeth remained in the mandible: Right, canine, first and second premolars, first, second, and third molars; Left, canine, second premolar, and first molar (Figure 11.2). There is an interproximal carie in the lower right second molar between the second and third molars. Using Hrdlicka'a (1952:53) criteria for dental wear, these teeth have Stage 4 wear.

The pattern of tooth wear is unusual. The teeth are worn off and polished on both the buccal and lingual sides, with the high point at the center of the tooth (Figure 11.2). This is not typical wear from chewing: "Wear of this type likely was associated with the habitual holding of objects between the front teeth rather than with the ordinary chewing of food [Stewart 1959:479]."

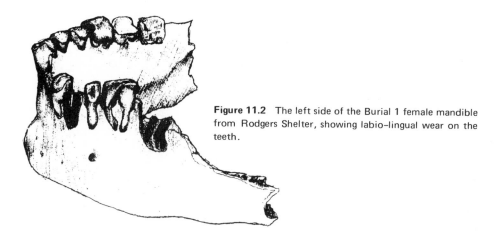

Figure 11.2 The left side of the Burial 1 female mandible from Rodgers Shelter, showing labio–lingual wear on the teeth.

Since this woman had lost her lower incisors, she was forced to hold objects with her canines, premolars, and the anterior edges of the first molars, as the wear on these teeth was in the center, with the enamel on the edges being the high point. Although not specifically referred to by Snow, this kind of wear seems to occur in the Archaic Indian Knoll population from Kentucky, where a similar but less well developed case is illustrated (Snow 1948:503, Fig. 40).

Stature could not be determined, since no long bones were complete enough to measure.

BURIAL 2

This interment was an individual in a tightly flexed position in a shallow pit that had been dug down between several large rocks. The grave was dug into Stratum 3 from a point just above the base of Stratum 4, and was between Burial 1 and the shelter wall.

The remains are those of a young male, on his right side, flexed, with his head directed to the north. The bones were placed in a plaster jacket and removed to the laboratory for excavation. The dark gray matrix filling the grave pit contrasted sharply with the surrounding reddish clay and gravel in Stratum 3. A number of fist-sized rocks were found beneath the bones when the burial cast was opened in the laboratory. The stones were in a horseshoe pattern, with the open end near the lower thoracic vertebrae. There were no associated artifacts.

The assignment of sex to a subadult is difficult; however, since the individual was approaching adulthood and all of the criteria used to determine sex consistently fell into the male range, the probability seems good that the individual was, in fact, male.

The innominate was largely depended on for sex determination. The sciatic notch is narrow (Krogman 1962:139), the pubic length is short, the sub-pubic angle is narrow, there is no buildup of bone on the sacroiliac joint, and there is no preauricular sulcus (Brothwell 1963:52). These criteria all suggest a male. The large frontal sinuses in the skull and the squareness of the chin (Hrdlicka 1952:130) are also indicative of a male. There is a prominent shelf on the anterior lower border of the mandible.

The head of the femur, which had not yet united, has a maximum diameter of 42 mm. This would place it in the "probable" female category if the individual had been an adult (Krogman 1962:144); however, since the head had not yet reached its full growth, we do not feel that this criterion is diagnostic. Anthropomorphic measurements are given in Table 11.1.

Age was determined by the state of the epiphyseal unions and by the pubic symphisis. The distal articular surface of the first metacarpal indicates incomplete union. Comparison of this stage of development with

Greulich and Pyle's (1959:107–111) standards for skeletal development of the hand and wrist suggests an age of 13–14 at the time of death. None of the epiphyses of the long bones are fused. McKern and Stewart (1957:44) state that, by 17–18 years of age, there was complete union of the head, greater trochanter, and lesser trochanter of the femur in 88% of their cases, with complete union of the distal epiphysis of the tibia in 89% of the cases.

The pubic symphyseal face was fragmentary, making an accurate reading difficult. Using McKern and Stewart's (1957:71–85) method, a component reading of 0, 0, 0 was obtained. This indicates a range of 0–17+ years, with a mean of 17.3 years.

The teeth are not badly worn and, using Hrdlicka's criteria, they have Stage 1 wear. All four third molars were present but had not erupted. The sockets for the upper right and lower left third molars are broken and missing. Because of the lack of space in the mandible, the lower left third molar probably would have been impacted when it erupted.

In summary, we suggest an age at death of about 14–16 years, probably in the early part of this range.

The estimated living stature is calculated at about 160 cm (5 ft 3⅜ inches), with a range of 157.1 to 164.7 cm (5 ft 1¾ inches to 5 ft 4½ inches). This was calculated using Trotter and Gleser's (1958:120) formula for Mongoloids: Stature = 2.15 (length of the femur in centimeters) +72.57±3.80. Since this formula should be used only with adult material, the stature calculated here is only an approximation.

PATHOLOGIES

The female from Rodgers Shelter has arthritic lipping on the fifth lumbar vertebra. Lumbar arthritis is also present in 60% of the Archaic Indian Knoll adult population (Steele 1948:498). Furthermore, 31% of the Indian Knoll females exhibit evidence of both arthritis and tooth decay (Steele 1948:502). Steele said that "a possible source of this virulent infection [arthritis] may have come from dental abscesses predominantly caused from extreme tooth wear . . . [1948:502]." The Rodgers Shelter female had extreme tooth wear, the probable cause of which has already been discussed. Her four lower incisors and the upper left molars were missing, and both regions were resorbed; she also had abcesses.

X-rays of the femur and tibia of the male from Rodgers Shelter indicate at least 11 lines of arrested growth (Figure 11.3). These lines suggest that he had been sick most of his life. The concentration of these lines between 5 to 9 cm from the distal end of the femur suggests a period of either prolonged illness or submarginal diet, possibly 5 to 7 years before death. This would correspond to the period of rapid growth during late childhood, and may indicate times when there was not enough food to supply the increased needs of the body.

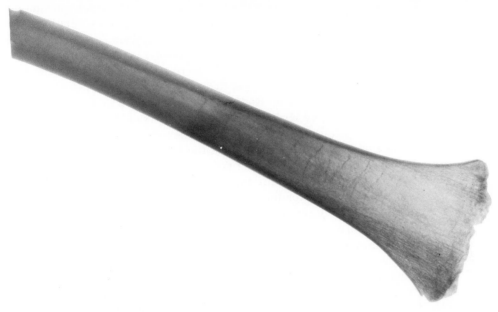

Figure 11.3 Lines of arrested growth in the distal femur
of the male burial from Rodgers Shelter.

DISCUSSION

The measurements and indices of Burial 1 were compared to the female
Archaic populations from Indian Knoll, Kentucky (Snow 1948) and Eva,
Tennessee (Lewis and Lewis 1961); those taken on Burial 2 were compared with the same measurements and indices for the male Archaic
populations at Indian Knoll, the Big Sandy component at Eva, and with
the Lansing Man burial, Kansas (Lewis and Lewis 1961; Bass
1973:99–104).

The male from Rodgers Shelter was brachycranic, a feature not
common in the other sites. The Indian Knoll population had a wide range
in cephalic indices, and the Rodgers Shelter male was near the top of this
range. The Rodgers Shelter male was, furthermore, more brachycranic
than any individual in the Eva population. Lansing Man was definitely
dolicranic.

As for postcranial measurements, the male from Rodgers Shelter was
14–16 years old, while measurements from the other sites were taken on
adults. Therefore, his measurements were expected to be on the low side
of the ranges from Indian Knoll and Eva, an expectation that was essentially confirmed. For example, the Rodgers Shelter male was within the
height range of the Eva population, although in the shortest part of the
range. Since the Rodgers Shelter male was only 14–16 years old, he had
not yet reached full height.

In comparing the Rodgers Shelter female with the female populations from Indian Knoll (Snow 1948) and Eva (Lewis and Lewis 1961), it was found that, for the most part, measurements were similar—more so than the measurements of the male, probably because the female was an adult.

Both burials from Rodgers Shelter were also compared with the Lansing Man (Hrdlicka 1907:49; Bass 1973:99–104). Although not of the same sex, the female skull from Rodgers Shelter is remarkably similar to the description given by Hrdlicka of the Lansing skull. Seen from the front, there is a sagittal ridge; from the side, there is a slight sloping from the glabella to a point halfway between the bregma and the lambda. From this point back there is a rapid reduction of this slope, which Hrdlicka (1907:49) described as "quite marked, but in no way abnormal. . . ."

The Rodgers Shelter female skull is a rugged skull for a female, but Snow (1948:413) described a "rugged female" type from Indian Knoll that displayed most of the characteristics of the Rodgers Shelter female—the large supraorbital ridges, the blunt eye orbits, and moderate mastoid processes. Burial 2 also had some alveolar prognathism. Snow (1948:439) found this to be characteristic of most female crania at Indian Knoll. The Rodgers Shelter female had a round bulbous forehead, guttered nasal furrows, and alveolar prognathism—as did eight individuals at Indian Knoll (Snow 1948:420). Snow suggested that these individuals represented a "variant of the more ordinary and typical form . . . [1948:420]."

CONCLUSIONS

Two human burials, that of an adult female and a teen-age male, were interred at Rodgers Shelter. Their stratigraphic position in the shelter and their anthropomorphic measurements indicate that they were Late Archaic Indians who were buried at the site 2500 to 3000 years ago; they compare favorably with Archaic populations from Indian Knoll, Kentucky; Eva, Tennessee; and Lansing Man, in Kansas.

One of the more important observations is the unusual wear on the teeth of the adult female. Wear of this type is not mentioned for most prehistoric populations in North America, but was noted by Stewart (1959:479) in the Shanidar Neanderthal skeleton. We agree with Stewart that this wear is due to the use of the teeth in holding objects, such as thongs. The young male from the shelter, to judge from lines of arrested growth in the long bones, had probably been ill or had suffered from malnutrition before puberty.

REFERENCES

Bass, W.M.
1973 Lansing Man: A half century later. *American Journal of Physical Anthropology* 38:99–104.

Brothwell, D.R.
  1963 *Digging up bones.* London: British Museum of Natural History.
Greulich, W.W., and W.I. Pyle
  1959 *Radiometric atlas of skeletal development of the hand and wrist,* 2nd
        edition. Stanford, California: Stanford Univ. Press.
Hrdlicka, A.
  1907 Skeletal remains suggesting or attributed to early man in North Amer-
        ica. *Bureau of American Ethnology,* Bulletin 33. Washington, D.C.
  1952 *Practical anthropometry,* 4th edition, edited by T.D. Stewart. Philadel-
        phia, Pennsylvania: Wistar Institute of Anatomy and Biology.
Krogman, W.M.
  1962 *The human skeleton in forensic medicine.* Springfield, Illinois: Charles
        C Thomas, Publisher.
Lewis, T.M.N., and M.K. Lewis
  1961 *Eva: An Archaic site.* Knoxville, Tennessee: Tennessee Univ. Press.
McKern, T.W., and T.D. Stewart
  1957 Skeletal age changes in young American males. Technical Report EP-45.
        Headquarters Quartermaster Research and Development Command.
        Natick, Massachusetts.
Snow, C.E.
  1948 Indian Knoll skeletons of site Oh2, Ohio County, Kentucky. University
        of Kentucky *Reports in Anthropology* 4(3-2):381–491.
Steele, D.G.
  1948 Homogeneity at Indian Knoll. University of Kentucky *Reports in An-
        thropology* 4(3-2):492–509.
Stewart, T.D.
  1957 Distortion of the pubic symphyseal surfaces in females and its effect on
        age determination. *American Journal of Physical Anthropology*
        15:9–18.
  1959 The restored Shanidar I skull. Annual Report of the Smithsonian In-
        stitution, 1958. Washington, D.C.
Trotter, M., and G.C. Gleser
  1958 A re-evaluation of estimation of stature based on measurements of sta-
        ture taken during life and of long bones after death. *American Journal
        of Physical Anthropology* 16:79–123.

12

The Dynamics of Cultural and Environmental Change at Rodgers Shelter, Missouri

R. Bruce McMillan

Chapters 9 and 10 provide descriptions of the range of variation in the subsistence remains and functional tool categories, and report these by correlative levels for the two major areas of the site—the shelter and main excavation. Correlative levels were designed to divide the deposits in each area into a number of arbitrary units that maintain chronological superposition (Table 7.2). These necessarily combined some arbitrary 6-inch excavation units in order to compensate for variance in strata thickness across the site and, thus, simplify intrasite comparisons.

To clarify the chronological trends in the overall cultural record it is useful to correlate the data from the shelter and main excavation areas by reducing the number of levels to 12 culture/time stratigraphic units (Table 12.1). *Culture/time stratigraphic units are chronologically discrete horizons that have been assigned absolute temporal limits and, based on subsistence data and activity indicators, contain levels that display some degree of cultural homogeneity when compared with units above or below them.* These units, which establish contemporaneity between levels from the shelter and main excavation, attempt to minimize as far as practicable the temporal span for each unit so as to allow for maximal explication of chronological changes in the record.

Table 12.1 gives the approximate temporal limits for each culture/time stratigraphic unit; the depositional units (Chapter 8) and their average aggradation rates; the general cultural affiliation for each unit; and a summary of the correlative levels that constitute each unit. It should be emphasized that the cultural chronology for the study locality still needs further refinement. Virtually all datable charcoal from Rodgers Shelter was submitted for radiocarbon analysis, yet there are no direct dates for Depositional Units F and G. The dates shown in boldface type (Table 12.1) are those for which we have radiocarbon determinations from Rodgers; the remaining dates are estimated by cross-dating Rodgers artifacts with stylistically similar materials from nearby dated sites (e.g., Falk 1969:48; Falk and Lippincott 1974:38; Vehik 1974:39; Wood 1967:118), and by calculation from datum depths and average sedimentation rates for depositional units (Table 12.1).

ANALYSIS OF CHRONOLOGICAL VARIATION

The cultural record at Rodgers Shelter is viewed here in terms of changes in activities as reflected by faunal and activity indicator frequencies rather than in terms of changes in artifact frequencies. This orientation is in keeping with the emphasis on explicating changing human behavior at the site, and correlating this change with corresponding environmental changes deduced for the locality. It is thought that changes in inferred human activities as documented by the faunal remains, artifact attributes, and observable features offer the best basis for analysis. Interpretations of the subsistence record will necessarily focus on the faunal record because of the inadequate sample of vegetal remains.

Frequencies of occurrence for 13 major categories of fauna and the indicators of 23 human activities are summarized according to the 12 culture/time stratigraphic units in Tables 12.2 and 12.3. It can be seen that Units 4, 10, and 12 exhibit little evidence of cultural activity between 3000 and 6300 B.P., 8600 and 9500 B.P., and prior to 10,500 B.P., respectively. While these units cannot be statistically analyzed, the paucity of remains in them is in itself important information bearing on the culture history of the study area; the significance of this is discussed later.

To understand changes in faunal procurement and other human activities we must first assess the importance of each activity relative to all other activities within each discrete time unit, then assess the importance of chronological changes in the relative frequency of the activities. One approach is to convert the raw counts of major faunal categories (elements) and activity indicators to percentages of the total occurrences recorded for each culture/time unit. Chronological change in each faunal category and activity is graphically illustrated by plotting percentages at the midpoint of each culture/time unit (Figure 12.1).

Figure 12.1 provides an excellent visual representation of changing activities and faunal frequencies, and also gives a simple basis for com-

TABLE 12.1 Culture/Time Stratigraphic Units at Rodgers Shelter

Culture/time stratigraphic unit	Temporal span	Depositional unit	Stratum	Average terrace aggradation rate	Cultural affiliation	Correlative level	
						Shelter	Main excavation
1	1000–1750 B.P.	G_2	4	3.6 cm/100 yrs	Woodland	1,2	1,2
2	1750–2500 B.P.	upper G_1	4	3.6 cm/100 yrs	Woodland/ Late Archaic	3,4,5	3,4
3	2500–3000 B.P.	lower G_1	4	3.6 cm/100 yrs	Late Archaic	6,7,8	5,6
4[a]	3000–**6300** B.P.[b]	F	3	1.9 cm/100 yrs	little occupation, unknown	9,10	7,8,9,10
5	**6300**–6700 B.P.	upper E	2	9.7 cm/100 yrs	Middle Archaic II	11,12,13	11,12
6	6700–**7000** B.P.	middle E	2	9.7 cm/100 yrs	Middle Archaic II	14,15,16	13,14
7[c]	**7000**–8000 B.P.	lower E	2	9.7 cm/100 yrs	Mixed Middle Archaic II/ Middle Archaic I	17,18,19	15,16
8	**8000**–**8200** B.P.	upper D	1	17.8 cm/100 yrs	Middle Archaic I	20	17,18
9	**8200**–8600 B.P.	lower D	1	17.8 cm/100 yrs	Middle Archaic I	21	19–25
10[a]	8600–9500 B.P.	lowest D, upper C	1	17.8 cm/100 yrs	little occupation, unknown		26–35
11	9500–**10,500** B.P.	lower C, B^1, B^2, B^3	1	17.8 cm/100 yrs	Dalton	22–24	36–41
12[a]	**10,500**–11,000 B.P.	A^1, A^2	1	17.8 cm/100 yrs	little occupation, unknown	25	42

[a]Culture/time units with little evidence of occupation. These units omitted in analysis of cultural and faunal remains.
[b]Dates in boldface type are established by C-14 analysis of Rodgers charcoal samples. Other dates are estimates.
[c]Unit 7 is a mixture of deflated cultural material eroded from Upper Unit D (8000–7500 B.P.) mixed with cultural material from lower Unit E (7500–7000 B.P.).

TABLE 12.2 Principal Subsistence (Meat) Species at Rodgers Shelter: Raw Counts[a]

Culture/ time unit	Fish	Aquatic turtle	Terrestrial turtle	Rabbit	Squirrel	Raccoon	Carnivore	Opossum/ skunk	Beaver/ muskrat	Other terrestrial rodents	Deer	Bison/ elk	Turkey	Total
1	4	3	2	10	2	1	—	4	3	1	23	—	6	59
2	—	10	18	8	1	3	1	6	3	5	64	—	8	127
3	1	6	5	1	—	1	—	—	1	2	23	—	2	42
4	1	—	—	—	—	—	—	1	—	—	2	—	1	5
5	5	15	34	82	11	10	2	—	5	10	58	—	7	239
6	18	28	95	273	76	18	6	8	11	19	121	—	20	693
7	23	35	82	406	155	36	11	3	18	17	256	3	38	1083
8	3	16	44	119	57	8	3	1	5	3	95	7	7	368
9	3	10	29	139	65	26	2	2	7	8	72	10	13	386
10	—	—	—	3	4	—	—	—	—	—	1	—	—	8
11	3	5	2	25	12	11	—	—	3	6	53	1	3	124
12	1	—	—	1	—	—	—	—	—	1	6	—	—	9
Totals	62	128	311	1067	383	114	25	25	56	72	774	21	105	3143

[a]For one-quarter-inch dry screening.

214

TABLE 12.3 Summary of Activity Frequencies at Rodgers Shelter: Raw Counts

Culture/time unit	Hunting	Specialized cutting	Generalized cutting	Specialized scraping	Generalized scraping	Perforating	Woodworking	Hammering	Pigment processing	Fishing	Containment	Precision flaking	Handstone pitting	Anvil pitting	Complex grinding	Simple grinding	Ornamentation	Stone pecking	Bone working	Stone heating	Fire maintenance	Ritual or ceremony	Caching	Totals
1	127	117	73	2	23	10	4	2	18	—	138	—	16	—	6	1	—	—	6	—	—	—	—	543
2	115	115	126	2	19	16	12	6	30	—	71	4	25	5	25	5	—	1	9	—	—	—	—	586
3	54	63	74	2	10	7	5	8	57	—	15	1	17	—	15	4	—	1	5	—	—	3	—	341
4	—	1	4	—	—	—	—	—	3	—	—	—	—	—	—	—	—	—	—	—	1	—	—	9
5	39	74	54	17	27	24	10	28	219	1	5	6	5	1	16	33	—	4	36	2	—	1	—	601
6	37	88	98	16	41	43	15	40	212	1	37	5	14	2	50	37	—	7	103	3	5	1	—	854
7	59	125	118	22	52	42	11	65	213	1	32	25	33	—	77	56	1	15	120	—	5	1	1	1074
8	10	25	27	6	15	4	2	12	38	—	23	6	14	—	27	17	—	4	31	1	1	—	—	262
9	7	10	22	2	5	2	2	6	18	—	3	2	5	—	12	6	—	1	5	1	3	—	—	112
10	—	—	3	—	—	—	—	—	3	—	—	—	—	—	1	—	—	—	—	—	1	—	—	8
11	9	9	12	5	2	1	5	—	4	—	—	3	—	—	1	—	—	—	2	—	6	—	—	59
12	—	—	1	—	2	—	—	—	—	—	—	—	—	—	—	—	—	—	—	—	—	—	1	4
Totals	457	627	612	74	196	149	66	167	815	3	324	52	129	8	231	159	1	33	317	6	22	4	1	4453

parisons with similar units at other sites. The use of percentages has disadvantages, however, since they provide no real measure of the significance of the data. For example, Figure 12.1 shows that hunting comprises 15.3% of the activity recorded in Unit 11 and 15.8% of all activity in Unit 3. One must ask, then, whether this means that hunting is of the same relative importance at each point in time. Contrary to one's first assumption, the answer is no, as is demonstrated in the following paragraphs.

Freshwater mussels were not included in Figure 12.1 because of the difficulty in equating valves with vertebrate remains. Instead, the numbers of mussel valves and their changing percentages as compared with faunal elements are shown in Table 12.4.

An alternative approach is to analyze changes in chi-square values[1] for each cell in the culture/time units by fauna and activity contingency tables (Tables 12.2 and 12.3). Chi-square values can then be listed for the frequency distributions of selected faunal classes and activity attributes (Tables 12.5 and 12.6). To further interpretation, cell values that are significantly less than those expected by chance are preceded by a minus sign to indicate significantly low occurrences as opposed to significantly high occurrences. Using a chi-square distribution table the actual frequency in any cell can be evaluated to see if it is significantly higher or lower than would be expected by chance. By scanning across the culture/time units in these tables, one can spot the faunal classes and cultural activities that are of greater relative importance at each temporal interval. Scanning up the columns provides a picture of changing activities and faunal procurement through time. A summary of these data is given in Table 12.7.

---

[1] Chi-square is a nonparametric statistic that measures deviation between an observed cell value and an expected cell value calculated on the basis of specified prediction criteria (Blalock 1972:275). Assuming that all variables are independent (this is not strictly fulfilled since frequencies of hunting and specialized cutting activities are by definition interrelated—Chapter 10), and suggesting as the null hypothesis that there is no more than a random chance relationship between the frequencies of various prehistoric activities and the proposed culture/time units, then cell frequencies expected under such random conditions can be calculated from marginal totals of rows and columns in Tables 12.2 and 12.3 (Blalock 1972:279). Chi-square values, then, can be calculated for each cell.

Two activities (caching and ornamentation) and three culture/time units (4, 10, and 12) are omitted from the chi-square tables because of exceptionally low totals for these columns and rows. No correction for continuity was made since Monte Carlo studies have demonstrated the lack of need for continuity corrections. Chi-square is a very conservative test of significance, even under conditions of extremely small expected cell values in both 2x2 and 2xN contingency tables (Grizzle 1967; Lewontin and Felsenstein 1965).

Cell values greater than 3.8 (boldface type) in Tables 12.5 and 12.6 indicate which of the observed cell frequencies deviate significantly from that expected by chance at the 0.05 level of confidence (3.84 or greater is a significant chi-square value at $p = 0.05$ and one degree of freedom). This is actually a very conservative measure of significance since the total chi-square value for a one degree of freedom, 2x2 contingency table would always be greater than 3.84, if that value was recorded for a single cell.

TABLE 12.4   Comparison of Frequency of Mussel Valves with Total Elements for Vertebrate Meat Species by Culture/Time Stratigraphic Units

Culture/ time unit	Mussels				Meat species		Grand total
	Shelter	Main excavation	Total	Percentage of grand total	Total elements[a] (Table 12.2)	Percentage of grand total	
1	463	519	982	94.0	59	6.0	1041
2	711	972	1683	93.0	127	7.0	1810
3	674	536	1210	96.6	42	3.4	1252
4	468	6	474	99.0	5	1.0	479
5	503	27	530	68.9	239	31.1	769
6	234	10	244	26.0	693	74.0	937
7	85	22	107	9.0	1083	91.0	1190
8	8	2	10	2.6	368	97.4	378
9	1	1	2	0.5	386	99.5	388
10	—	—	—	0.0	8	100.0	8
11	26	—	26	17.3	124	82.7	150
12	—	—	—	0.0	9	100.0	9

[a]From one-quarter-inch screening.

It should be stressed that the chi-square values provide only a measure of statistically significant variation in cultural or faunal attributes at the intrasite level, and that chi-square significance does not measure the strength of association between variables. Also, it should be noted that the likelihood of statistical significance increases with greater overall table sample size, and that chi-square cell values are generally higher in table rows and columns having low marginal totals.

In order to gain some measure of the interrelationship among variables listed in the chi-square tables, the data in Tables 12.5 and 12.6 were entered in a R mode principal components analysis (program FACTOR, Veldman 1967:206–236). Four factors with eigenvalues greater than 1.0 were rotated by the varimax criterion; the rotated factor loadings are given in Table 12.8. All four factors are bipolar, having both significant high positive and high negative loadings. Rotated factor scores are plotted by culture/time units in Figure 12.2.

Factor 1 is comprised primarily of variables representing activities rather than fauna, and may represent shifts in the settlement strategy. One pattern that dominates Culture/Time Units 5–9 is exemplified by a lack of emphasis on hunting, lack of specialized cutting, and the dearth of turkey, opossum, skunk, and fish; and high frequencies for grinding, hammering, pecking, bone working, precision flaking, and pigment processing. This pattern is indicated by high positive scores in Figure 12.2. Perhaps the pattern reflects a seasonal, long-term occupation accompanied by plant-processing and tool-maintanance activities.

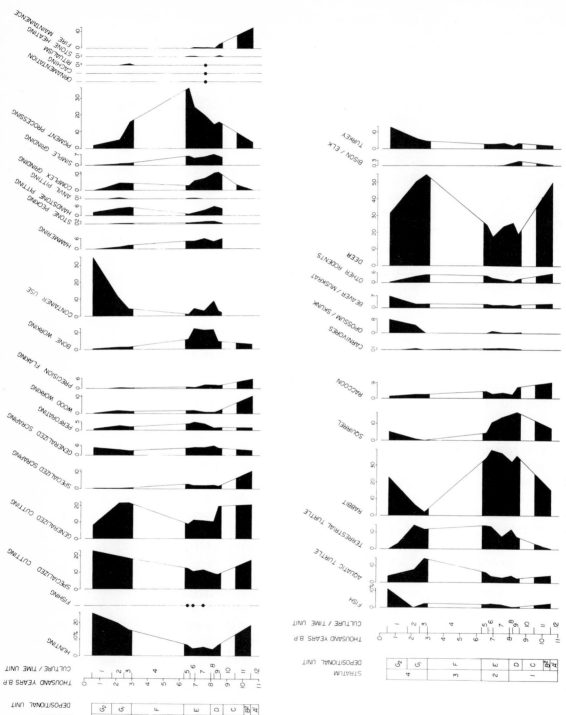

Figure 12.1 Frequencies for cultural activities and fauna by culture/time unit at Rodgers Shelter.

TABLE 12.5 Principal Subsistence (Meat) Species at Rodgers Shelter: Chi-Square Values[a][b]

Culture/time unit	Fish	Aquatic turtle	Terrestrial turtle	Rabbit	Squirrel	Raccoon	Carnivore	Opossum/skunk	Beaver/Muskrat	Other terrestrial rodents	Deer	Bison/elk	Turkey
1	**7.2**	-2.4	-2.6	**-5.1**	-3.7	-0.6	-0.5	**27.7**	3.6	-0.1	**5.1**	-0.4	**8.3**
2	-2.4	**4.4**	2.3	**-28.7**	**-13.5**	-0.6	0.0	**25.8**	0.2	1.5	**34.7**	-0.9	3.4
3	0.0	**10.6**	0.2	**-12.4**	**-5.1**	-0.2	-0.3	-0.3	0.1	1.1	**15.7**	-0.3	0.3
5	0.0	2.8	**4.4**	0.0	**-10.9**	0.2	0.0	-1.8	0.1	**3.8**	0.0	-1.6	-0.1
6	1.6	0.0	**9.8**	**-5.8**	-0.8	-2.1	0.0	1.3	-0.2	0.7	**-14.1**	**-4.7**	-0.4
7	0.2	-2.0	0.0	3.7	**4.2**	-0.3	0.6	-3.4	-0.1	-2.4	-0.3	-2.5	0.1
8	-2.4	0.1	1.5	-0.3	3.4	-2.2	0.0	-1.2	-0.4	-3.4	0.3	**8.3**	-2.3
9	-2.6	-2.2	-2.3	0.4	**7.0**	**10.1**	0.4	-0.3	0.0	-0.1	**-5.4**	**21.1**	0.0
11	0.2	0.0	**-8.7**	**-7.0**	-0.6	**9.2**	-1.0	-1.0	0.3	2.7	**16.8**	0.0	-0.3

[a]For one-quarter-inch dry screening.
[b]Significant chi-square values (greater than 3.8) are in boldface type.

TABLE 12.6 Summary of Activity Frequencies at Rodgers Shelter: Chi-Square Values[a]

Cultural/time unit	Hunting	Fishing	Specialized cutting	Generalized cutting	Specialized scraping	Generalized scraping	Perforating	Woodworking	Precision flaking	Bone working	Containment	Hammering	Stone pecking	Handstone pitting	Anvil pitting	Complex grinding/crushing	Simple grinding	Pigment processing	Ritual or ceremony	Stone heating	Fire maintenance
1	**90.1**	-0.4	**21.2**	0.0	**-8.7**	0.0	-3.7	-2.1	**-6.4**	**-27.8**	**243.6**	**-16.7**	**-4.0**	0.0	-1.0	**-17.5**	**-17.5**	**-66.4**	-0.5	-0.7	-2.5
2	**49.3**	-0.4	**12.5**	**26.6**	**-6.2**	-1.7	-0.7	1.2	-1.2	**-25.9**	**18.5**	**-11.7**	-2.6	3.7	**14.7**	-1.0	**-12.2**	**-55.4**	-0.6	-0.8	-2.6
3	**10.1**	-0.2	**4.6**	**16.3**	-2.4	-1.6	-1.7	0.0	-2.3	**-15.4**	**-4.0**	-1.8	-0.9	**5.0**	-0.6	-0.4	**-5.5**	-0.4	**23.5**	-0.5	-1.5
5	**-8.5**	0.9	-1.4	**-9.5**	**4.8**	0.0	-0.7	0.1	-0.2	-1.2	**-34.5**	1.3	-0.1	**-8.9**	0.0	**-7.4**	**6.1**	**108.8**	-0.5	1.7	-2.7
6	**-29.6**	0.3	**-8.8**	-2.9	0.2	-0.3	**7.1**	0.4	-2.5	**32.5**	**-10.4**	1.9	0.1	**-4.7**	-0.1	-0.7	1.3	**20.2**	-0.8	2.9	0.3
7	**-24.0**	0.1	**-4.6**	**-5.4**	0.9	0.5	1.0	-1.5	**12.3**	**24.5**	**-27.4**	**15.0**	**6.2**	0.1	-1.9	**8.2**	**8.8**	1.5	0.0	-1.5	0.0
8	**-10.7**	-0.2	**-3.9**	-2.1	0.6	1.1	-2.6	-0.9	2.9	**8.0**	0.8	0.6	2.2	**5.3**	-0.5	**13.2**	**6.1**	-2.0	-0.2	-0.4	0.0
9	-1.8	-0.1	-2.1	3.0	0.0	0.0	-0.8	-0.1	0.4	-1.1	-3.3	0.7	0.0	0.9	-0.2	**6.8**	1.0	-0.3	-0.1	-0.4	**12.3**
11	1.4	0.0	0.1	1.9	**16.3**	-0.1	-0.5	**19.3**	**7.7**	-1.2	**-4.3**	-2.2	-0.4	-1.7	-0.1	-1.4	-2.1	**-4.3**	-0.1	-0.1	**123.4**

[a]Significant chi-square values (greater than 3.8) are in boldface type.

TABLE 12.7 Summary of Significant Activities and Faunal Classes by Culture/Time Units[a]

Culture/time unit	Significant positive values		Significant negative values	
	Activities	Fauna	Activities	Fauna

1. Woodland
 	
1000–1750 B.P.
	containment
	hunting
	specialized
	  cutting
		opossum/
		  skunk
		turkey
		fish
		deer
			pigment processing
			bone working
			complex grinding/
			  crushing
			simple grinding
			hammering
			specialized scraping
			precision flaking
			stone pecking
				rabbit

2. Woodland–Late Archaic
 	
1750–2500 B.P.
	hunting
	generalized
	  cutting
	containment
	anvil pitting
	specialized
	  cutting
		deer
		opossum/
		  skunk
		aquatic
		  turtle
			pigment processing
			bone working
			simple grinding
			hammering
			specialized scraping
				rabbit
				squirrel

3. Late Archaic
 	
2500–3000 B.P.
	ritual/ceremony
	generalized
	  cutting
	hunting
	handstone
	  pitting
	specialized
	  cutting
		deer
		aquatic
		  turtle
			bone working
			simple grinding
			containment
				rabbit
				squirrel

5. Middle Archaic II
 	
6300–6700 B.P.
	pigment
	  processing
	simple grinding
	specialized
	  scraping
		terrestrial
		  turtle
		other terrestrial
		  rodents
			containment
			generalized cutting
			handstone pitting
			hunting
			complex grinding/
			  crushing
				squirrel

6. Middle Archaic II
 	
6700–7000 B.P.
	bone working
	pigment
	  processing
	perforating
		terrestrial
		  turtle
		rabbit
			hunting
			containment
			specialized cutting
			handstone pitting
				deer
				bison

7. Middle Archaic II/ Middle Archaic I 7000–8000 B.P.	bone working hammering precision flaking simple grinding complex grinding/ curshing stone pecking	squirrel	containment hunting generalized cutting specialized cutting	

[a] Based on chi-square values.

TABLE 12.7 (continued)

		Significant positive values		Significant negative values	
	Culture/time unit	Activities	Fauna	Activities	Fauna
8.	Middle Archaic I 8000–8200 B.P.	complex grinding/ crushing bone working simple grinding handstone pitting	bison	hunting specialized cutting	
9.	Middle Archaic I 8200–8600 B.P.	fire maintenance complex grinding/ crushing stone heating	bison raccoon squirrel		deer

11.	Dalton
	
	9500–10,500 B.P.
		fire maintenance
		woodworking
		specialized
		  scraping
		precision flaking
			deer
			raccoon
				containment
				pigment processing
					terrestrial
					  turtle
					rabbit

A mutually exclusive pattern is indicated by high negative scores on Factor 1, which represent hunting, specialized cutting, and containment activities associated with turkey, opossum, skunk, and fish remains. Notably absent are tool-maintenance activities and vegetal processing (Table 12.8). Perhaps this pattern illustrates short-term occupation, with the site used as a transient hunting camp.

Factor 2 largely points out contrasting faunal procurement strategies (Table 12.8). Positive scores and loadings indicate emphasis on deer and aquatic turtles associated with stone-pitting and generalized-cutting activities. This procurement base is contrasted with the emphasis on squirrel and rabbit in units with negative scores (Figure 12.2).

Factor 3 points out an association of fire-maintenance, specialized-scraping, and woodworking activities with raccoon remains. This pattern occurs only in Culture/Time Unit 11, the Dalton occupation.

Dichotomous patterns are revealed by Factor 4, where pigment-processing and perforating activities peak at the top of Unit E, and with bison and squirrel remains and handstone pitting peaking in Culture/Time Unit 9 in Unit D.

The data from the factor analysis, when taken with the chi-square data summarized in Table 12.7, then, provide a basis for interpreting changing adaptations during the human history at Rodgers Shelter. As an aid to identifying the discrete cultural units represented in the sequence, the rotated factor scores were subjected to a weighted average cluster analysis (program BMDP2M, Engleman and Fu 1971) in order to compare and contrast the similarity between each of the culture/time units. The results of this analysis, presented in the form of a dendrogram, clearly illustrate five major cultural units (Figure 12.3).

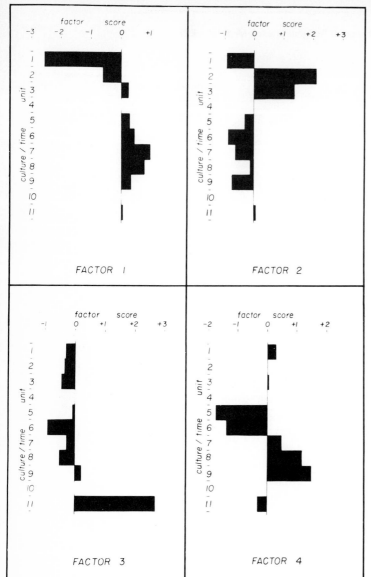

FACTOR 1

FACTOR 2

FACTOR 3

FACTOR 4

Figure 12.2 Factor scores by culture/time units.

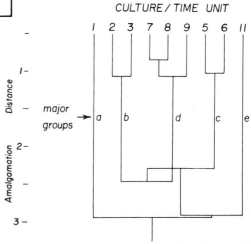

CULTURE / TIME UNIT

Figure 12.3 Dendrogram showing results of clustering of nine culture/time stratigraphic units on four factor scores.

TABLE 12.8 Varimax Rotated Factor Loading Matrix for Twenty-Nine Activity and Fauna Variables on Nine Culture/Time Units, Rodgers Shelter[a]

Variable	Factor 1	Factor 2	Factor 3	Factor 4	Percentage of communality
Turkey	**-.96**	.02	-.12	.03	93.0
Hunting	**-.95**	.25	-.02	.17	99.0
Containment	**-.94**	-.21	-.10	.18	96.6
Specialized cutting	**-.92**	.32	-.02	.14	96.7
Opossum/skunk	**-.87**	.29	-.19	.06	88.6
Fish	**-.74**	-.43	-.06	-.26	80.3
Simple grinding	**.89**	-.36	-.01	-.06	93.5
Hammering	**.87**	-.32	-.03	.00	86.2
Complex grinding	**.83**	.05	-.07	-.48	94.0
Stone pecking	**.79**	-.30	-.06	.18	75.3
Bone working	**.73**	**-.53**	-.11	-.18	86.4
Precision flaking	**.58**	-.07	.48	.24	63.2
Pigment processing	**.58**	-.26	.00	**-.57**	72.1
Generalized cutting	-.23	**.89**	-.05	.21	89.0
Deer	-.30	**.88**	.29	.07	95.3
Aquatic turtle	.12	**.79**	-.17	-.26	73.8
Anvil pitting	-.21	**.75**	-.09	-.04	61.5
Handstone pitting	-.03	**.51**	-.15	**.77**	88.4
Rabbit	.37	**-.91**	-.09	-.07	97.1
Squirrel	.38	**-.63**	.12	**.61**	91.8
Fire maintenance	.05	-.01	**.97**	-.05	94.2
Woodworking	.07	.12	**.94**	-.17	93.2
Specialized scraping	.48	-.15	**.81**	-.26	98.0
Raccoon	.07	-.14	**.77**	.29	70.3
Terrestrial turtle	.25	-.03	**-.79**	-.48	92.6
Bison/elk	.15	-.18	.09	**.73**	58.9
Perforating	.43	-.23	-.18	**-.51**	53.1
Ceremony/ritual	.10	.48	-.15	.04	26.7
Stone heating	.21	-.41	-.04	-.08	22.4
Percentage of variance, unrotated factors	34.5	20.5	14.6	10.9	Total = 80.5%

[a]Values greater than 0.50 in boldface type.

CHANGING PATTERNS OF HUMAN ADAPTATION

The cultural units segregated in the cluster analysis represent five discrete adaptive patterns for the human record at Rodgers Shelter. From the oldest to the youngest, these horizons are labeled Dalton, Middle Archaic I, Middle Archaic II, Late Archaic, and Woodland. The estimated dates given for the cultural units are an attempt to define temporally each component at Rodgers Shelter.

Dalton (10,500–9500 B.P.)

The earliest definable cultural pattern is one of ephemeral campsites found near the base of Terrace 1b and just above the bedrock floor of the shelter (Culture/Time Unit 11). Open hearths were well preserved on the terrace since the aggrading floodplain effectively buried each living surface, leaving it virtually intact. The various Dalton occupation floors beneath the overhang, however, were not as clear-cut and could not be separated from one another.

The debris associated with the terrace campsites was scattered around individual open fireplaces, the concentrated area of scatter usually not exceeding 10 m in diameter. Faunal remains suggest these early occupants were procuring a variety of large and small game. Although hunting, as an activity at Rodgers, does not appear to have been as important as it was in the later horizons, both deer and raccoon have significant values in the Dalton horizon, and hunting was obviously basic to the subsistence system. It is important to point out that all of the major fauna represented in the later horizons, excluding prairie species, appear in this early manifestation. The analysis of plant remains proves that hickory nuts and black walnuts were also a part of the Dalton subsistence base.

Specialized scraping activities (hide preparation?) and the working of wood with adzes suggest that these temporary camps were more than simple overnight hunting stations; instead, they are proposed to be transient settlements accommodating small bands. During the periods these early groups were stopping at Rodgers Shelter they were mobile, spending probably less than a week at a time there. At this time, we simply do not know how other components in the overall Dalton settlement system in western Missouri may have compared with or complemented the manifestations at Rodgers Shelter.

Middle Archaic I (8600–7000 B.P.)

Culture /Time Units 7, 8, and 9 include remains representing an Archaic adaptive pattern in which the shelter was inhabited for longer durations (seasonally?) over centuries. The pattern varies considerably from that represented by the preceding Dalton horizon. The shelter now served as a base camp for people carrying out a wide range of subsistence and domestic pursuits reflected by the debris from numerous manufacturing, processing, and maintenance activities (Table 12.7). Activity indicators suggest that the processing of plant materials and the manufacturing and maintanance of tools were especially important.

The significant lack of evidence for hunting and butchering (specialized cutting) as major activities during this horizon correlates well with the sharply reduced percentages of deer remains. Although not found in great numbers, the presence of bison bones is important in the Middle Archaic I horizon since remains of these large herbivores do not occur in any of the other horizons. Still, the overall faunal evidence indicates that bison and other prairie species, which were now available to some extent in the locality, were only procured incidentally; the system focused more on the procurement of smaller game. Squirrels were especially important compared with other periods, and probably represent an exploitation of the bottomland forests. Hickory nuts, walnuts, and hackberries were probably taken from the same zones.

The length or season(s) of occupation is still unknown, but it is important to note that no storage or cache pits were found in connection with the Middle Archaic I horizon.

Middle Archaic II (7000–6300 B.P.)

Originally, the Middle Archaic at Rodgers Shelter was described as a continuum spanning over two millennia, in which there was a gradual decline in deer hunting and milling activities with a concomitant shift to the procurement of smaller game animals, focusing on rabbits and squirrels (McMillan 1971). The more recent analyses have suggested, however, that there are two separate patterns in the Middle Archaic; this is nicely demonstrated by the cluster analysis (Figure 12.2). The physical mixing caused by deflation in Unit 7 tended to obscure the change between the two horizons. Although it is now recognized that there is some mixing in Culture/Time Unit 7, the bulk of the assemblage in that unit is more closely related to Middle Archaic I.

The Middle Archaic II pattern is in many ways similar to the earlier Middle Archaic horizon in that the shelter continued to be used as a seasonal(?) base camp for a wide range of subsistence and domestic activities. The lack of evidence of major hunting activity and the dearth of deer remains (when compared with other horizons) was still one of the salient features of the Middle Archaic II. There was a shift to even greater reliance on rabbits and other small rodents, and away from squirrels, which may reflect focusing on zones outside the bottomland forest. For the first time, freshwater mussels were utilized on more than an incidental basis.

Many of the processing, maintenance, and manufacturing activities prevalent in the Middle Archaic I horizon continued, but activities related to plant processing (complex grinding, crushing) were far less important during this period. The most significant activity during this time was the processing of hematite pigment, obtained from local raw materials; the shelter was an important station for this industrial activity. As with the earlier Middle Archaic horizon, no evidence of storage or cache pits was found in Units 5 and 6.

Late Archaic (3000–2000 B.P.)

Following a hiatus of almost 3 millennia, the shelter was reoccupied by Late Archaic populations around 3000 B.P. There is again evidence of the residents' having carried out a diversified range of activities on the site, but these are sharply divergent from the Middle Archaic patterns. Deer hunting became extremely important during the Late Archaic, with an accompanying focus on the aquatic resources of turtles and mussels. The major contrast with the Middle Archaic is the change from a focus on small game procurement to the hunting of deer. This is not only reflected by a sharp increase in the percentage of deer remains, but by the far greater incidence of projectile points and hafted cutting tools, which are interpreted here as hunting indicators.

There are also differences from the Middle Archaic, in the domestic and tool-maintenance activities as shown in Table 12.7. More evidence for ceremony or ritual was found in this horizon, and the only two primary burials came from this zone (Chapter 11). Storage pits were again noticeably absent; had they been present, they would have been very easily detected, since they would have intruded into the underlying sterile Unit G (Stratum 3).

Woodland (1750–1000 B.P.)

Culture/Time Unit 1 contained remains attributed to a Woodland occupation, and Woodland materials were mixed with those from the Late Archaic horizon in Unit 2. The Woodland occupation is identified as a habitation component. It is related to the Fristoe Burial Complex as defined by Wood (1961, 1967) for this area of Missouri.

Projectile points and hafted cutting tools indicate that hunting and butchering were important, if not the principal activities carried out at the site during this period. In fact, there is a dearth of indicators for other kinds of activities in this Fristoe assemblage. Ceramics were present for the first time and provided containers for the transportation or storage of food.

During the Late Woodland Fristoe occupation of Rodgers Shelter the site was once again used as a transient settlement station, this time for hunting deer and turkey, and other food-procurement activities. The data suggest that both fishing and mussel collecting were also important subsistence pursuits. If indeed the shelter functioned as a hunting and procurement camp, it was probably linked to base settlements located on the open-air terraces elsewhere in the area.

A few sherds (less than 1% of the sample) show Middle Woodland affinities (Fig. 10.11n). However, they are too rare to postulate a Middle Woodland component; rather, they may be trade sherds. There were no nonceramic artifacts that could be attributed to a Middle Woodland occupation.

ENVIRONMENTAL CHANGE AND CULTURAL ADAPTATION

There may have been a number of interrelated cultural and environmental factors that produced the changes observed in the cultural record. Based on depositional changes, faunal distributions, and changes in activity patterns, some hypotheses are advanced here to account for these changes. First, it is necessary to look at the environmental dynamics for this area along the southern border of the Prairie Peninsula during the past 10,000 years.

We propose that there was a gradual but major shift from a forest-edge environment to one containing greatly reduced amounts of arboreal habitat beginning with the time interval represented by Culture/Time Unit 9 (8200–8600 B.P.) and continuing through Culture/Time Unit 4, up to about 3000 B.P. It is further proposed that following the deposition of Stratum 3 (Depositional Unit F), perhaps as early as 4000 years ago, there was a gradual return to mixed plant communities that could be classified as forest edge. This proposed model is quite similar to that described by Wright (1968:84) for the northeastern edge of the Prairie Peninsula.

The dynamics for such a shift have been demonstrated by the instability of modern plant communities, and are revealed for the study area in the original land surveys (Chapter 2). During pioneer times, much of the study locality described as barrens was apparently grassland that was succeeding to forest. Thus, during past climatic regimes more conducive to grassland, it is probable that the reverse would be true. In fact, there may have been periods when, except for floodplain habitats and areas of greater relief, the entire western flank of the Ozarks was dominated by grassland.

Studies of the sedimentary processes at Rodgers Shelter (Chapter 8) have demonstrated a gradual change from more distant upland erosion to local hillside erosion, and this has been linked to changing environmental conditions concomitant with changing hillslope vegetation cover (Ahler 1973; McMillan and King 1974:119).

The major period of aggradation of Terrace 1b was the time when there should have been vast tree kills in the path of an encroaching prairie. It is conceivable that if there were periods when great numbers of trees were expiring in the face of adverse climatic factors, there could have been greater erosion on the uplands with added deposition on the floodplain. It is interesting to note that, by the time there is faunal evidence for prairie in the area, alluviation had subsided and Terrace 1b had stabilized.

Subsequent to 7000 years ago, there may have been less vegetational cover on the hill above the shelter, as indicated by an alluvial fan of hillside debris deposited at the foot of the bluff. Later, during the period the shelter was abandoned, there must have been times when the hillside was virtually denuded of vegetation, contributing to mass movements of colluvium, perhaps in the form of mudslides. This may reflect a time of extreme dessication of the study locality.

The faunal evidence also suggests that the environment in the Rodgers Shelter locality changed during the mid-Holocene. Although it is nearly impossible to delineate *minor* fluctuations between the forest edge–prairie border from faunal analysis, there is sound evidence for a gradual trend to greater areas of grassland at the expense of the woody communities, beginning about 8600 B.P. The faunal data suggest that this trend peaked between 8000 and 7000 B.P., although it probably continued for another three millennia during the period that Unit F (Stratum 3) was being deposited at Rodgers Shelter. Unfortunately, there is no vertebrate record for this essentially sterile colluvial horizon. The faunal evidence for prairie expansion is an increased number of grassland vertebrates, with the greatest variety of species present between 8500 and 6500 B.P. (Figure 12.4). During this time, there was a concomitant decline in the frequency of forest species, especially raccoon. There was also a significant reduction in deer, which usually prefer forest-edge habitats. It is important to remember that the proposed shifts probably reflect only upland vegetation; changes in the bottomland habitats would have been less severe.

The increased emphasis on small game (rabbits, squirrels, and other small rodents) during the same period that grassland species increased probably reflects the de-emphasis of deer hunting, perhaps again for environmental reasons.

During a period when the upland oak–hickory forest was being replaced by grassland, cottontails and small rodents could be supported and find forage in brushy areas along ravines or hollows and on some hillsides. Bottomland forests, which would have been less affected than the upland forests, would have continued to provide suitable habitats for squirrels. In this case, the landscape would continue to provide a high capacity for cottontails and rodents, but would simultaneously greatly reduce the effective deer habitat.

Recent wildlife studies on deer in the western Ozarks have stressed the importance of acorn mast as the principal food of deer in this region (Korschgen 1962:166). Furthermore, research on the food availability for deer during drought years has demonstrated that both mast yields and vegetative browse were lowest during periods of low rainfall (Segelquist and Green 1968:336), and that die-offs occurred following these food shortages (Segelquist *et al.* 1969).

It is suggested here, then, that if there was a greater incidence of severe and prolonged droughts during the early to mid-Holocene that was contributing to the reduction of available food supply (especially acorn mast), it would have had a demonstrated effect on deer populations.

The hypothesis that greater proportions of the landscape again supported forest after about 3000 B.P. is evidenced by the increased frequencies of deer, turkey, and raccoon, and the accompanying disappearance of all grassland vertebrate species (Figure 12.1).

In sum, it is hypothesized that there was a gradual shift during the mid-Holocene from a forest edge to a prairie biotype and back. It is believed that a vegetational change of this magnitude had a pronounced effect on the past human populations in western Missouri and accounts in

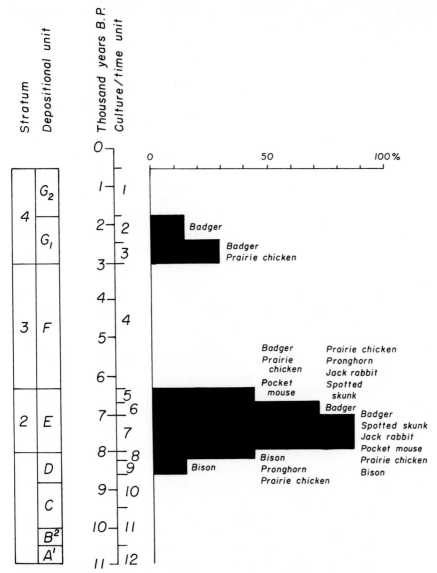

Figure 12.4 Frequency by percentage of seven grassland species through time at Rodgers Shelter.

part for the changes in subsistence and settlement strategies seen in the archaeological record.

The Rodgers Shelter sequence is instructive in that it is a case study for an area where changing paleoenvironmental conditions directly affected prehistoric food-procurement systems and settlement patterns during the mid-Holocene. During the earliest period, the Dalton horizon, the area was apparently forested and a wide range of plant and animal food was known. There was, however, a focus on hunting certain game, especially deer. Although little is known about the overall settlement system of these early people, at Rodgers the occupations represent the remains of small transient bands.

There are two important variables that may have contributed to the differences between the Middle Archaic and the Dalton horizons. These are: (1) that there was a general population increase over that of the Dalton horizon based on the greatly increased area utilized for living space, and (2) that Middle Archaic populations were facing a deteriorating environment where increased incidence of severe drought was helping to transform much of the area's arboreal habitats to grass.

A reduced emphasis on deer hunting and the increase of diversity of species taken, especially small game, during the Middle Archaic was a more costly system when measured against energy expenditure per calorie return. We believe that this "less efficient system" was a necessary stress response, however, set in motion by a deteriorating effective environment.

The change in strategies during the Middle Archaic, defined through changes in activities, may also be environmentally linked. For example, the major industrial activity performed at the site during Middle Archaic II times, the processing of hematite pigment, became important at a time when sparse hillside cover and erosion would have provided optimal conditions for securing the mineral.

The virtual abandonment of Rodgers Shelter after 6300 B.P. for 3000 years may not have been a sudden cultural response. There appears to have been decreasing occupational evidence throughout Depositional Unit E, although declining debris density is not a direct measure of occupational intensity unless one can adequately control for depositional rate. Nevertheless, we believe there was a trend toward fewer occupations, beginning a few centuries before the site was finally abandoned. Presently, it is unknown whether there was merely an adjustment in the local settlement system that excluded Rodgers Shelter or whether the entire area was abandoned. Sites currently known in the Pomme de Terre basin dating from this period (6000–3000 B.P.) are rare at best.

The Late Archaic adaptation reflects a return to environmental conditions supporting deer herds and, concomitantly, to a procurement system designed to exploit these animals. There was also increased use of aquatic resources, although it is not known if this is related to changes in the stream itself following the hypsithermal. This Late Archaic pattern was established by the time it appeared at Rodgers Shelter; when and where it was first established is still unknown. By 2700 B.P. there were contemporary, related sites that appear to have been functionally different from the settlement based at Rodgers. This is suggested by the presence of subsurface pits and postmolds (structures?) at the nearby Thurman site (Falk and Lippincott 1974).

The Late Woodland occupation represents a new level of organization. Rodgers Shelter is believed to have served as a hunting and fishing camp for peoples who have been described as semisedentary horticulturalists (Wood 1967:125). We are not certain how early cultigens reached the area; presently there is evidence from Boney Spring (Chapter 6) for domestic squash *(Cucurbita pepo)* in the Early Woodland at 1900 years ago (King and McMillan 1975).

Comparing the Rodgers Shelter study with other long Archaic sequences in the American Midwest (e.g., Fowler 1959; Klippel 1971; Asch *et al.* 1972) demonstrates that there are as many contrasts as there are parallels between these different regional environmental and cultural histories. We believe that in order to arrive at adequate explanations for the causes of the long period of stability before food-procurement systems moved on to food production, we need far more detailed case studies like these. This has been the first step for such a model for the western margin of the Missouri Ozarks.

REFERENCES

Ahler, S.A.
  1973 Post-Pleistocene depositional change at Rodgers shelter, Missouri. *Plains Anthropologist* 18(59):1–26.
Asch, N.B., R.I. Ford, and D.L. Asch
  1972 Paleoethnobotany of the Koster Site: The Archaic horizons. *Reports of Investigations* No. 24. Illinois State Museum, Springfield, Illinois.
Blalock, H.M., Jr.
  1972 *Social statistics*, 2nd edition. New York: McGraw Hill.
Engleman, L., and S. Fu
  1971 *BMDP2M cluster analysis on cases.* Health Sciences Computing Facility, University of California, Los Angeles. Xeroxed.
Falk, C.
  1969 Archeological salvage in the Kaysinger Bluff Reservoir, Missouri: 1966. Report to the National Park Service, Midwest Region. Omaha, Nebraska.
Falk, C.R., and K.A. Lippincott
  1974 Archeological investigations in the Harry S. Truman Reservoir, Missouri: 1967–1968. Manuscript submitted to the National Park Service, Midwest Region. Omaha, Nebraska.
Fowler, M.L.
  1959 Summary report of Modoc Rock Shelter 1952, 1953, 1955, 1956. *Report of Investigations* No. 8. Illinois State Museum, Springfield, Illinois.
Grizzle, J.E.
  1967 Continuity correction in the chi-square test for 2 x 2 tables. *American Statistician* 21:28–32.
King, F.B., and R.B. McMillan
  1975 Plant remains from a Woodland storage pit, Boney Spring, Missouri. *Plains Anthropologist* 20(68):111–115.
Klippel, W.E.
  1971 Prehistory and environmental change along the southern border of the Prairie Peninsula during the Archaic Period. Ph.D. dissertation, Department of Anthropology, University of Missouri, Columbia.

Korschgen, L.J.
1962 Foods of Missouri deer with some management implications. *Journal of Wildlife Management* **26**(2):164–172.

Lewontin, R.C., and J. Felsenstein
1965 The robustness of homogeneity tests in 2 x N tables. *Biometrics* **21**:19–33.

McMillan, R.B.
1971 Biophysical change and cultural adaptation at Rodgers shelter, Missouri. Ph.D. dissertation, Department of Anthropology, University of Colorado, Boulder.

McMillan, R.B., and J.E. King
1974 Evidence for Holocene biogeographic change in Missouri's western Ozarks. *American Quaternary Association Abstracts*, Third Meeting: 119. Madison, Wisconsin.

Segelquist, C.A., and W.E. Green
1968 Deer food yields in four Ozark forest types. *Journal of Wildlife Management* **32**(2):330–337.

Segelquist, C.A., F.D. Ward, and R.G. Leonard
1969 Habitat–deer relations in two Ozark enclosures. *Journal of Wildlife Management* **33**(3):511–520.

Vehik, R.
1974 Archeological investigations in the Harry S. Truman Reservoir area: 1970. Manuscript submitted to the National Park Service, Midwest Region, Omaha, Nebraska.

Veldman, D.J.
1967 *Fortran programming for the behavioral sciences.* New York: Holt.

Wood, W.R.
1961 The Pomme de Terre reservoir in western Missouri prehistory. *The Missouri Archaeologist* **23**:1–131.
1967 The Fristoe Burial Complex of southwestern Missouri. *The Missouri Archaeologist* **29**:1–127.

Wright, H.E., Jr.
1968 History of the prairie peninsula. In *Quaternary of Illinois*, edited by R.E. Bergstrom. University of Illinois College of Agriculture, Special Publication 14. Urbana, Illinois.

V
Synopsis and Epilogue

13

A Summary of Environmental and Cultural Change in the Western Missouri Ozarks

R. Bruce McMillan and W. Raymond Wood

The purpose of the present study has been to offer a preliminary model for the paleoecology of the western Ozark Highland for the past 35,000 years, and an interpretation of how man adapted to and exploited the Ozarks for the more than 10,000 years he occupied the area. This model, based on the work of many specialists, is the product of an inter-disciplinary research program spanning the decade 1963–1974.

The study focuses on a series of localities in and near an abandoned entrenched meander of the Pomme de Terre River—Breshears Bottoms—on the mosaic ecotone between the prairies of western Missouri and the oak–hickory forests of the northwestern Ozark Highland. The river bottomlands—and most of the sites—in the study locality are scheduled to be inundated by the Harry S. Truman Reservoir, now under construction by the U.S. Army Corps of Engineers.

The Pomme de Terre River, a north-flowing affluent of the Osage River, forms a sinuous border between the Salem and Springfield plateaus in west–central Missouri. Their relatively undissected uplands are areas of low relief, but streams have cut deeply into them, creating deep valleys bordered by areas of steep relief, including many high bluffs, some of them containing rock overhangs such as Rodgers Shelter. The narrow, terrace-stepped valley floors contain broad streams of clear running water.

The climate of west–central Missouri is quite variable, being affected by both the continental Pacific air masses, and by maritime tropical air from the Gulf of Mexico. The study locality lies along the southern margin of the Prairie Peninsula—the wedge-shaped mid-continent area of tall grass prairies—in an area having low winter rainfall and snowfall, and occasional summer droughts that have a heavy impact on ecotones such as this one.

There are abundant natural resources in the area, and both man and his animal prey depended on the floral resources of the prairies to the west, the oak–hickory forests to the east, and the mosaic ecotone in the study locality. Fauna was abundant, with the study locality rich in animals adapted to the variegated nearby plant communities. Major lithic resources included cherts and sandstones, for chipped and ground stone tools, and hematite and galena, which provided raw material for less utilitarian purposes. Hematite, especially, seems to have been an important product produced in—and possibly exported from—the study locality in Middle Archaic II times.

Historic documentation and data from U.S. Federal Land Surveys provide the basis for an early historic phytogeographic model for the study locality. Several vegetation zones for this period—now heavily modified by Euro–American settlement practices—are identified:

1. upland prairies, on the undulating and lightly dissected plateaus on stream divides;
2. bottomland prairies, which in the study locality occurred only in two abandoned stream meanders;
3. oak barrens, or grasslands, in hilly country that contained scattered trees and brush;
4. oak–hickory forest, dominating the more highly dissected terrain;
5. bottomland forest, a highly diversified flora dependent on the bottomland drainage along streams.

Historic records support the proposition that, at the time of Euro–American settlement, the oak–hickory forest was encroaching on the grasslands near Rodgers Shelter.

The Ozark Highland, a structural dome and one of the oldest land surfaces in North America, was elevated above sea level during the Pennsylvanian period, some 300 million years ago. It has undergone several periods of uplift and subsequent erosion since that time. The Pomme de Terre River is entrenched 100 m or more into the northwest margin of this dome. Bedrock in the locality is chiefly dolomite of Ordovician age. There are several abandoned, entrenched meanders along the lower reaches of the river. One of them, Breshears Bottoms, is a horseshoe-shaped valley containing three terraces. The oldest one, Terrace 2, stands some 12 m above the bed of the stream; the compound Terrace 1 is some 3.5 m above the river bed; and Terrace 0 is the modern floodplain.

Terrace 2 formed sometime prior to 40,000 years ago, during the Wisconsinan stage, following the abandonment of the meander, and was abandoned by about 28,000 B.P. Four artesian springs are embedded in this terrace: Jones, Kirby, Trolinger, and Koch. Radiocarbon dates and pollen spectra from them show that a nonarboreal pollen and pine zone was established by 40,000 B.P., and existed until 25,000–22,000 B.P. This time correlates with the mid-Wisconsinan interstade, probably the Farmdalian substage. The vegetation in the study locality at that time is interpreted as open pine parkland, similar to present conditions in southern Manitoba. Faunal remains from the springs are dominated by mastodon, horse, and muskox.

Terrace 1 is divided into an earlier Terrace 1a, and a later Terrace 1b, and includes the period 28,000 to 1000 B.P. Terrace 1a is correlated with the late Woodfordian substage; the interval between Terrace 1a and 1b with the Twocreekan substage; and Terrace 1b with the Valderan substage and the post-Valderan period. Terrace 0 was created by degradation of the river after 1000 B.P.

Spruce pollen became dominant with the beginning of late Wisconsinan full glacial conditions, some 25,000–22,000 B.P., when Terrace 1a was beginning to form. Older pollen spectra in the full glacial period are dominated by spruce—but between 16,500 and 13,500 B.P., spruce declines somewhat, and deciduous tree pollen rises. Fauna associated with this apparent climatic improvement include giant beaver, ground sloth, tapir, horse, and deer.

Terrace 1b, originally defined on the basis of deposits in Rodgers Shelter, has now been identified in other parts of the valley. At Rodgers, the terrace is presumed to have begun to form about 11,000 B.P., for there is a date of 10,500 B.P. not far above its base there. Comparative data suggest that the modern oak–hickory forest was established by about 12,000 B.P., so the entire Archaic and Woodland cultural sequence is based on essentially modern floral communities.

No significant archaeological or paleobotanical data have yet been found in Terrace 0.

Archaeological remains were found in three of the springs investigated: Trolinger, Boney, and Koch. In each case, however, the tools associated with fossil mammals were restricted to the spring conduit or feeder: The association between man and mastodon in each of these cases is therefore presumably spurious. The possibility of the contemporaneity of man and mastodon, first initiated by Koch's work along the Pomme de Terre River in 1840, is given no support by this work.

Some of the material in the spring conduits had its origin in occupations around the margin of the spring. The excavated material and surface specimens from Koch Spring suggest a long history of transient occupations around the spring from about 8000 B.P. well into the Christian Era. A more intensive occupation took place at Boney Spring. An Early Woodland component there included hearths, a storage pit containing squash seeds, and the grave of a young adult male, dating to about 2000 B.P.

The major archaeological work in the Pomme de Terre valley was at Rodgers Shelter, where work was carried out between 1963 and 1968. This shelter looks out over a high terrace (Terrace 1b), part of which was beneath the shelter overhang itself. Incorporated in the 9 m of deposits was a record of human activity that spanned the Holocene (Figure 13.1). Excavations were concentrated both beneath the shelter and on the terrace in front of the overhang.

Four major strata were obvious in the field and, later, through mechanical analyses of the sediments, these were further subdivided into eight depositional units. These units reflect a gradual change in the source of materials forming and capping the terrace. Earlier, most sediments were silts deposited as alluvium by the Pomme de Terre. Later, however, when river deposition ceased, the accumulation came from debris washing down from the hill above. These changes in depositional patterns are hypothesized as being related to changing Holocene climatic conditions that initially affected upland biota and, later, vegetation in the vicinity of the site.

The subsistence record at Rodgers Shelter demonstrates a long history of changing emphases in the exploitation of local resources. Hickory nuts, walnuts, and hackberries seem to have been exploited throughout the sequence, although none were ever abundant. As one might expect along an ecotone, there was considerable variety in the fauna exploited. In all, 44 terrestrial vertebrate species and 9 varieties of fish were identified. Although most species were those preferring forest edge or forest habitats, the remains of a number of prairie species clustered in the mid-Holocene zones dating between 6300 and 8200 years ago.

The analysis of artifacts was approached from a functional standpoint. By focusing on attributes that reflected the use of 31 artifact classes and features, 23 different activities that were performed at one time or another at the site were defined. These were basically subsistence and domestic activities related to food procurement; food processing; and tool, utensil, and clothing manufacture and/or maintenance.

There were two human burials at Rodgers, that of an adult female and a teen-aged male. Both of them were primary and flexed, in shallow pits. X-rays of the male's femur and tibia show numerous lines of arrested growth, suggesting he had been sick most of his life, with at least one period of prolonged illness or submarginal diet. The stratigraphic position of both burials, and their morphology, indicate they are Late Archaic Indians buried about 2500 to 3000 B.P. They compare favorably with Archaic populations in other parts of eastern United States.

For purposes of analyzing the temporal changes in the subsistence and artifactual data, the levels were combined into 12 culture/time stratigraphic units, which integrated contemporary units across the site. Statis-

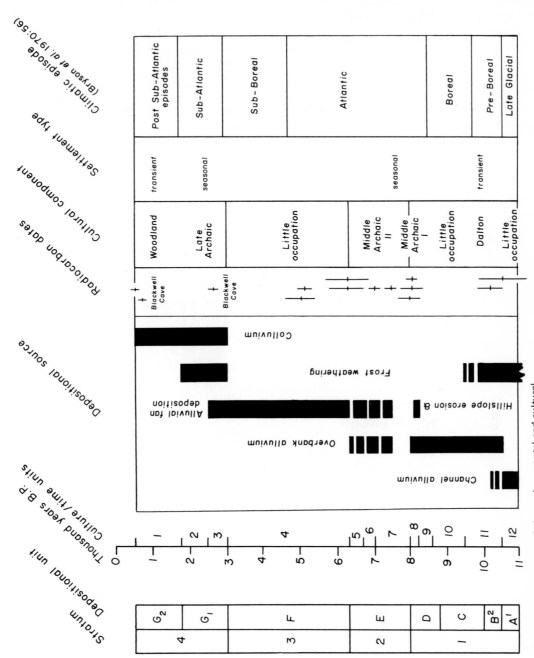

Figure 13.1 Summary of the environmental and cultural records at Rodgers Shelter.

239

tical analyses of these units identified five basic cultural patterns: Dalton, Middle Archaic I, Middle Archaic II, Late Archaic, and Woodland. Analyses of the activities and fauna from each of these units demonstrated changing adaptive patterns, which are interpreted as being closely linked to environmental changes for this area during the Holocene.

The model for Holocene environmental change is based primarily on faunal evidence and geomorphological data. It argues that the area was probably forested during the early Holocene, but, beginning about 8500 B.P., the Prairie Peninsula gradually moved southeast. We believe that between 5000 and 8000 years ago much of the region that supports trees today was covered with prairie. This had a demonstrated effect on the Middle Archaic populations, and caused them to turn to a foraging, more generalized economy that was probably less efficient (energy versus calorie return) than the deer-hunting activities of the earlier and later periods.

The shelter was used as only a transient settlement during its earliest history, and again when Late Woodland peoples occupied it as a hunting and fishing camp. Throughout most of the Archaic, however, it was occupied for longer periods of time, perhaps on a seasonal basis. The site was unoccupied between 3000 and 6000 years ago.

The model developed from these studies at Rodgers Shelter and at the nearby springs—one of changing human adaptations and environmental change—is a first step, and will provide a series of hypotheses for testing during future studies of man–land relationships in the western Ozark Highland.

REFERENCES

Bryson, R.A., D.A. Baerreis, and W.M. Wendland
    1970 The character of late-glacial and post-glacial climatic changes. In *Pleistocene and Recent environments of the Central Great Plains*, edited by W. Dort, Jr., and J.K. Jones, Jr. Lawrence, Kansas: Univ. Press of Kansas.

14

Models in Western Missouri Paleoecology and Prehistory: The Future

W. Raymond Wood, R. Bruce McMillan, and James E. King

For the past decade the interdisciplinary research team working in the western Missouri Ozark Highland has continued to refine and sophisticate its strategies for investigating changes in the past biota and the integral role the environment played in shaping the course of human experience since the end of the Pleistocene. Fortunately, most of the principal investigators have been able to spend the field seasons together. Through frequent and continuing dialogue we have all gained a far greater appreciation of the problems of each individual discipline which, in turn, has created a bond of common interests.

Although the principal personnel of the program have worked closely, it has been difficult, and in some cases impossible, to complete all phases of the study on schedule. Thus, some studies planned for inclusion in this volume are still in progress (e.g., studies of the lithic debitage, freshwater mussels, and terrestrial gastropods). These problems, relating to the disparity between the aims and results of large interdisciplinary projects, have been articulated by others (Struever 1968; Brown and Struever 1973: 261–263). In addition, new lines of inquiry are now needed to answer questions raised by the research described earlier.

The principal contributors to this volume have continued their active research interests in the western Missouri Ozark Highland, with current and future research designed to test the hypotheses generated by the earlier studies. Foremost among these are the completion of a number of analyses of materials already available or soon to be excavated from Rodgers Shelter. Proposals for funding this work have been prepared and submitted to the appropriate federal agencies in order to mitigate the impact of the Harry S. Truman Reservoir on this National Register site.

A descriptive report of the formal attributes of the artifacts from Rodgers Shelter is presently being prepared and will be indispensible for identifying chronologically related components at other area sites. More detailed functional analyses of the artifacts through the study of microscopic wear patterns are also planned to augment Ahler's (1971) pilot study and the more cursory treatment given the total assemblage here. Furthermore, plans are in preparation to see that technological studies of chipped stone artifacts, including flaking debris, are completed. New studies of the freshwater mussels and terrestrial gastropods will be made, analyses that simply were not completed by the person who initially agreed to do them. Also, through more intensive examination of existing faunal remains, the seasonal aspects of occupation at Rodgers Shelter will be more thoroughly investigated.

Further excavations are now underway at Rodgers Shelter in a control block originally left there for the application of later and more refined field techniques. These excavations are designed to obtain a more consistent sample of floral and faunal microscale remains, many of which were lost with the recovery techniques employed during the earlier years of the project.

Perhaps the most serious problem in the interpretation of data from Rodgers Shelter has been the lack of contrastive data from other area sites; that is, analyses of materials from other sites in many cases have not been approached from a functional standpoint comparable to that used at Rodgers. Any interpretation based on a single site is patently biased since evidence for activities carried out at other locations is for the most part missing. We realize this bias but believe that now, equipped with the chronological model and classificatory schemes developed for Rodgers Shelter, we are in a better position to structure investigations at other sites.

A thorough survey of the study locality, as part of a reconnaissance of the greater Harry S. Truman Reservoir flood pool, is therefore scheduled.Rodgers Shelter provides a provocative but fragmentary idea of the adaptive strategies of western Missouri human populations through time: The survey is designed to round out gaps in the existing data. One goal of the survey is to identify and define settlement types—that is, sites that share a "particular configuration of exploitative and maintenance activities [Struever 1968:135]" for each of the time/stratigraphic units in the study area. The identification of activity patterns at other sites will be facilitated, in part, by detailed functional studies of tools from Rodgers Shelter, as well as through further development of the concept of "activity indicators" as defined in Chapter 10.

As part of the survey, a systematic terrace-coring and backhoe-trenching program will be used to find buried sites not otherwise exposed. For instance, the Paleo–Indian period is poorly known, not only in the study area, but in western Missouri in general. One reason for this is that many of their sites are in river valleys at the bases of terraces such as Terrace 1b. One of the cores collected in 1973, from Breshears Bottoms about 1.5 km southeast of Rodgers Shelter, yielded charcoal and flakes at a depth of nearly 9 m. Work here and in similar localities should augment the meager data on early Holocene cultures in the area, as well as much of the Middle Archaic period, which is apparently represented largely by sites buried in Terrace 1b deposits.

To aid in stratifying the survey area, a full-time zoologist and botanist, using original land survey data, will develop models of the past plant and animal communities, so that the spatial and seasonal concentrations of prime resources can be identified and quantified. The most difficult task will be identifying the changes in these resource configurations back through time from our temporal datum, the time of the original land surveys. This will be absolutely essential, however, in order to stratify the study area for archaeological investigation of components of the Archaic horizons.

To help clarify these paleoenvironmental dynamics, there is need for a postglacial pollen chronology that overlaps the cultural sequence from Rodgers Shelter. Current work at Phillips Spring (23HI216) on the Pomme de Terre River, 3.5 km southeast of Rodgers Shelter, may provide this record. In addition, another spring a few kilometers south of the study area is known to contain pollen-bearing sediments of postglacial age. Work is planned at this and other springs to expand our knowledge of environmental change during the Holocene.

It is equally important to understand the nature of the late Pleistocene environments, for they form the setting for man's initial occupation and exploitation of the area. A good beginning has been made in comprehending the period from about 40,000 to 13,500 B.P., but many details are still lacking. Work at Jones Spring, now underway, holds great promise. The faunal deposit there contains not only horse and bison, but mammoth and mastodon as well. These Pleistocene proboscideans are normally interpreted as occupying distinctive environments. An explanation for their co-occurrence at Jones Spring is at present unclear, but fieldwork now in progress should provide data on ecological niche separation for the two animals. The excavations at Boney Spring were so conducted that the spatial relationships of skeletal elements within the deposit could be determined, for the processes operating on an animal after death are important not only to the interpretation of the paleontological record, but of the paleoenvironmental record as well. Current research by Saunders (1975) explores this relationship. Saunders also plans to reevaluate and analyze Koch's original Pomme de Terre fossil collections, now in the British Museum.

A general outline of the terrace system in the Pomme de Terre River valley has been proposed, but further work is necessary to detail the relationships within this system, as well as the relationships of the springs themselves to the terraces. The accumulation of fossil materials in the springs is related to specific periods in spring history, which in turn are apparently tied to the Pomme de Terre River discharge. The general scarcity of postglacial deposits may be due, in part, to changes in the hydrological regime of the area at the end of the Pleistocene. The program described earlier as part of the archaeological survey to core the valley's terrace system systematically will illuminate some of these questions, at the same time that it refines the terrace sequence.

A project bibliography follows that outlines the continuing contributions of the interdisciplinary research team who, working together, hope to contribute to a better understanding of the paleoecology and prehistory of the western Ozark Highland.

REFERENCES

Ahler, S.A.
   1971 Projectile point form and function at Rodgers shelter, Missouri. Missouri Archaeological Society *Research Series* No. 8. Columbia, Missouri.
Brown, J.A., and S. Struever
   1973 The organization of archeological research: an Illinois example. In *Research and theory in current archaeology*, edited by C. Redman. New York: Wiley.
Saunders, J.J.
   1975 Late Pleistocene vertebrates of the western Ozark Highland, Missouri. Ph.D. dissertation, Department of Geosciences, University of Arizona, Tucson.
Struever, S.
   1968 Problems, methods and organization: a disparity in the growth of archeology. In *Anthropological archeology in the Americas*, edited by B.J. Meggers. Washington, D.C.: The Anthropological Society of Washington.

PROJECT BIBLIOGRAPHY

Wood, W.R., and R.B. McMillan
   1967 Recent investigations at Rodgers shelter, Missouri. *Archaeology* 20:52–55.
Mehringer, P.J., Jr., C.E. Schweger, W.R. Wood, and R.B. McMillan
   1968 Late-Pleistocene boreal forest in the western Ozark Highlands? *Ecology* 49:567–568.
McMillan, R.B.
   1970 Early canid burial from the western Ozark Highland. *Science* 167:1246–1247.

Mehringer, P.J., Jr., J.E. King, and E.H. Lindsay
1970 A record of Wisconsin-age vegetation and fauna from the Ozarks of western Missouri. In *Pleistocene and recent environments of the Central Great Plains*, edited by W. Dort, Jr., and J.K. Jones, Jr. Pp. 173–183. Lawrence, Kansas: Univ. Press of Kansas.

Wood, W.R., and J.E. King
1970 Wisconsinan vegetational and faunal history in the Ozark Highlands, Missouri. *American Quaternary Association Abstracts*, First Meeting:156. Bozeman, Montana.

Ahler, S.A.
1971 Projectile point form and function at Rodgers shelter, Missouri. *Missouri Archaeological Society Research Series*, No. 8. Columbia, Missouri.

McMillan, R.B.
1971 Biophysical change and cultural adaptation at Rodgers shelter, Missouri. Ph.D. dissertation, Department of Anthropology, University of Colorado, Boulder.

McMillan, R.B.
1971 Ozark Pleistocene springs. Illinois State Museum *The Living Museum* 33:28–31.

McMillan, R.B.
1971 Spring bogs—nature's time capsules. *Midwest Museums Conference Quarterly* 31:15–19.

McMillan, R.B.
1972 Pleistocene springs in Missouri. *The Explorer* 14(3):22–24.

King, J.E.
1972 Late Pleistocene biogeography of the western Missouri Ozarks. Ph.D. dissertation, Department of Geosciences, University of Arizona, Tucson.

Ahler, S.A.
1973 Post-Pleistocene depositional change at Rodgers shelter, Missouri. *Plains Anthropologist* 18:1–26.

Ahler, S.A.
1973 Chemical analysis of deposits at Rodgers shelter, Missouri. *Plains Anthropologist* 18:116–131.

King, J.E.
1973 Late Pleistocene palynology and biogeography of the western Missouri Ozarks. *Ecological Monographs* 43:530–565.

Bass, W.M. III, and R.B. McMillan
1973 A Woodland burial from Boney Spring, Missouri. *Plains Anthropologist* 18:313–315.

McMillan, R.B., and J.E. King
1974 Evidence for Holocene biogeographic change in Missouri's western Ozarks. *American Quaternary Association Abstracts*, Third Meeting: 119. Madison, Wisconsin.

King, F.B., and R.B. McMillan
1975 Plant remains from a Woodland storage pit, Boney Spring, Missouri. *Plains Anthropologist* 20(68):111–115.

Van Devender, T.R., and J.E. King
1975 Fossil Blanding's Turtles, *Emydoidea blandingi* (Holbrook), and the late Pleistocene vegetation of western Missouri. *Herpetologica* 31 (in press).

Saunders, J.J.
1975 Late Pleistocene vertebrates of the western Ozark Highland, Missouri. Ph.D. dissertation, Department of Geosciences, University of Arizona, Tucson.

VI
APPENDICES

Appendix A

Potential Food Plants of the Western Missouri Ozarks

Frances B. King

The list of 206 plants that follows is a compilation of potential food plants of the western Missouri Ozark region (Table A.1). It includes all plants listed by Steyermark (1963) as occurring in the study area that are also listed in the references cited in Table A.1 as being edible. This is not an attempt to produce a hypothetical ethnobotany but, rather, an attempt to define the region's potential plant resources as a basis for future ethnobotanical research.

Gilmore (1919) lists 167 plants used by the Indians of the Missouri River region. Of these, he records approximately 50 native species as sources of food or beverages. His study, however, was made at a time when long association with European culture (and the introduction of cultigens) had already greatly reduced reliance on wild plants.

Yarnell (1964) estimates that at least 20% of about 1973 vascular plants in the Great Lakes region were used aboriginally, more than 7% of them as food. If these percentages are extrapolated to the Ozarks region, some 418 of the 2092 taxa reported by Steyermark (1959, 1963) for the Ozarks were utilized by the Indians, and probably at least 146 of them were used as food.

These potential food plants have been tabulated by season of availability and edible parts (Table A.2). Season of availability is generalized since it differs for each species; however, the widest variety of plant foods is available in the spring (mainly greens) and in the fall (fruits, seeds, and nuts). Fewer species of edible plants are available in the early summer and fewer still in the winter and early spring, although some plants were undoubtedly dried and stored for later use. Beverage plants are also listed according to season of availability in order to show the large number of available plants.

REFERENCES

Fernald, M.L., and A.C. Kinsey
  1958 *Edible wild plants of eastern North America*. Revised by R.C. Rollins. New York: Harper & Brothers.
Gilmore, M.R.
  1919 Uses of plants by the Indians of the Missouri River Region. Bureau of American Ethnology, *Annual Report* **33**:43–154.
Medsger, O.P.
  1939 *Edible wild plants*. New York: Macmillan.
Morton, J.F.
  1963 Principal wild food plants of the United States. *Economic Botany* **17**(4):319–330.
Steyermark, J.A.
  1959 *Vegetational history of the Ozark forest*. University of Missouri Studies, Columbia, Missouri.
  1963 *Flora of Missouri*. Ames, Iowa: Iowa State Univ. Press.
Yanovsky, E.
  1936 Food plants of the North American Indians. *Miscellaneous Publication* 237. U.S. Department of Agriculture, Washington, D.C.
Yarnell, R.A.
  1964 Aboriginal relationships between culture and plant life in the Upper Great Lakes region. *Anthropological Papers* **23**, Museum of Anthropology, University of Michigan.

TABLE A.1 Potential Food Plants of the Western Missouri Ozarks

Plant	Part eaten	Habitat	Season	Source[a]
Acer (4 species) (Maple)	sap (sugar, seasoning), bark (bread)	bottomland, oak-hickory forest, bluffs	early spring	Sty. 1019 Yav. 41
Aesculus glabra (Buckeye)	seeds (after roasting)	bottomland, bluffs	fall	Sty. 1022
Agastache nepetoides (Giant hyssop)	leaves (tea), seeds	woodland, bottomland	spring, fall	Sty. 1277 Mor. 320
Alisma plantago—aquatica (Water plantain)	roots and stems	marsh, slough borders	spring (root) fall (stem)	Sty. 58 FKR 89
Allium canadense (Wild garlic)	bulbs, entire plant	open woodland, prairie	late winter, spring	Sty. 428 Yav. 11
Allium mutabile (Wild onion)	bulbs	limestone glades, prairie	spring, late fall	Sty. 428 Yav. 11
Allium stellatum (Wild onion)	bulbs	limestone glades, bluffs	spring, late fall	Sty. 429 Yav. 11
Amaranthus spp., esp. *retroflexus* (Pigweed)	leaves, seeds	disturbed ground	spring (leaves) fall (seeds)	Sty. 623 Gil. 86
Ambrosia trifida (Horse weed)	seeds	bottomland	fall	Sty. 1538
Amelanchier arborea (Shadbush)	fruits leaves (tea)	oak-hickory forest, bluffs	spring	Sty. 802
Amorpha canescens (Lead plant)	leaves (tea)	glades, prairie	spring	Sty. 901 Gil. 93
Amphicarpa bracteata (Hog peanut)	fruits	bottomland	fall	Sty. 954
Anemonella thalictroides (Rue anemone)	roots	open woodland	spring	Sty. 704 Med. 252
Apios americana (Ground nut)	roots, seeds	thickets, bottomland	spring, fall	Sty. 947 Mor. 320
Aquilegia canadensis (Columbine)	roots	oak-hickory forest, bluffs	?	Sty. 678 Yav. 25
Aralia racemosa (Spikenard)	roots, young tips	oak-hickory forest	spring	Sty. 1112 Yav. 47
Arisaema atrorubens (Jack-in-the-pulpit)	corm	oak-hickory forest, bottomland	spring, fall	Sty. 384 FKR 112
Arisaema dracontium (Green dragon)	corm	oak-hickory forest, bottomland	spring, fall	Sty. 384 FKR 112
Artemisa ludoviciana (White sage)	seeds	prairie, glades	late summer, fall	Sty. 1610 Yav. 59
Asarum canadense (Wild ginger)	root stock	oak-hickory slopes, bottomland	spring, summer	Sty. 572 Yav. 20

[a]FKR = Fernald, M.C., and A.C. Kinsey (1958)
Gil. = Gilmore, M.R. (1919)
Med. = Medsger, O.P. (1939)
Mor. = Morton, J.F. (1963)

Sty. = Steyermark, J.A. (1963)
Yav. = Yanovsky, E., (1936)
Numbers following abbreviations indicate page references.

Plant	Part eaten	Habitat	Season	Source[a]	
Asclepias incarnata (Swamp milkweed)	young shoots, leaves, buds	bottomland, prairie, slough borders	spring, summer	Sty. Yav.	1206 53
Asclepias syriaca (Milkweed)	stems, leaves, buds, immature fruit pods	oak-hickory forest	spring, summer, fall	Sty. Yav.	1207 53
Asclepias tuberosa (Butterfly weed)	shoots, buds, pods, roots	prairie, barrens	spring, summer	Sty. Yav.	1203 53
Asimina triloba (Pawpaw)	fruits	bottomland	fall	Sty. Yav.	671 26
Astragalus caryocarpus (Ground plum)	green fruits	glades, prairie	fall	Sty. Yav.	910 36
Astragulus mexicanus (Ground plum)	green fruits	glades, prairie, barrens	fall	Sty.	910
Blephilia ciliata (Ohio horse mint)	basal shoots and root, leaves	glades,	spring,	Sty.	1294
Bumelia lanuginosa (Chittim-wood)	fruits	glades, barrens	late summer	Sty. Yav.	1174 52
Callirhoe digitata (Fringed poppy mallow)	root	glade, prairie	?	Sty. Yav.	1050 43
Campanula americana (Tall bellflower)	young plants	bottomland	spring	Sty.	1432
Cardamine bulbosa (Bitter-cress)	leaves	bottomland	spring	Sty. FKR	750 221
Carpinus caroliniana var. *virginiana* (Blue beech)	nuts	bottomland, bluffs	fall	Sty.	527
Carya (7 species) (Hickory)	nuts	bottomland, oak-hickory forest	fall	Sty. Yav.	516 16
Ceanothus americanus (New Jersey tea)	leaves (tea)	glades, prairie	summer	Sty. Yav.	1030 42
Ceanothus ovatus (Redroot)	leaves (tea)	prairie	summer	Sty.	1031
Celtis occidentalis (Hackberry)	fruit, seeds	bottomland	fall	Sty.	558
Cenchrus longispinus (Sandbur)	seeds	bottomland, sandy areas	fall	Sty. FKR	240 106
Cercis canadensis (Redbud)	flowers and young fruits	oak-hickory forest, bluffs	spring	Sty.	878
Chenopodium album (Lambsquarter)	shoots, seeds, leaves	disturbed ground	spring, fall, summer	Sty. Yav.	612 22

TABLE A.1 (continued)

Plant	Part eaten	Habitat	Season	Source[a]	
Cirsium altissimum (Thistle)	stems, roots	disturbed ground, open woodland	spring, summer	Sty. Mor.	1622 320
Claytonia virginica (Spring beauty)	roots, corms, young plants	oak-hickory forest, prairie, bottomland	spring	Sty. Yav.	636 24
Comandra richardsiana (Bastard toadflax)	fruit	oak-hickory forest, prairie, barrens	late summer	Sty.	572
Commelina diffusa (Day-flower)	shoots, leaves	bottomland, prairie,	spring, summer	Sty. FKR	398 122
Corylus americana (Hazelnut)	nuts	oak-hickory forest, barrens	late summer, fall	Sty. Gil.	524 74
Crataegus mollis (Summer haw)	fruit	oak-hickory forest, open woods	fall, winter	Sty. Yav.	816 31
Crataegus pruinosa (Frosted haw)	fruit	oak-hickory forest, barrens	fall,	Sty. Yav.	818 31
Crataegus uniflora (One flower hawthorne)	fruit	open woods	fall, winter	Sty. Yav.	804 31
Cryptotaenia canadensis (Honewort)	roots, stems, leaves	bottomland	spring, summer	Sty.	1135
Cunila origanoides (Dittany)	leaves (tea)	barrens	spring, summer	Sty.	1300
Cyperus esculentus (Yellow nut grass)	Tubers	sandy bottomland, prairie, gravel bars	spring, late fall	Sty. FKR	264 108
Cypripedium calceolus (Small yellow lady slipper)	rootstocks	oak-hickory forest	?	Sty. FKR	470 145
Daucus pusillus (Wild carrot)	roots	glades, prairie	spring, summer	Sty. Yav.	1147 48
Dentaria laciniata Muhl. (Toothwort)	rootstocks	bottomland	spring	Sty. Yav.	751 27
Dicliptera brachiata	shoots, leaves	bottomland	spring	Sty.	1380
Diospyros virginiana (Persimmon)	fruit, seeds, leaves (tea)	glades, bottomland, barrens	fall	Sty. Yav.	1176 52
Echinochloa muricata, est. var. *microstachya* and var. *occidentalis* (Barnyard grass)	seeds	bottomland, gravel bars	summer, fall	Sty. FKR	234 104
Eclipta alba (Yerba de tajo)	plants	borders of sloughs, moist fields and valleys	?	Sty.	1554
Elymus canadensis (Canada wild rye)	seeds	prairie, bottomland, bluffs, barrens	summer, fall	Sty.	130

253

Plant	Part eaten	Habitat	Season	Source[a]	
Elymus glaucus (Blue wild rye)	seeds	bluff ledges	summer, fall	Sty. Yav.	128 8
Epilobium coloratum (Willow herb)	shoots, leaves (tea)	bottomland	spring, summer	Sty. Mor.	1099 323
Erigenia bulbosa (Harbinger of spring)	tuberous roots	oak-hickory forest, bottomland	spring	Sty.	1129
Erythronium albidum (White dog tooth violet)	bulbs, leaves	oak-hickory forest, bottomland	spring, fall	Sty. Yav.	434 13
Erythronium americanum (Yellow adder's tongue)	bulbs, leaves	oak-hickory forest, bluffs, bottomland	spring,	Sty. FKR	433 132
Festuca octoflora (Six-weeks fescue)	seeds	glades, prairie, barrens	fall	Sty.	89
Fragaria virginiana (Wild strawberry)	fruit, leaves (tea)	prairie, barrens	summer	Sty. Yav.	824 31
Galium aparine (Cleavers)	shoots, leaves	oak-hickory forest, bottomland	late spring, early summer	Sty.	1389
Gleditsia triacanthos (Honey locust)	pulp around seeds	upland slopes, bottomland	fall to spring	Sty. Yav.	873 36
Glyceria striata (Fowl meadow grass)	seeds	wet bottomland, slough borders	summer	Sty. FKR	96 93
Gymnocladus dioica (Kentucky coffee tree)	seeds	bottomland	fall, winter	Sty. Gil.	872 90
Hedeoma pulegioides (Pennyroyal)	leaves (tea)	barrens	summer	Sty.	1296
Helianthus annuus (Common sunflower)	seeds	disturbed ground, bottom-land prairie	fall	Sty. Yav.	1568 61
Helianthus Maximiliani (Maximilian sunflower)	tubers	glades, rocky prairie, bluffs	fall	Sty. Yav.	1572 61
Helianthus petiolaris (Prairie sunflower)	seeds	disturbed ground	fall	Sty. Yav.	1569 61
Helianthus tuberosus (Jerusalem artichoke)	tubers	wet prairie, wet bottomland, sloughs	late summer, fall	Sty. Gil.	1575 131
Heracleum maximum (Cow parsnip)	root, stems	bottomland	late spring, early summer	Sty.	1147
Humulus Lupulus (Hops)	young shoots	oak-hickory wooded slopes	spring	Sty. Yav.	566 20
Hydrophyllum appendiculatum (Woollen breeches)	young shoots	oak-hickory forest	spring	Sty. Yav.	1234 53

Plant	Part eaten	Habitat	Season	Source[a]	
Hydrophyllum virginianum (Waterleaf)	tips of stems, leaves	base of bluffs, bottomland	spring	Sty. Yav.	1234 53
Ipomoea pandurata (Wild potato vine)	roots	bottomland	fall to spring	Sty. Yav.	1216 53
Juglans cinerea (Butternut)	sap (sugar), nuts	bottomland	fall, spring	Sty. Yav.	511 17
Juglans nigra (Black walnut)	nuts	oak-hickory forest, bottomland	fall	Sty. Gil.	510 74
Lactuca floridana (Wild lettuce)	young shoots	bottomland	spring	Sty.	1643
Lepidium virginicum (Pepper grass)	unripe seed pods, shoots	glades, prairie	spring, fall	Sty.	738
Lilium michiganese (Michigan lily)	bulbs	wooded slopes, prairie	summer	Sty. FKR	432 132
Lindera Benzoin (Spice bush)	fruit, stems, leaves (tea)	base of bluffs, bottomland	spring to fall	Sty.	718
Lithospermum incisum (Yellow puccoon)	roots	prairie, barrens	?	Sty. Yav.	1247 54
Monarda fistulosa (Wild bergamot)	leaves (tea)	glades, prairie bottomland	spring to fall	Sty.	1291
Monarda Russeliana (Horsemint)	leaves (tea)	glades, barrens	spring to fall	Sty.	1290
Monotropa uniflora (Indian pipe)	plant	oak-hickory	summer	Sty.	1156
Morus rubra (Red mulberry)	fruit	oak-hickory forest, open areas	summer	Sty. Yav.	562 20
Nelumbo lutea (American lotus)	tubers, seeds, leaf stalks, young leaves	oxbow lakes and bottomland ponds	fall to early spring (tubers), summer, fall (seeds)	Sty. Yav.	668 25
Nuphar luteum (Yellow pond lily)	rootstocks, seeds	borders of streams, slough	fall to early spring	Sty.	665
Oenothera biennis (Evening primrose)	new roots, seeds	disturbed ground, glades, prairie	fall to early spring (roots), fall (seeds),	Sty. Yav.	1101 47
Onoclea sensibilis (Sensitive fern)	fiddleheads	wet bottomland	spring, summer	Sty.	27
Opuntia compressa (Prickly pear)	fruit, stems	glades, prairie, barrens	summer	Sty. Gil.	1086 104
Osmorhiza claytoni (Sweet cicely)	roots, branches	oak-hickory forest, ravines	summer	Sty. Yav.	1126 49
Osmorhiza longistylis (Sweet cicely)	roots, branches	oak-hickory forest, ravines	summer	Sty.	1126

TABLE A.1 (continued)

Plant	Part eaten	Habitat	Season	Source[a]	
Osmunda cinnamonea (Cinnamon fern)	center of crown	oak-hickory forest	spring	Sty. FKR	20 76
Oxalis violacea (Violet wood sorrel)	leaves	glades, prairie, barrens	spring	Sty.	959
Panax quinquefolius (Ginseng)	leaves (tea, emergency food)	oak-hickory forest	summer	Sty.	1114
Panicum spp. (Panic grass)	seeds	oak-hickory slopes, prairie	fall	Sty. FKR	206 104
Parthenocissus quinquefolia (Virginia creeper)	fruit, stalks	oak-hickory forest, ravines, bluffs	fall, spring	Sty. Yav.	1034 42
Passiflora incarnata (Maypops)	fruit	bottomland, disturbed ground	late summer, fall	Sty.	1083
Pedicularis canadensis (Wood betony)	shoots, leaves	barrens, prairie	spring	Sty. Yav.	1366 57
Petalostemon candidum (White prairie clover)	roots, leaves (tea)	barrens, prairie, glades	summer	Sty. Gil.	900 17, 94
Petalostemon purpureum (Purple prairie clover)	roots, leaves (tea)	barrens, prairie, glades	summer	Sty. Gil.	900 17, 94
Phalaris caroliniana (Canary grass)	seeds	prairie, disturbed ground	late summer, fall	Sty. Gil.	188 31, 87
Phaseolus polystachios (Wild bean)	seeds	barrens, bluff base	late summer, fall	Sty. Yav.	950 38
Physalis (6 species) (Ground cherry)	fruit	bottomland, oak-hickory forest, prairie	fall	Sty. Yav.	1314 56
Phytolacca americana (Pokeweed)	shoots	disturbed ground/ oak-hickory forest	spring	Sty. Yav.	630 23
Pilea pumila (Gray clearweed)	shoots, leaves	oak-hickory forest, bottomland	spring	Sty.	570
Plantago spp., esp. *P. Rugelii, P. cordata* (Plantain)	petioles, leaf blades	bottomland	spring	Sty.	1382
Platanus occidentalis (Sycamore)	sap (sugar)	oak-hickory slopes, bottomland	spring	Sty.	790
Podophyllum peltatum (May apple)	fruits	oak-hickory forest	late summer	Sty. FKR	711 206
Polanisia dodecandra var. *trachysperma* (Clammy-weed)	young plants	glades, bluffs	spring	Sty. Yav.	769 28

Plant	Part eaten	Habitat	Season	Source[a]
Polygonatum biflorum (Solomon's seal)	shoots, rootstocks	oak-hickory forest	spring, fall	Sty. 442 FKR 1137
Polygonatum canaliculatum (Solomon's seal)	rootstocks, leafy shoots	oak-hickory forest, bottom-land, barrens	spring, fall	Sty. 442
Polygonum aviculare (Knotweed)	seeds (starvation food)	disturbed ground	fall and winter	Sty. 587 Yav. 20
Polygonum pensylvanicum (Pinkweed)	seeds	swamps, sloughs, streams, gravel bar	fall	Sty. 590
Pontederia cordata (Pickerel weed)	fruits, stems, seeds, leaves	swamps, sloughs, bottomland	spring, late summer, fall	Sty. 401 FKR 125
Populus deltoides (Cottonwood)	bark	bottomland	spring	Sty. 507 Yav. 16
Potamogeton spp. (Pondweed)	rootstocks	ponds and springs	?	Sty. 50 FKR 85
Prunella vulgaris (Self heal)	plant	prairie, bottomland	spring	Sty. 1279 Yav. 55
Prunus (7 species) (Wild plum)	fruit	oak-hickory forest	summer	Sty. 860 Gil. 87
Psoralea esculenta (Prairie turnip)	roots	glades, prairie, barrens	summer	Sty. 897 Gil. 92
Pteridium aquilinum (Bracken fern)	fiddleheads	barrens	spring	Sty. 21 FKR 71
Pyrus ioensis (Wild crab)	fruit	oak-hickory forest, bottomland	fall	Sty. 799 Gil. 86
Quercus (5 species) (Oak)	acorns	oak-hickory forest, bottomland	fall	Sty. 535 Yav. 18 Gil. 75
Rhus aromatica (Fragrant sumac)	fruit (drink), roots	barrens	summer	Sty. 1003
Rhus copallina (Dwarf sumac)	fruit (drink), roots	oak-hickory forest, prairie, barrens	summer,	Sty. 1000 Yav. 40
Rhus glabra (Smooth sumac)	fruit (drink), roots	prairies, barrens	summer, fall	Sty. 1000 Yav. 40
Ribes cynosbati (Prickly gooseberry)	fruit	bluffs	summer	Sty. 785
Ribes missouriense (Wild gooseberry)	fruit	forest borders and barrens	summer	Sty. 785
Robinia pseudo-acadia (Black locust)	seeds and flowers	disturbed ground, bottomland	late spring, fall	Sty. 907 Yav. 39

Plant	Part eaten	Habitat	Season	Source[a]	
Rubus (4 species) (Blackberry)	fruit, leaves (tea)	bottomland, thickets	summer	Sty.	841
Rubus (2 species) (Dewberry)	fruit, leaves (tea)	prairies, barrens, thickets	summer	Sty. Yav.	838 34
Rubus occidentalis (Black raspberry)	fruit, leaves (tea)	bluffs, barrens, thickets	summer	Sty. Gil.	836 84
Rudbeckia laciniata (Wild goldenglow)	young stems	sloughs, bottomland	spring	Sty. Yav.	1557 63
Rumex altissimus (Pale dock)	shoots, leaves, seeds	sloughs, thickets, bottomland	spring, fall	Sty.	578
Rumex verticillatus (Swamp dock)	shoots, leaves	wetlands	spring	Sty.	578
Sagittaria latifolia (Duck potato)	tubers	ponds, slow streams	late summer, fall	Sty. FKR	66 87
Sambucus canadensis (Elderberry)	fruit	open woods, bottomland	late summer, fall	Sty.	1418
Sassafras albidum (Sassafras)	twigs, leaves, bark from root	glades, bottomland, barrens	all year (root), spring (twigs and leaves)	Sty.	717
Satureja arkansana (Savory)	leaves (tea)	open woods, bottomlands	summer	Sty.	1298
Scirpus validus (Great bulrush)	rootstocks, pollen, seeds	wet prairie, sloughs	spring, summer, fall	Sty. FKR	292 110
Setaria geniculata (Prairie foxtail)	seeds	glades, prairies	summer, fall	Sty. FKR	237 105
Silphium laciniatum (Compass plant)	stem	glades, prairie	summer	Sty.	1550
Sium suave (Water parsnip)	roots	bottomland forest and prairie, sloughs	spring, summer	Sty.	1138
Smilacina racemosa (False solomon's seal)	roots, berries, young shoots	oak-hickory forest	spring, late summer	Sty. FKR	440 135
Smilax Bona-nox (Catbrier)	rootstocks, young shoots	glades, bottomland, barrens, thickets	spring, fall, winter	Sty. Yav.	452 14
Smilax herbacea (Carrion flower)	fruit, young shoots	oak-hickory forest, barrens	spring, summer	Sty. FKR	451 138
Smilax tamnoides (Bristly greenbrier)	rootstocks	oak-hickory forest, bottomland	fall to spring	Sty. Yav.	452 14
Solanum americanum (Black nightshade)	young stems, berries, leaves	base of bluff and bottomland	spring, summer, fall	Sty.	1312

Plant	Part eaten	Habitat	Season	Source[a]
Solidago missouriensis (Goldenrod)	leaves (tea or greens)	prairie, oak-hickory forest	summer	Sty. 1488 Yav. 63
Sparganium americanum (Bur-reed)	tubers	bottomland lakes and sloughs	late fall	Sty. 49 FKR 85
Spiranthes gracilis (Slender ladies' tresses)	rootstocks	prairie, oak-hickory forest	?	Sty. 480
Spiranthes vernalis (Ladies' tresses)	rootstocks	prairie	?	Sty. 480 FKR 145
Sporobolus spp. (Dropseed)	seeds	prairie, forest openings	fall	Sty. 161 FKR 96
Staphylea trifolia (American bladder-nut)	seeds	oak-hickory forest, bottomland	fall	Sty. 1011 Yav. 41
Tilia americana (Basswood)	flowers, sap, fruit, bark	bottomland, oak-hickory slopes	spring	Sty. 1044 Yav. 43
Tradescantia spp. (Spiderwort)	shoots, leaves	oak-hickory forest, bottomland	spring	Sty. 392 FKR 124
Trillium sessile (Wake robin)	shoots, leaves	oak-hickory slopes, bottomland	spring	Sty. 444 FKR 138
Triosteum perfoliatum (Common horse gentian)	fruit (coffee)	barrens	summer, fall	Sty. 1411
Typha latifolia (Cat-tail)	rootstocks, new shoots, seeds, pollen	sloughs marshes, ponds	fall to spring, early summer	Sty. 46 FKR 82 Yav. 6
Ulmus rubra (Slippery elm)	bark (tea, cooked veg.)	bottomland, bluff areas	spring	Sty. 555 Yav. 51
Urtica dioica (Nettle)	young shoots	bottoms, waste ground	spring	Sty. 567
Uvularia grandiflora (Bellwort)	young shoots, roots	oak-hickory forest	spring	Sty. 424 FKR 126
Vaccinium stamineum (Deerberry)	fruit	oak-hickory forest, barrens	summer	Sty. 1162
Vaccinium vacillans (Lowbush blueberry)	fruit	barrens, bluff areas, glades	summer	Sty. 1164
Valerianella radiata (Corn salad)	leaves	prairies, bottoms	spring	Sty. 1421

Plant	Part eaten	Habitat	Season	Source[a]	
Verbena hastata (Blue vervain)	leaves, seeds	bottomland, slough margins	spring, summer	Sty. Gil.	1258 111
Veronica comosa (Water speedwell)	leaves	vicinity of springs	spring	Sty.	1356
Viburnum prunifolium (Black haw)	fruit	bottomland, oak-hickory slopes	fall	Sty. Yav.	1415 58
Viburnum rufidulum (Southern black haw)	fruit	glades, bluff areas, bottomland	fall	Sty.	1415
Vitis (4 species) (Grape)	fruit	oak-hickory forest, glades, bluff areas	summer, fall	Sty.	1037

TABLE A.2 Edible Plants of the Western Missouri Ozarks, Arranged by Season of Availability and Edible Parts

	Late winter— Early spring	Spring	Late spring— Early summer	Summer	Late summer— Early fall	Fall	Late fall— Early winter	Winter	Total
	—Feb—	—Mar—	—Apr—May—	—June—July—	—Aug—Sept—	—Oct—	—Nov—	—Dec—Jan	
Cambium	5	3							8
Sap	6	1							7
Pollen		2							2
Flowers		3							3
Tubers and roots	8	21	10	10	10	18	10	7	94
Greens		51	12	12	4	1			80
Fruit	1	5	4	18	26	32	6	4	96
Seeds			2	7	15	29	7		60
Nuts					1	16	5		22
Totals	20	86	28	47	56	96	28	11	372
Beverage Plants	1	14	24	28	20	5	1		93

Appendix B

Forest Density and Nut Production Potential for the Rodgers Shelter Area

Frances B. King

Original United States Federal Land Survey data have been used with increasing frequency to describe presettlement vegetation. The only major previous work in western Missouri is that of Howell and Kucera (1956); no studies are available for the study locality. Consequently, presettlement tree frequency and density are here reconstructed for the bottomland, oak–hickory, and barrens vegetational zones (Chapter 2) within a 10-km radius of Rodgers Shelter. The area of each of the major vegetational zones was computed with a planimeter from the 1945 Fristoe, Missouri, U.S.G.S. 15′ quadrangle map.

The original land surveys recorded two types of data, collected in different ways. The notes from each section corner record the nearest tree in each of the four adjoining quarter sections, while at the quarter section corners only the two nearest trees were recorded; frequently, they were in adjoining sections. These two procedures are basically different sampling techniques, and therefore must be treated differently in computing forest density. Plant ecologists, well aware of the problems of working with original land survey data, have developed a number of procedures for making these data equivalent with one another and with data from modern forest studies.

When measuring the distance from the section corner to the nearest tree in each of four quarter sections, the average of the four distances is equal to the square root of the mean area of each tree (Cottam *et al.* 1953; Cottam and Curtis 1956). It is therefore easy to determine the number of trees per acre by squaring the average distance (*d*) to determine the mean area per tree, and then dividing it into the number of square feet in an acre (43,560).

$$\text{density} = \frac{43560}{d^2}$$

However, unlike section corners, the quarter section data cannot be averaged for a true distance between trees, since an average from only two trees would be biased toward too short a distance and would therefore lead to an erroneously high tree density. Consequently, in working with quarter section data, the distance between two trees is calculated from the general formula for finding the third side of a triangle when *a* and *b* are two sides of the triangle and *C* is the enclosed angle: $-2ab \cos C$. This distance is then multiplied by a factor (*x*) that is a linear function of the angle of exclusion. For a complete discussion of the determination of density data from quarter section survey notes, see references to the random pairs method in Cottam and Curtis (1949, 1955, 1956), and Cottam *et al.* (1953). Using the corrected distances, tree density is then computed as it was for section corners:

$$\text{density} = \frac{43560}{(xd)^2}$$

Section corner and corrected quarter section distances were combined from the Federal Land Survey notes and averaged to compute tree density. Once the tree density was computed, the total number of trees within a 10-km radius of Rodgers Shelter was calculated by multiplying the tree density of each vegetational zone by the area occupied by that zone (Table B.1).

TABLE B.1   Vegetation within Ten Kilometers of Rodgers Shelter[a]

Vegetation zones	Percentage	Acres	km²	Hectares	Intertree distance	Tree density/hectares	Total trees
Bottomland	12	9,311	37.68	3,786	70.34±7.88	21.74 (8.80/acre)	81,935.90
Oak-hickory	20	15,519	62.80	6,280	56.78±5.51	33.38 (13.51/acre)	209,650.26
Barrens	60	46,557	188.40	18,840	90.44±11.20	13.17 (5.17/acre)	248,135.98
Prairie	(8)	—	—	—	—	—	—
Total							539,722.14

[a] r = 10 km.
$\pi = 3.14 \ (10)^2 = 314 \ \text{km}^2 = 314,000,000 \ \text{m}^2 = 31,400 \ \text{ha (hectares)} = 77,589 \ \text{acres}$.

TABLE B.2 Estimated Numbers of Various Tree Species within Ten Kilometers of Rodgers Shelter[a]

Species	Barrens Number	Barrens Percentage	Oak–Hickory Number	Oak–Hickory Percentage	Bottomland Number	Bottomland Percentage	Total Number	Total Percentage
Post oak (*Quercus stellata*)	143,918	58.0	95,601	45.6	—	—	239,519	44.5±9 [b]
Black oak (*Quercus velutina*)	47,146	19.0	36,898	17.6	15,568	19.0	99,612	18.5±10
Black jack oak (*Quercus marilandica*)	11,910	4.8	16,772	3.5	—	—	28,682	5.3±5.5
White oak (*Quercus alba*)	12,903	5.2	45,074	21.5	—	—	57,977	10.7±5.7
Northern red oak (*Quercus rubra*)	992	0.4	4,612	2.2	1,762	2.15	7,366	1.4±2.9
Bur oak (*Quercus macrocarpa*)	4,466	1.8	1,886	0.9	3,523	4.3	9,875	1.8±3.6
Pin oak (*Quercus palustris*)	2,233	0.9	2,725	1.3	—	—	4,958	0.9±1.9
Chinkapin oak (*Quercus prinoides* var. *acuminata*)	6,452	2.6	4,612	2.2	5,162	6.3	16,226	3.0±4.6
Black hickory (*Carya texana*)	7,692	3.1	7,547	3.6	3,523	4.3	18,762	3.5±4.7
White hickory (*Carya tomentosa*)	—	—	339	0.4	3,523	4.3	3,862	0.7±2.1
Shellbark hickory (*Carya laciniosa*)	992	0.4	339	0.4	1,762	2.15	3,093	0.6±2.3
Hickory (*Carya* spp.)	3,226	1.3	339	0.4	—	—	3,565	0.7±1.1
Black walnut (*Juglans nigra*)	—	—	339	0.4	1,762	2.15	2,101	0.4±1.7
White walnut (*Juglans cinerea*)	—	—	--	—	1,762	2.15	1,762	0.3±1.0
Walnut (*Juglans* spp.)	992	0.4	—	—	—	—	992	0.2±0.6
White elm (*Ulmus americana*)	992	0.4	—	—	8,685	10.6	9,677	1.8±2.9
Red elm (*Ulmus rubra*)	—	—	—	—	3,523	4.3	3,523	0.7±1.5
Elm (*Ulmus* spp.)	2,233	0.9	—	—	—	—	2,233	0.4±0.9
White ash (*Fraxinus americana*)	—	—	—	—	1,762	2.15	1,762	0.3±1.0
Ash (*Fraxinus* spp.)	—	—	—	—	1,762	2.15	1,762	0.3±1.0
Box elder (*Acer negundo*)	—	—	—	—	1,762	2.15	1,762	0.3±1.0
Sugar maple (*Acer saccharum*)	992	0.4	—	—	1,762	2.15	2,754	0.5±1.7
River maple (*Acer saccharinum*)	—	—	—	—	1,762	2.15	1,762	0.3±1.0
Maple (*Acer* spp.)	—	—	—	—	5,162	6.3	5,162	1.0±1.7
Hackberry (*Celtis occidentalis*)	—	—	—	—	8,685	10.6	8,685	1.6±2.2
Sycamore (*Platanus occidentalis*)	—	—	—	—	6,965	8.5	6,965	1.3±2.0
Willow (*Salix* spp.)	992	0.4	—	—	1,762	2.15	2,754	0.5±1.7
Totals	248,131	100.0	217.083	100.0	81,939	100.0	547,153	100.0

[a]Taxonomy based on Steyermark (1963).
[b]Confidence interval at the 95% level.

The total number of trees of each species was determined by multiplying the frequency (in percentage) of each species (Table 2.3) by the number of trees estimated for each zone (Table B.2). Finally, the total number of trees of each species within 10 km of Rodgers Shelter was computed by adding together the numbers of trees of each species in all vegetation zones. It is this total on which potential nut production is estimated.

Average potential nut yields in bushels were calculated by taking the total number of trees of each of the important nut-producing species and multiplying that total by an estimated yield from published sources (USDA 1948, 1965). Yield is affected by a number of factors, particularly the size of the tree and forest density. Trees in an open forest have less

TABLE B.3 Potential Nut Production[a]

Species	Total number of trees within 10 km of Rodgers Shelter				Years between crops[b]	Years between good yields[b]	Total estimated yield (bushels)[c]
	Barrens	Oak-hickory	Bottom-land	Totals			
Post oak							
(Quercus stellata)	143,918	95,601	—	239,519	1	2-3	60,000-359,278
Black oak							
(Quercus velutina)	47,146	36,898	15,568	99,612	2	2-3	12,451 – 74,709
Black jack oak							
(Quercus marilandica)	11,910	16,772	—	28,682	2	—	3,585 – 21,511
White oak							
(Quercus alba)	12,903	45,074	—	57,977	1	4-10	14,494 – 86,965
Northern red oak							
(Quercus rubra)	992	4,612	1,762	7,366	2	2-5	920 – 5,525
Bur oak							
(Quercus macrocarpa)	4,466	1,886	3,523	9,875	1	2-3	2,468 – 14,812
Pin oak							
(Quercus palustris)	2,233	2,725	—	4,958	2	—	619 – 3,718
Chinkapin oak							
(Quercus prinoides var. acuminata)	6,452	4,612	5,162	16,226	1	—	4,056 – 24,339
Black hickory							
(Carya texana)	7,692	7,547	3,523	18,762	1	—	—
White hickory							
(Carya tomentosa)	—	—	3,523	3,523	1	2-3	7,046 – 10,569
Shellbark hickory							
(Carya laciniosa)	992	339	1,762	3,093	1	2	7,732
Black walnut							
(Juglans nigra)	—	339	1,762	2,101	1	2-3	4,202 – 6,303
White walnut							
(Juglans cinerea)	—	—	1,762	1,762	1	2-3	3,524 – 5,286

[a]Taxonomy based on Steyermark (1963).
[b]Based on data from USDA 1948:Table 164.
[c]Based on estimated yields of ¼-1½ bu for oaks, 1½-2 bu for white hickory, 2-3 bu for shellbark hickory, 1-several bu for black walnut, and ¼-1 bu for white walnut (USDA 1943:301; USDA 1965:559, 589-590, 609, 633).

competition and therefore tend to be larger and more productive than trees in a closed canopy forest. Some tree species reach peak production early in life and produce less as they become older, while others maintain a constant production rate throughout their lives. In addition, disease and insect infestations can greatly reduce productivity; however, these factors are too variable to be estimated.

Nut production is also affected by the length of a tree's reproductive cycle. The acorns of red and black oaks require 2 years to mature, and thus only one-half of the trees produce acorns each year. Hickories and walnuts, on the other hand, produce a crop every year that averages one to three bushels per tree. Many oaks produce an average yield of approximately one-quarter bushel per tree (USDA 1948, 1965). Disregarding these variables, estimated potential nut yields are given in Table B.3.

REFERENCES

Cottam, G., and J.T. Curtis
   1949 A method for making rapid surveys of woodlands by means of pairs of randomly selected trees. *Ecology* **30**:101–104.
   1955 Correction for various exclusion angles in the random pairs method. *Ecology* **36**:767.
   1956 The use of distance measures in phytosociological sampling. *Ecology* **37**:451–460.
Cottam, G., J.T. Curtis, and W.B. Hale
   1953 Some sampling characteristics of a population of randomly dispersed individuals. *Ecology* **34**:741–747.
Howell, D.L., and C.L. Kucera
   1956 Composition of presettlement forests in three counties of Missouri. *Bulletin Torrey Botanical Club* **83**:207–217.
Steyermark, J.A.
   1963 *Flora of Missouri.* Ames, Iowa: The Iowa State Univ. Press.
USDA
   1948 Woody Plant Seed Manual. United States Department of Agriculture, *Miscellaneous Publication* 654. U.S. Government Printing Office, Washington, D.C.
   1965 Silvics of Forest Trees of the United States. United States Department of Agriculture, *Handbook* 271. U.S. Government Printing Office, Washington, D.C.

Index